Money Rules

A volume in the series

CORNELL STUDIES IN POLITICAL ECONOMY

edited by Peter J. Katzenstein

A full list of titles in the series appears at the end of the book.

MONE¥
RU£ES

THE NEW POLITICS OF FINANCE IN BRITAIN AND JAPAN

Henry Laurence

CORNELL UNIVERSITY PRESS

ITHACA AND LONDON

First published 2001 by Cornell University Press

Printed in the United States of America

Library of Congress Cataloging-in-Publication Data

Laurence, Henry, b. 1963
    Money rules : the new politics of finance in Britain and Japan / Henry Laurence
      p. cm. — (Cornell studies in political economy)
    Includes index.
    ISBN 0-8014-3773-3
    1. Finance—Great Britain.   2. France—Japan.   I. Title.   II. Series.
    HG186.G7 L28 2001

332'.0941—dc21
00-0011357

Cornell University Press strives to use environmentally responsible suppliers and materials to the fullest extent possible in the publishing of its books. Such materials include vegetable-based, low-VOC inks and acid-free papers that are recycled, totally chlorine-free, or partly composed of nonwood fibers. Books that bear the logo of the FSC (Forest Stewardship Council) use paper taken from forests that have been inspected and certified as meeting the highest standards for environmental and social responsibility. For further information, visit our website at www.cornellpress.cornell.edu.

Cloth printing   10 9 8 7 6 5 4 3 2 1

Contents

Preface   vii
1 Financial Reform in Britain and Japan   I
2 Regulatory Politics and Financial Markets   26
3 Globalization and National Politics   41
4 Financial Reform in the United Kingdom   65
5 Japanese Financial Deregulation in the 1980s   103
6 Japanese Finance in the 1990s: Creating a "Free, Fair
   and Global" Market   145
   Conclusion: The New Politics of Financial Interdependence   188
   Index   203

Preface

The Japanese economy has been mired in recession since 1991. Japanese banks are still struggling through one of the worst bad-debt problems in world history. Many analysts, both Japanese and foreign, are arguing that the only long-term solution to both the slowdown and the financial crisis is *jiyuka*: the liberalization of the economy. Every week seems to bring fresh calls for reform, and in the Diet (parliament) parties vie with one another to propose the most sweeping deregulation. One of the most important proposals for reform came in November 1996, with the announcement by Prime Minister Hashimoto Ryutaro that Japan would undertake a fundamental reform of its financial system in a fashion modeled on the reforms undertaken in Britain in 1986. The British reforms centered on the complete deregulation of the London Stock Exchange and were known, somewhat grandiosely, as the "Big Bang." The reforms announced by Hashimoto are similar in nature, involving the liberalization of the Tokyo Stock Exchange and other moves toward a "Free, Fair, and Global" marketplace. Among many specific proposals are the abolition of fixed brokerage commissions; the elimination of barriers between different sectors of the financial services industry; liberalization of the rules governing foreign exchange and other financial transactions; and the general relaxation of restrictions on the issuing, trading, and investing of various financial instruments. The phrase "the Japanese Big Bang" (*Biggu Ban* in Japanese) is in constant use.

I was working as a fund manager for the Bank of Tokyo International in London in 1986, when I was younger and considerably slimmer, and witnessed the London Big Bang at first hand. At the time, my Japanese colleagues and I watched from the sidelines as the British financial community prepared itself hurriedly for reform. The expression "running around like headless chickens" came to mind more than once as we watched the frantic preparations. Clearly, many British firms experienced difficulty in coming to terms with the fact that what had previously been a very insular and protected market was being blown wide open to national and international competition. A small, cozy cartel of brokering partnerships would now be competing head-to-head with bigger British banks and with much, much bigger American, Japanese, and European financial institutions. I remember asking my Japanese colleagues if and when the same thing would happen in Tokyo. The reply was always the same: never. The Japanese financial community didn't want reform. The all-powerful Ministry of Finance (MOF) didn't want reform. The Japanese government didn't want it and would never allow it. If I had read the scholarly literature at the time (which, being a banker, I had not), I would have found that the academic community concurred that financial liberalization was very unlikely to happen in Japan. The two countries were poles apart in terms of history, culture, tradition, and political and economic situations. Moreover, if anyone had made the suggestion in 1985 that Japan, the economic success story of the past three decades, had anything to learn about economic management from Britain, widely regarded as the economic basket case of the OECD, then that person would undoubtedly have been laughed off campus.

To make the same point in terms acceptable to social scientists, these events present a puzzle for scholars of comparative political economy. Conventional wisdom is that Japan has a highly successful system of economic management responsible for the postwar Japanese economic miracle. Britain, by contrast, suffers from the British disease of poor economic management and subsequently poor economic performance. Yet in 1996 the Japanese prime minister announced that Japan must follow the British example. To put the questions bluntly: What do the miraculous Japanese have to learn from the diseased British about economic management? Why does the Japanese government assert the need to reform along British lines?

I argue that the fundamental cause of the reforms in Japan, as in Britain, has been the increased integration of the world economy since the 1980s and, in particular, the ways in which financial markets have become, to use an overworked word, globalized. Britain and then Japan reacted similarly to a common external change in circumstances. However, the key agents of reform have been domestic Japanese economic actors, in particular those Japanese firms that have exploited the new opportunities presented by the globalization of finance to escape from the restrictive and tightly controlled regulatory regime of their home country. Their exit, or in some cases merely the threat of their exit, from the domestic arena was the most important single factor, although by no means the only one, that prompted the Japanese authorities to overhaul their entire financial system.

The financial reforms announced in 1996 are part of a fundamental change in the structure of the Japanese political economy. They may be seen as one important step in a series of reforms in the 1990s that have had the cumulative effect of bringing the Japanese financial system closer into line with, although by no means identical to, the Anglo-Saxon model of capitalism. This book explains how the changes came about.

My first thanks and my greatest intellectual debt belong to Susan J. Pharr. She first encouraged me to leave the world of investment banking and join the world of academia, a decision I have never regretted. Right from the start, she has been exceptionally helpful both intellectually and practically, and endless in her enthusiastic support. Jim Alt, Lawrence Broz, and Robin Radin also played major roles in the development of this project and provided essential guidance, advice, and encouragement. While at Harvard I also benefited enormously from the comments and constructive criticism of many others, including Ronald Dore, Jeff Frieden, Dave Johnson, Junko Kato, Yuen Fung Khong, Lisa Martin, Stephan Haggard, Joel Hellman, Robert Keohane, Andrew Moravcsik, Ken Oye, Ezra Vogel, Brian Woodall, and Mike Yoshino. Steve Vogel deserves particular thanks for his support and encouragement, given freely and generously despite our differing conclusions about the subject matter. I also owe much thanks for the intellectual rigor and candor of my friends and colleagues Brian Burgoon, Martha Chang, Jon Crystal, Raj Desai, Tim Frye, Michael Hiscox, Sid Mitter, Page Fortna, Jeff Taliaferro, Kip Wennerlund, and Stewart Wood. My father, Tony Laurence, read and reread the whole book and takes most of the credit for the degree to which it is actually readable. Charlotte Laurence, Paula Maute, and Susan Ransom also gave prodigious service in editing and preparation.

Much of the research for this study took the form of a series of trips to Britain and Japan to conduct interviews. Many people whose time was infinitely more valuable than my own were generous in their help. I should particularly like to thank Steven Axilrod, Nils Taube, James Ekins, Toshio Ogahara, and Fabio Savoldelli. In Japan, research would have been impossible without the help of James and Safia Minney, Hiroshi Okumura, Fumio Iida, Takeshi Eguchi, Kojiro Shiraishi, Takako Hikotani, and many of my old friends and colleagues at the Bank of Tokyo, especially Michi Watanabe, Fumi Otsuka, Shigeru Hayashi, and my old boss and mentor, Kikuo Nagaoka. Thanks are due also to my parents-in-law, Tony and Cynthia Lamport, who have been very supportive of this project. My parents, Tony and Nicola Laurence, deserve my special thanks and deepest appreciation for all of their interest, help, and encouragement.

I received vital financial support for research and travel from the John D. and Catherine T. MacArthur Foundation, the Mellon Foundation, the Freeman Foundation, and especially Harvard University's U.S.–Japan Relations Program, where Frank Schwartz and Wen-Hao Tien gave critical moral and institutional support. Saori Horikawa, Cizuka Seki, and Qiao Qiao Wang gave invaluable research assistance. Bowdoin College provided a wonderful setting and vital financial and institutional support for the final drafting. At Cornell University Press, I am deeply indebted to Peter Katzenstein and an anonymous reader for their brilliant commentaries, and to Roger Haydon for his infectious enthusiasm and good cheer. Finally, the biggest thanks of all go to my wife, Sarah, and our children Colin and Gemma. Colin and Gemma have patiently (and sometimes not so patiently) put up with my long absences while I traveled or worked on the manuscript and often fell quietly but soundly asleep as I read them early drafts. My wife, Sarah, has been a wonderful source of constant encouragement and emotional support, as well as being my sternest and most helpful intellectual critic. I dedicate this work to her.

HENRY LAURENCE

Brunswick, Maine

Chapter 1

Financial Reform in Britain and Japan

How has economic internationalization affected domestic politics in advanced industrialized democracies?[1] This book examines the impact of capital mobility on financial regulation in Japan and Britain. It argues that both countries restructured their domestic capital markets in response to the explosive growth in international finance beginning in the mid-1970s. Two aspects of these reforms are noteworthy. First, both countries undertook similar responses to economic globalization, and as a result regulatory structures in these countries have converged. This convergence is striking given how differently the two countries had previously regulated their markets. Second, although the trend has been mostly toward liberalization, there has also been a shift toward increased regulation and a tightening of standards in a number of practices.

The main driving force of reform has come from holders of mobile capital assets, who enjoy increased political leverage as a result of the globalization of finance. Internationalization has given these actors new opportunities to pick and choose the countries they will do business in. They prefer those whose national regulations are most attractive. If mobile-asset holders find their home country's regulations burdensome, thanks to financial internationalization, they can now do business in another country. This exit option has systematically altered the dynamics of domestic political competition in similar ways in these and other countries, and subsequent regulatory reforms have systematically favored the holders of mobile assets.[2]

The shift in political power toward holders of mobile assets challenges several important tenets of political science theory. This book will make three important contributions to the understanding of regulatory politics. First, the shift marks the ascendancy of consumer interests over producer interests. The direction of this shift represents a fundamental challenge to the traditional Stigler-Peltzman model of regulatory capture, which asserts that regulatory policies will typically be implemented for the benefit

---

[1] In this book, the term "internationalization" is used to refer to an increase in the number of cross-border economic transactions relative to domestic transactions.

[2] The idea that consumers have three strategies in dealing with producers—exit, voice, and loyalty—was put forward by Albert O. Hirschman, *Exit, Voice, and Loyalty* (Cambridge: Harvard University Press, 1971). In this book I apply the concepts to the political as opposed to the economic marketplace. I discuss the concepts further in chapter 2.

of producer groups at the expense of consumers.[3] A vital but usually implicit assumption of most existing models of regulatory politics is that exit is not an option for any of the actors. Political battles over the distribution of the costs and benefits of regulation have winners and losers, and the losers have no choice but to abide by the outcomes. Internationalization means that economic actors with mobile assets but who are politically weak no longer have to suffer the consequences of rent-seeking by more politically powerful groups. They can simply do business in another country. In other words, *internationalization has not merely altered the* distribution of political power in individual countries, but has fundamentally altered the landscape in which political battles are fought. This has profound implications not only for the Stigler-Peltzman model, but for all models of regulatory politics that underestimate the possibility of exit by important actors.[4]

The second implication of this book concerns an enduring puzzle in the literature on international political economy: If holders of mobile assets can leave and do business in other countries more easily than they can lobby to change regulations, why do they not always leave if regulations are not to their liking? Holders of mobile assets should have fewer incentives to lobby and engage in battles over regulatory policy than holders of immobile assets because the latter are stuck with the consequences of national regulatory policies and therefore have far greater incentives to lobby for favorable regulation. Given that economic integration will widen this difference in incentives, one expects internationalization to be accompanied by an increase in regulatory policies favoring the holders of less-mobile assets.

The puzzle is that the opposite has happened. Why? In this book I explore the underlying political processes of regulatory reform in an interdependent world and find a surprising new dynamic. The loudest and most persistent lobbying for regulations that favor the holders of mobile assets is undertaken not by these actors themselves, but by the holders of less-mobile assets, who rely on them for business. The threat that holders of mobile assets will exit a country because of its unattractive regulatory structure is enough to prompt the holders of less-mobile assets to demand regulatory reform—even if that means abolishing or amending regulations that currently favor the holders of less-mobile assets. We see, for example, cartels of bankers or brokers demanding to be broken up. Their task is made easier by the fact that policymakers, both politicians and bureaucrats, often have their

[3] This model is also known as the economic theory of regulation in George Stigler, "The Theory of Economic Regulation," *Bell Journal of Economics* 2 (1971): 113–121; Sam Peltzman, "Toward a More General Theory of Regulation," *Journal of Law and Economics* (August 1976): 211–240. Stigler's model draws on Olson's theory of collective action and stresses differences in the ability of producer and consumer groups to organize. See Mancur Olson, *The Logic of Collective Action* (Cambridge: Harvard University Press, 1965).

[4] James Q. Wilson, *The Politics of Regulation* (New York: Basic Books, 1974) is the classic text in this field.

own interests either in trying to prevent mobile-asset holders from leaving the country or in attracting mobile asset holders from abroad. We can hence begin to understand the mechanisms by which increased international capital mobility translates into domestic policy outcomes. Paradoxically, the major proponents of regulatory reform are often not the major beneficiaries of it.

Finally, the book examines the policy preferences of capitalists with internationally mobile assets, who are usually but wrongly assumed to want fewer regulations. Many scholars predict a competition in deregulatory laxity as nations compete to attract internationally mobile business by deregulating their economies.[5] In fact, this has not always happened. On the contrary, states have competed in many areas by strengthening their regulations, particularly over issues of investor protection. In other words, an understanding of the increased power of mobile-asset holders must be accompanied by an understanding of the preferences of these actors, in particular their preference for greater rather than less regulatory protection.

This book sheds new empirical light on a number of contemporary debates. At the broadest level, it is about the nature of economic competition between countries.[6] More specifically, the book builds on recent work in international political economy that has asserted the importance of global forces on domestic politics.[7] One particularly relevant question is the degree to which "hot money"—that is, internationally mobile financial capital—now represents a systemic constraint on national sovereignty.[8] The book also looks at current regulatory politics in both Britain and Japan, in particular the changing nature of business-government relationships in

---

[5] See, for example, Ralph Bryant, *International Financial Mediation* (Washington, D.C.: Brookings, 1987). An important exception is David Vogel, *Trading Up: Consumer and Environmental Regulation in a Global Economy* (Cambridge: Harvard University Press, 1995), who argues that increased trade has led to higher standards of environmental and consumer protection regulation.

[6] See Douglas North and Robert Thomas, *The Rise of the Western World: A New Economic History* (Cambridge: Cambridge University Press, 1973); Douglas North, *Structure and Change in Economic History* (New York: Norton Press, 1981); and Lawrence Broz, "Rent-Seeking and the Organization of the Fiscal-Military State," *Harvard University Center for International Affairs Working Paper* 94, no. 1 (1994). The debate is well summarized and discussed in Jack Knight, *Institutions and Social Conflict* (Cambridge: Cambridge University Press, 1992).

[7] This is the second image reversed literature of which Peter Gourevitch, "The Second Image Reversed: The International Sources of Domestic Politics" (*International Organization* 32 [1978]: 881–911) is the classic statement. Some of the recent work includes Robert Keohane and Helen Milner, eds., *Internationalization and Domestic Politics* (Cambridge: Cambridge University Press, 1996).

[8] Proponents of the hypothesis that international capital mobility does indeed represent such a structural constraint include Michael Webb, "International Economic Structures, Government Interests and International Coordination of Macroeconomic Adjustment Policies," *International Organization* 45, p. 1991; *The Political Economy of Policy Coordination: International Adjustment since 1945* (Ithaca: Cornell University Press, 1995); and David Andrews, "Capital Mobility and State Autonomy," *International Studies Quarterly* 38 (1994): 193–218.

financial markets.[9] Perhaps the most significant finding for the field of Japanese studies is that the hitherto all-powerful Japanese Ministry of Finance has been forced into a defensive and essentially reactive role by factors beyond its control, culminating in an attack on its existence. This view challenges theories that identify the bureaucracy as the locus of power in Japan.[10]

The relevance of the project is clear. Financial markets are "the infrastructure of the infrastructure," at the very heart of any modern economy.[11] Any changes will have important repercussions for the rest of the economy both distributionally and in terms of national economic performance.[12] In addition, financial services are a major industry in their own right, accounting for approximately 15 percent of total employment in Britain, and close to 6 percent in Japan.

This chapter first provides an overview of the reforms I seek to explain, which will be discussed in greater detail in later chapters. Next I elaborate on the main argument: that the internationalization of finance has resulted in regulatory reforms that have systematically favored holders of internationally mobile assets, who are the largest consumers of financial services. I discuss the actors—institutional investors and large corporate borrowers— their regulatory preferences, and, most important, the mechanisms by which increased internationalization results in policies that benefit them. In particular I stress the role of the providers of financial services—banks and brokers—as lobbyists for regulatory reforms that chiefly benefit their largest customers. The final sections discuss research methods and outlines the remainder of the book.

[9] See Michael Moran, *The Politics of the Financial Services Revolution* (London: Macmillan Press, 1991); and Peter Hall, *Governing the Economy: The Politics of State Intervention in Britain and France* (Cambridge: Polity Press, 1986) on relations between the British government and the city. For the politics of financial regulation in Japan, see Frances McCall Rosenbluth, *Financial Politics in Contemporary Japan* (Ithaca: Cornell University Press, 1989); Louis Pauly, *Opening Financial Markets: Banking Politics on the Pacific Rim* (Ithaca: Cornell University Press, 1989); Andrew Carl Sobel, *Domestic Choices, International Markets* (Chicago: University of Chicago Press, 1994); and Steven Vogel, *Freer Markets, More Rules: The Paradox of Liberalization* (Ithaca: Cornell University Press, 1996).

[10] The debate over who governs Japan is still defined by Chalmers Johnson, *MITI and the Japanese Economic Miracle* (Stanford: Stanford University Press, 1982); with challenges to Johnson's view of bureaucratic dominance coming from Richard Samuels, *The Business of the Japanese State* (Ithaca: Cornell University Press, 1987) and Mark Ramseyer and Frances Rosenbluth, *Japan's Political Marketplace* (Cambridge: Harvard University Press, 1993).

[11] Philip Cerny, ed., *Finance and World Politics* (Aldershot: Edward Elgar Press, 1993), 10.

[12] See John Zysman, *Governments, Markets, and Growth* (Ithaca: Cornell University Press, 1983) on how financial market structure affects economic performance; and Jeffry Frieden, "Invested Interests: The Politics of National Economic Performance in a World of Global Capital," *International Organization* 45, no. 4 (1991): 425–451, for the distributional consequences of financial reform.

I. Financial Reform in Britain and Japan

From 1945 until the early 1970s, the capital markets of the world were domestic in orientation and well insulated from one another.[13] Financial services in both Britain and Japan were provided by government-sanctioned cartels. But beginning with the first eurocurrency issues in the late 1950s and early 1960s, international offshore markets for capital developed that were outside the jurisdiction of any one national regulatory authority and to which certain borrowers and lenders could turn. These international markets grew rapidly in the 1970s and 1980s.[14] Floating exchange rates, high inflation, increased cross-border trade, and advances in telecommunications and computing technology stimulated huge growth in cross-border financial flows.[15] For example, between 1973 and 1989 the stock of international loans grew from $175 billion (or 5 percent of aggregate GNP for all industrialized countries) to $2,490 billion (or 17 percent of aggregate GNP).[16] Most countries tried to maintain regulatory barriers between domestic and international markets, but these barriers gradually eroded. The result was that by the early 1980s it had become much easier for citizens or firms from almost any country to engage in financial transactions in other markets, although it was still possible to distinguish domestic from international markets.[17] This increased integration presented new and serious challenges to domestic regulators and policymakers.

In the 1980s both Britain and Japan radically reformed their national securities markets. The reforms were typically referred to as instances of deregulation or liberalization, but neither term is strictly accurate. While both governments abolished many existing regulations and cartelistic practices such as price-fixing, they introduced new rules or strengthened existing ones in other areas such as fraud prevention. In both countries the pat-

---

[13] For background, see David Meerschwam, *Breaking Financial Boundaries: Global Capital, National Deregulation, and Financial Service Firms* (Boston: Harvard Business School Press, 1991); and Samuel Hayes and Philip Hubbard, *Investment Banking: A Tale of Three Cities* (Boston: Harvard Business School Press, 1990). It is necessary to point out that the postwar period of closed national markets is by no means normal. Historically, there have been many periods in which capital was far more internationally mobile—most famously in the late nineteenth and early twentieth centuries, when the British financed a large part of America's industrial development and Baring Bank nearly went bust as a result of over-leveraged lending in Latin America.

[14] Ralph Bryant, *International Financial Mediation* (Washington, D.C.: Brookings Institution, 1987), 74. See also International Monetary Fund (IMF), *Determinants and Systemic Consequences of International Capital Flows* (Washington, D.C.: International Monetary Fund, 1991).

[15] The political aspects of this are addressed by Susan Strange, *Casino Capitalism* (Oxford: Blackwell, 1986), and Eric Helleiner, *States and the Reemergence of Global Finance: From Bretton Woods to the 1990s* (Ithaca: Cornell University Press, 1994), among others.

[16] IMF, *Determinants and Systemic Consequences*, 5.

[17] Which could either be a genuinely offshore market, such as the euromarkets, or another national market—that is, a Japanese investor buying U.S. Treasury bonds directly in New York. This distinction is developed in chapter 2.

tern of reforms was similar in that what was deregulated and what was more tightly regulated varied more by the specific regulatory issue concerned than by country.[18] This similarity is very marked despite the fact that the two countries are at opposite ends of the spectrum in terms of the organization of financial markets and of more general styles of regulation. As John Zysman observed, the two countries did not simply have different forms of financial system, they practically defined these forms, the United Kingdom as a competitive capital market and Japan as a government-administered credit-based system.[19] Ronald Dore, a sociologist, uses the two countries to define the competing styles of Anglo-Saxon versus Asian or Japanese-style capitalism.[20] The laissez-faire Britain of Margaret Thatcher could not have had a more different regulatory ideology than Japan's bureaucratic and interventionist developmental state.[21] Yet these distinctions do a poor job of predicting policy outcomes in the issue of financial market reform. The Thatcher government imposed one of the most far-reaching sets of new regulations on British capital markets in history, and the Japanese bureaucracy has been in the process of slowly but surely *dismantling* the regulatory structure of the financial system that had, according to John Zysman, Dore, and others, been directly responsible for Japan's postwar economic success. What explains these apparent anomalies? This book accounts for the fact that these two very different countries chose to implement the same pattern of policy reforms and also explains the pattern itself. To do so, it is first necessary to consider in more detail the reforms themselves.

Britain

Britain has been a major center for international finance since the seventeenth century, and in the postwar period London was host to some of the most exuberant developments in the eurocurrency markets.[22] Surprisingly,

[18] There were, of course, differences in both the degree and the method of reform across countries, as is emphasized by Vogel, *Freer Markets, More Rules*, and Sobel, *Domestic Choice, International Markets*. Briefly, my response is that these differences in detail are less significant substantively than are the similarities and, given the traditionally wide differences between the two countries in terms of regulatory policy, are less surprising theoretically.

[19] Zysman, *Governments, Markets, and Growth*.

[20] Ronald Dore, *Taking Japan Seriously: A Confucian Perspective on Economic Issues* (London: Athlone, 1987).

[21] The classic statement of bureaucratic dominance in Japan is of course Johnson, *MITI and the Japanese Miracle*. The particulars of his model have been challenged in a variety of ways; see, for example, Samuels, *Business of the Japanese State*; and Michio Muramatsu and Ellis Krauss, "The Conservative Policy Line and the Development of Patterned Pluralism," in *The Political Economy of Japan*, vol. 1, *The Domestic Transformation*, ed. Kozo Yamamura and Yusukichi Yasuba, (Stanford: Stanford University Press, 1987), 516–555. Even so, it is relatively uncontroversial that Japan has always been one of the more heavily regulated of the advanced industrial democracies, with one of the highest levels of government involvement in the economy.

[22] The euromarkets, sometimes called the off-shore markets, are those markets in which financial instruments such as stocks, bonds, or the currencies themselves are traded outside of their national jurisdiction. They are discussed in more detail in chapter 3.

however, the London Stock Exchange (LSE), serving as the main market for domestic British securities, remained insular and isolated until the 1980s.

In 1986 the British government liberalized the LSE. Previously the LSE had comprised a cartel of small member firms divided functionally between brokers, who took orders for securities from the public, and jobbers, who acted as wholesalers for stock, but were not permitted to deal directly with investors. No outsiders, either foreigners or even other British institutions such as the High Street (commercial) banks, were allowed to trade listed shares except through member firms. Service charges were controlled by a system of fixed commissions on brokerage trades. A single reform, somewhat grandiosely dubbed the Big Bang, abolished these arrangements and opened the exchange to competitive market forces. This reform was one of the centerpieces of Thatcherite deregulation, although it was one in which Thatcher herself took little personal interest. The Big Bang increased openness and market access to any participant. It dismantled the system of functional segregation and abolished price controls. Separate reforms increased the number and diversity of financial products such as futures, options, and other derivatives that could be traded, and liberalized the restrictions on trading them. Most significant was the establishment of the London International Financial Futures Exchange (LIFFE) in 1981.

The cumulative effects of these reforms were predictable: the number and size of participants in the market grew, competition increased, and average transaction costs fell. It is important to note, however, that the reforms benefited larger financial institutions significantly more than small firms and individual investors. To illustrate, the old system of fixed commissions had cross-subsidized private investors at the expense of institutional investors; liberalization resulted in lower trading costs for large customers, but much higher costs for small ones.

More or less simultaneously, however, the Financial Services Act of 1986 introduced stricter rules governing business practices. Standards of professional conduct were raised by the introduction of new examinations and licenses for all industry participants. To give one example, brokers were required to pass a registered representatives examination before they were allowed to trade or give advice to clients. Transparency and disclosure laws were tightened; for example, brokers were required to time-stamp deal tickets for clients in order to be able to demonstrate that they had traded at the best prevailing price. Market makers were obliged to publish constant firm prices for any stocks that they had declared that they would trade.[23] The obligations of intermediaries to their clients were, in many cases for the first time, defined fully and formally. The new law imposed criminal sanctions for misconduct. For example, it became illegal for

[23] A firm price is one at which the market maker is obliged to deal, as opposed to an indicative price, also known as a level, at which the market maker may choose to deal.

a broker to "churn" a client's account by making unnecessary trades to gain commission revenues. Potential conflicts of interest were addressed by regulations requiring financial services companies to isolate their different departments from each other using "Chinese walls," known in America as "fire walls."[24] To illustrate, a firm's brokerage department, which gives stock recommendations to clients, should be kept entirely separate from the trading department, since knowledge about the firm's own trading positions could undermine the brokers' obligation to give unbiased advice. In particular, the possibilities of fraud or market manipulation were taken very seriously, and many measures were taken to protect the rights of shareholders. Insider trading is perhaps the most obvious unfair business practice. It was criminalized in 1980, with stiffer penalties and broader definitions being added thereafter. It is interesting, however, that various other practices that are logically just as unfair, such as share-support operations during takeovers, were allowed to stand.[25] It soon became apparent, in fact, that the new concern for investor protection extended far more to institutional investors than to individuals.

A centerpiece of the reforms was the introduction of a new structure of regulatory supervision. Informal self-regulation by practitioners was replaced by a series of formally organized self-regulatory organizations (SROs), all subordinate to a new regulatory agency, the Securities and Investments Board (SIB), created by the Financial Services Act in 1986. The SIB was modeled on America's Securities and Exchange Commission (SEC). Its main role was to be a watchdog to ensure that firms complied with the new rules. Its establishment demonstrated a marked determination by the government to police the markets more strongly than hitherto.

In summary, then, reform in Britain developed in two different directions. Deregulation occurred in some areas including market access, intra-market competition, price controls, and product diversity. At the same time, strict new regulations were introduced in other areas, including professional standards and conduct, transparency and disclosure, investor protection, and the protection of shareholder rights.

Japan

A similar pattern of reforms became evident in Japan in the 1980s. There was liberalization in the same issue areas of price and competition, and stricter regulation in areas of transparency, market supervision, and in-

[24] The concepts of moral hazard and conflict of interest are discussed in greater detail in chapter 2.

[25] Share-support operations usually involve groups of investors coordinating their buying programs to keep the price of a share artificially high during a takeover, with the result that the company making the takeover attempt has to pay more for it. Alternatively, the company making the takeover can also attempt to use a share-support operation to make its offer appear more attractive to the shareholders of its target.

vestor protection. Japan's financial system prior to the 1970s was one of the most heavily regulated and uncompetitive of any comparable economy.[26] The Ministry of Finance (MOF) exercised unrivaled domination over private intermediaries.[27] However, Japan undertook reforms throughout the 1980s to make its markets more open and competitive. The Tokyo Stock Exchange (TSE), previously a cartel similar to the LSE, was opened up in 1986 to allow six foreign companies to become full members. Sixteen more foreign members were admitted in 1988. Reforms lowered commission rates for all stock exchange trading and deregulated them entirely for large institutional trades. Markets for financial futures and other derivatives were introduced: trading in Japanese government bond futures began in Tokyo in 1985, and the Nikkei Stock Index future was introduced in 1987. The Tokyo International Financial Futures Exchange (TIFFE) was established in 1989.

The major barrier to internal competition had long been Article 65 of the Japanese Securities and Exchange Law of 1947. This rule was modeled on the U.S.'s Glass-Steagall Act, which separates investment from commercial banks. As with the U.S. law, Article 65 has been steadily eroded, blurring the once clear divisions between securities companies and banks. The subsidiaries of certain banks are now allowed to trade and underwrite securities, and subsidiaries of securities companies have been allowed into banking. Other forms of functional segmentation, such as those defining which firms are allowed to conduct foreign exchange, fund management, or trust banking business, have been weakened or scrapped.

In short, in common with the British, the Japanese have considerably liberalized market access, intramarket competition, price controls, and product diversity. Most commentators agree that, while differences still remain, Japan's market is far more competitive than it was in the 1980s and that it much more closely resembles Britain's and America's.[28]

At the same time, the Japanese government introduced new regulations and began to enforce more seriously existing ones governing transparency, disclosure, and investor protection. For example, the threshold at which a firm must publicly declare a stake in another firm has been lowered dramatically to 5 percent. Competitive examinations for industry professionals were introduced in the 1980s and are being taken seriously. Conflict-of-interest problems have also been addressed: fire walls to separate different departments of the same firm were made mandatory in 1987. The preven-

---

[26] For background, see Steven Bronte, *Japan's Financial Markets* (London: Euromoney Publications, 1982), or Royama Shoichi, *Nihon no Kinyu Shisutemu* [Japan's financial system] (Tokyo: Toyo Keizai Shimbunsha, 1985).

[27] Kawakita Takako, *Okurasho: Kanryō Kikō no Chōten* [Ministry of Finance: Pinacle of the bureaucratic system] (Tokyo: Kodansha, 1989).

[28] See, for example, Shinkai Yoichi, "The Internationalization of Finance in Japan" in *The Political Economy of Japan*, vol. 2, *The Changing International Context*, ed. Inoguchi Takashi and Daniel Okimoto (Stanford: Stanford University Press, 1988), 249–275.

tion of fraud and the protection of property rights have also been the subject of regulation. Insider trading was criminalized in 1989.[29] This action was particularly startling in a country where, prior to the 1980s, the practice of insider dealing had been commonplace and had never been regarded as particularly unethical. Many previously commonplace forms of market manipulation have been prohibited, including the practice of price ramping. The practice of fund managers guaranteeing large clients a set rate of return and compensating them for portfolio losses has also been banned.[30]

As in Britain, the traditional informal system of regulatory oversight has been called into question. Unlike British self-regulation, the Japanese have historically relied on close but informal oversight and guidance by the MOF. Yet scandals in the late 1980s revealed considerable public dissatisfaction with this arrangement. A new bureaucratic agency, the *Shoken torihiki kanshi i inkai* (Securities and Exchange Surveillance Commission, SESC), which, similar to Britain's SIB, was modeled in large part on America's SEC, was established in 1992. It provides a more formal and independent supervision of the markets.

In short, as in Britain, there has been a move toward tighter regulation in areas of professional standards, transparency and disclosure, and investor protection, especially on issues of protecting property rights and preventing conflicts of interest and fraud.

Reform and Mobile-Asset Holders

There has been a clear trend in Britain and Japan since the 1980s toward greater openness of markets to both users of financial services, including borrowers and investors, and to service providers, including banks and securities companies; greater intramarket competition between different service providers; greater variety and complexity of financial instruments that may be traded; more price competition; and higher standards for the protection of shareholder rights and for investor protection, especially by means of formal regulation. This concern includes a shift toward greater transparency requirements, such as stricter disclosure rules as the basis for safety and soundness regulation, and a decreased tolerance of fraud or market manipulation. Finally, both countries established new regulatory bodies to police and oversee their markets. These trends are summarized in Table 1.1.

The interests of one particular interest group, the consumers of mobile financial services, have been best served by these reforms, which have simultaneously promoted competition and increased standards of transparency and investor protection. This group of consumers includes both large institutional investors and large corporate borrowers. They have ben-

---

[29] See Nihon Keizai Shimbunsha, *Insaida Tengoku: Kenshō Nihon Kabushiki Shijo* [Insiders' paradise: The Japanese stock markets] (Tokyo: Nihon Keizai Shimbun, 1988).

[30] A price ramp involves a coordinated buying program by a broker or a group of speculators that pushes the price of a selected stock up artificially in the short term.

Table 1.1. Trends in securities market reform, 1980–1999

Issue Area	Description	Example	Reform U.K.	Reform Japan	Trend
Market access	Who is allowed to trade in the market?	Stock exchange membership	Big Bang 1986	*Biggu Ban* opens TSE, 1996	Liberalizing
Intramarket competition	In which business areas can different firms participate?	Segregation of commercial and investment banking	Abolition of single capacity	Erosion of Article 65	Liberalizing
Product diversity	What financial instruments may be traded, and by whom?	Trading of futures, options and other derivatives	LIFFE established 1982	TIFFE established 1989	Liberalizing
Price controls	Are prices set by regulation or by the market?	Fixed *vs.* negotiated brokerage commissions on stock trades	Fixed commissions abolished in 1986	Fixed commissions abolished in 1996	Liberalizing
Consumer protection	What constitutes fraud, and what is acceptable business practice?	Permissibility of insider trading	Insider trading criminalized in 1980	Insider trading criminalized in 1989	Stronger regulations
Regulatory oversight	Who oversees the market?	Which regulatory agency is responsible for enforcing laws?	SIB, 1986	SESC, 1992; FSA, 1998	Stronger regulations

Note: Abbreviations: FSA, Financial Supervisory Agency; LIFFE, London International Financial Futures Exchange; SESC, Securities and Exchange Surveillance Commission; SIB, Securities and Investments Board; TIFFE, Tokyo International Financial Futures Exchange; TSE, Tokyo Stock Exchange.

efited most through increased competition in financial services, which has had the most significant effect of lowered costs on large and international transactions. Increased competition has come through a dramatic reduction in the intermarket and intramarket barriers among sellers of financial services, through a steady expansion of the variety of products on offer, and through systematic attempts to encourage greater depth and liquidity in secondary markets for these products. On the downside, there has been a concurrent increase in externalities such as systemic risk. Unrestricted trading, whether it be in currencies or derivatives, can be hazardous not just to the health of individual firms, but to the stability of the entire financial system, as the 1998 collapse of the U.S. hedge fund Long Term Capital Management, the 1996 fall of Baring Brothers in Singapore, and the 1997–98 East Asian currency crisis all demonstrate. However, the costs of insuring against such risks are borne, at least in part, by governments and therefore by taxpayers, while the benefits of unrestricted trading accrue solely to the private firms.

On the other side of the regulatory coin, safety and soundness regulations have also been reformed in the interests of large mobile-asset investors. Investor protection is decreasingly provided by structure and increasingly by government-administered regulation (e.g., through heightened disclosure requirements). The result of this shift is that all taxpayers, rather than the consumers of financial services, bear the costs of regulation. In general, the shift in safety and soundness regulation has been toward strengthening the power of the shareholders (the most-mobile-asset group) at the expense of management, labor, and less-mobile-asset holders such as bank lenders. One example has been fraud rules, which have vastly strengthened the property rights of a shareholders vis-à-vis other groups.[31]

Small investors, paradoxically, have generally either lost out or done less well from the reforms. In both Britain and Japan, small investors have been the beneficiaries of the traditional regulatory structures, benefiting both from cross-subsidization and from the structural regulatory protection given by functional segmentation and high barriers to entry. In some instances it is true that small investors have also benefited from increased competition or from improvement in regulatory structures, but usually they have benefited relatively less than the big institutions. In other cases, notably with trading costs on the LSE, small investors are worse off not just relatively, but in absolute terms: They are paying more than before for the same services. In both countries, endless financial scandals show that the new regulations have not adequately replaced the old structural protections that were abolished in the name of efficiency.

---

[31] The logic of the prohibitions on insider trading, for example, is that private corporate information should be the property of shareholders and not, for example, of the managers or employees of the corporation. This does not produce an objectively more fair outcome, merely one in which profit opportunities have been transferred from corporate managers to the group of most-mobile-asset holders—institutional investors.

II. The Argument

The pattern of reforms described in the preceding section is best explained by the increased internationalization of finance, which has systematically benefited the holders of mobile assets at the expense of regulators and the holders of less-mobile assets. Internationalization clearly allows some economic actors to exit one political marketplace and enter another if regulations or policies are not to their liking.[32] This clearly enhances the ability of these mobile-asset holders to influence the regulatory process both in their home countries and abroad. Robert Keohane and Helen Milner, political scientists, state: "Those who can exit can use the threat of exit to magnify their political influence, or 'voice.'"[33] If this is true, it might be expected that regulatory reforms should favor the holders of more-mobile assets at the expense of the holders of less-mobile assets. In other words, power has shifted in favor of "the managers and owners of financial assets and transnational corporations."[34]

To demonstrate how this power shift takes place, I show in the following sections how traditional models of regulatory politics make the crucial assumption that actor voice rather than actor exit is the key influence on policy outcomes. I then present a simplified model of the Stigler-Peltzman economic theory of regulation, which includes that assumption. This model is indeed able to explain regulatory policies in both Britain and Japan until the 1970s, when political marketplaces were closed in the sense that few economic actors had the option of leaving the country. In both countries, governments sanctioned uncompetitive cartels that benefited banks and brokers at the expense of the users of services. Following this discussion I explore the difference that globalization, or a shift to more-open political marketplaces, would make to models of regulatory politics in general and to financial markets in particular. Finally I offer two measures of asset mobility and elaborate on the distinctive policy preferences of the holders of mobile and immobile assets.

Regulatory Politics in Closed Political Markets

In traditional theories of regulatory politics, there is usually only one political arena in which bargains are struck. In a democracy, this arena is usually the parliament. Actors such as political parties and interest groups compete with one another for the prizes of favorable regulatory policies. The amount

[32] See for example, David Dollar and Jeffry Frieden, "The Political Economy of Financial Deregulation in the United States and Japan," in *La finanza americana fre euforia e crisi*, ed. Giacomo Luciani (Rome: Olivetti, 1989), 74–102; Frieden, "Invested Interests"; James Alt and Michael Gilligan, "The Political Economy of Trading States: Factor Specificity, Collective Action Problems, and Domestic Political Institution," *Journal of Political Philosophy* 2 (1994): 165–192, and Keohane and Milner, *Internationalization and Domestic Politics*.

[33] Keohane and Milner, *Internationalization and Domestic Politics*, 29–30.

[34] Paulette Kurzer, *Business and Banking: Political Change and Economic Integration in Western Europe* (Ithaca: Cornell University Press, 1993), 20.

of their political resources determines their success. Political resources come in the form of votes, money, or ideas, and much of the literature on regulatory politics focuses on identifying which resources are most efficacious and under what circumstances. Resources aside, the ability of actors to lobby effectively is further affected by their ability to organize and overcome collective-action problems, and this capability is in turn affected by their number, geographic concentration and institutional access to policymakers. An important but often implicit assumption of such theories is that the political marketplace is closed, and that all of the actors must abide by all of the regulatory outcomes. In the political marketplace, to use the typology of Albert Hirschman, an economist, exit is not an option, or at any rate a very costly one, so voice is consequently important. The key to explaining regulatory outcomes under these assumptions is to determine who has the most political resources and therefore the loudest voice.[35] George Stigler suggests that producer groups will be favored over consumers due to their superior organizational ability. This is a function of their relatively higher concentration, smaller number, and proportionately greater stakes in the outcome, which allow them to overcome collective-action problems and lobby effectively.

Regulatory Politics in Interdependent Markets

The effect of internationalization has been to allow the consumers of financial services, both borrowers and lenders, to escape the constraints of the regulators and the clutches of the producer cartels. This means that the old power imbalance between regulators and intermediaries over consumers has become increasingly irrelevant. It was not so much that the political power of the consumers increased, as that their need for political power decreased. In fact, it was the intermediaries who were often at the forefront of lobbying efforts to persuade regulators to rewrite regulations that were unacceptable to their biggest customers. The regulators went along with such requests partly because this was the least bad option available to them, and partly because they also had motivations to attract mobile-asset holders. Which consumers in particular benefited the most from the reforms? In the issue of securities regulation, both borrowers and investors benefited, but actors of both groups holding the largest and most mobile assets benefited most.[36]

---

[35] This is the essence of Stigler's model. Producer groups will be favored due to their lobbying power, which is a function of their higher relative concentration, small number, and proportionally greater stakes, which allow them to overcome collective-action problems and lobby effectively. Thus regulations will favor them at the expense of less politically powerful actors such as consumers or taxpayers. See Stigler, "The Theory of Economic Regulation."

[36] The idea is present in Rosenbluth's study of the effects of the euromarkets on Japanese banking deregulation. She writes that "banks were forced by their own self-interest to relax domestic issuance rules because corporations had the alternative of the Euromarket. The changes, in other words, did not reflect either declining political influence of banks or independent MOF planning." Rosenbluth, *Financial Politics in Contemporary Japan*, 163. In this respect I am not proposing a new idea, but am testing its implications against new evidence and across different countries.

Mobile Assets

How does one measure mobility? Jeffry Frieden suggests looking at the specificity of the assets in question: the more specific the asset, then the less mobile it is.[37] Capital is more mobile than labor, which is more mobile than land. Among capital assets, direct investments such as production plants are less mobile than portfolios of stocks, bonds, or currencies. Assets for which there are large, liquid markets, such as dollar denominated bonds, confer the greatest mobility of all. The abstract nature of financial transactions also makes consumers of financial services more mobile than producers, since consumers incur fewer of the fixed costs of establishing a physical presence in all of the markets in which they wish to transact. For example, a brokerage wishing to operate in Singapore needs to acquire office space, dealing equipment, local staff, and so on. An investor wishing to buy stocks quoted in Singapore needs only a phone to do so from anywhere in the world.

In financial markets, mobility is also a function of size because many of the costs of transaction in international markets are high and fixed. Therefore international transactions will be relatively cheaper if they are done on a large scale. Consider a couple of simple examples. On the borrowing side, a small unknown company making its first eurobond issue will pay a relatively higher price than a large multinational company with a strong international reputation. On the investing side, a large pension fund with a high volume of trading will pay relatively less in brokers' commissions than a single investor making a few small trades.

If mobility is a function of asset specificity and size, then the most mobile lenders will be large portfolio investors, also known as institutional investors, a group that includes insurance companies, pension funds, mutual and hedge funds, and the trading and fund management departments of investment banks. The most mobile borrowers will be large multinational corporations. More precise and country-specific details of these actors are provided in later chapters.

Preferences of Mobile-Asset Holders

What are the distinctive interests of the holders of more-mobile assets? As do all consumers, they prefer lower prices for and greater choice in the products or services they are buying. However, as potential customers in new markets, they will also be particularly concerned with issues of cross-national harmonization, transparency, and strong protection of property rights. Their preferences will thus be for the following mix of regulatory outcomes.

1. Lower transaction costs. They desire greater competition among intermediaries, which will drive down service charges. Greater competition can be encouraged by lower barriers to entry to the securities industry, and lower functional barriers within it. Large consumers with greater buying

---

[37] Frieden, "Invested Interests."

power will probably prefer to negotiate prices with intermediaries rather than operate in a system of fixed prices.

2. More choice. The ability to diversify and spread risk is vital for portfolio investors, and therefore they should want both increased market access and greater diversity in the financial instruments that they can trade. Borrowers benefit from a greater array of financing options to match their borrowing needs.

3. Clarity and predictability of rules and regulations. Part of the costs of investing or borrowing in a new market or with a new instrument are the search costs associated with becoming acquainted with the rules and business practices of the local marketplace. Those who wish to transact in new markets, both investors and borrowers, usually prefer foreign market rules and regulations that are as formalized and plain as possible, so that they are not put at a competitive disadvantage in relation to local actors. They will also have some interest in the standardization of regulations across countries, since this too will lower search costs.

4. Strong consumer-protection measures. Investors will look for the stringent protection of property rights. Foreign investors or borrowers are at a natural disadvantage when transacting with locals, so those who wish to enter foreign markets have strong incentives to demand that their rights as consumers be protected.

Note that consumer protection in item 4 can be provided in a variety of ways, each of which distributes the costs and benefits of the regulation somewhat differently. For example, structural safeguards against abuse such as the functional segmentation of markets provide excellent and universal safeguards against conflicts of interest, but result in diminished competition and higher costs for all consumers. However, if the same conflict-of-interest problems are addressed by a system of increased regulatory surveillance and stiff criminal penalties for transgressors, then relatively more of the cost will be borne by the state, and relatively less by the actual consumers.

To illustrate the differential effect of investor protection regulation on different classes of investor, consider a classic instance of investor protection: the prohibition on insider trading. The popular misconception is that a ban on this practice primarily benefits ordinary investors. In fact, the real beneficiaries of such a prohibition are more likely to be professional liquidity traders and institutional investors.[38] These professionals engage in relatively more short-term trading than ordinary investors and are therefore

---

[38] See, for example, Jonathan Macey, *Insider Trading: Economics, Politics and Policy* (Washington, D.C.: American Enterprise Institute, 1991); Dan Bernhardt, Burton Hollifield, and Eric Hughson, *Investment and Insider Trading*, Social Science Working Paper 830 (Pasadena: California Institute of Technology, 1993); David Haddock and Jonathan Macey, "Controlling Insider Trading in Europe and America: The Economics of the Politics," in *Law and Economics and the Economics of Legal Reregulation*, Graf van der Schwelenburg and Golan Skogh (Dordrecht: Kluwer Academic, 1988), 155–165; and Henry Laurence, "Inside Track," *The Economist*, 6 August 1994, 8.

more vulnerable to trading losses at the hands of the better-informed. Conversely, professional traders are best able to exploit the short-term arbitrage possibilities that arise when insider trading is banned. To illustrate, imagine that a company announces a takeover bid that sends its share price rocketing. The people who can most easily cash in on this price jump are the traders who constantly track price movements and monitor news services and who have the technical capacity to deal immediately, not the ordinary investors who don't follow the market on a minute-by-minute basis. The benefits of a ban on insider trading for private investors who are not frequent traders are, thus, relatively few. The legal and bureaucratic costs of enforcing the ban, however, can be high and are borne by the state.[39] The costs to intermediaries of complying with the prohibition may also be high and will be spread equally among all of the intermediaries' customers, professionals and small investors alike. In fact, the view that a ban on insider trading may not be in society's best interests is becoming more popular, at least in Britain. The Labour Party's city spokesman, Alistair Darling, announced in 1996 that he would consider scrapping Britain's insider trading laws if doing so would encourage long-term investment at the expense of short-term speculative investment.[40]

Preferences of Immobile-Asset Holders

Immobile-asset holders may be divided into two groups, producers (sellers) of services, and consumers of services. In finance, the immobile-asset producers are the financial intermediaries: the banks, brokers, and securities houses. These are the actors who the Stigler-Peltzman model of regulatory capture predicts will be able to secure favorable regulation. In their cases, favorable regulation will include high barriers to competition both from inside the industry and outside, which allow producers to capture rents. Sure enough, in the period of closed international markets from the 1940s to the 1970s, financial services in both Britain and Japan were characterized by cartelistic or oligopolistic practices, exactly as the Stigler-Peltzman model would predict. The details varied but in both cases producer groups were favored over consumers of all sizes. In the absence of financial openness, there is no reason to suppose that the banks and brokers would have preferred any other outcome.

While the major beneficiaries of financial regulation in the preinternationalization era were producers, small consumers of financial services benefited rather more than large users. Small investors and small borrowers generally benefit more from regulatory structures that afford automatic protections against problems of moral hazard and adverse selection. Often

---

[39] At least, this is true in Britain and Japan. In the United States, the government-incurred costs of enforcing financial regulations such as insider trading have been offset in recent years by the tidy profit that the SEC has been able to turn on its fines.

[40] Anthony Harris, "At Long Last, a Darling Idea from Labour," *The Times* (London), 1 May 1996, 6.

structural protection takes the form of functional segmentation in the financial services industry: different firms provide different services rather than having a universal system in which one company provides all services under one roof. The separation between brokers and jobbers on the U.K. stock exchange, discussed in chapter 4, is one such protection. The division between investment and commercial banks affords another such structural protection. Protection against conflicts of interest is provided automatically, so the information asymmetries between individual consumers and large corporate providers of investment services are not a problem. On the other hand, such functional segmentation is inefficient in the sense that the markets are not as streamlined or consolidated as they could be. Thus, the downside of the quest for greater market efficiency, which benefits large users of financial services, is typically a loss of structural protection benefiting small users.

Small users of financial services usually also benefit from the imposition of price controls, which often result in cross-subsidization of small consumers by large ones. This is because financial services is a business in which marginal revenues rise much more quickly than do marginal costs as trading volumes increase. The costs to a bank or brokerage firm of holding a deposit or settling a trade are very similar whether the transaction amount is $100 or $100,000. However, the returns to the bank from the $100,000 trade will be significantly higher. Therefore, in the absence of regulation, financial service providers will find it much more profitable to attract large institutional business than retail business. This will be reflected in price structures that force retail consumers to pay a much higher rate for their services.

Last, a word on what small-scale consumers don't care about. There is no reason for them to care about the harmonization of their country's regulations with those of other countries, since they will probably never need to transact in another country. Moreover, they will be relatively less concerned about increasing the depth and liquidity of futures and options markets, which have high relative transaction costs because they will not usually be planning to use such markets.

We might expect that internationalization will result in the potential migration of mobile-asset holders to jurisdictions with regulations that provide the benefits discussed. In the field of financial services, these mobile-asset holders will seek regulatory structures that encourage greater competition, increased access to markets, greater product choice, and lower transaction costs. They will also seek enhanced investor protection, and greater clarity and formality of rules and regulatory structures. Hence we might expect individual nation-states to reform their markets in a way that meets this pattern of preferences. States might undertake such reforms either to attract new business from abroad, to prevent the flight of existing domestic business, or both. As the case studies in this book reveal, financial internationalization was indeed followed by a series of reforms that closely matched this pattern of mobile-asset actor preferences.

Mechanisms for Change

So how did globalization translate into increased political power for economically mobile users of financial services? There are various related, but
analytically distinct, pathways of influence through which mobility was
turned to political advantage.

Threat of Exit

The first broad group of mechanisms centers on the political consequences of internationalization and in particular on the opportunity it gives
some actors to escape domestic regulations and conduct business in new jurisdictions. This threat of exit plays into political outcomes in a variety of
ways, which can be separated into two broad categories. The first category
contains those cases in which patterns of influence run directly from mobile-
asset holders such as international investors to policymakers. The second
category contains cases in which the new political influence of mobile-asset
consumers of services is indirect and is facilitated through the efforts of financial service providers. In these cases, it is immobile-asset producers who
lobby policymakers on behalf of mobile-asset consumers, whose business
the service providers want to keep or to win.

In the category of direct patterns of influence, there are three distinct
pathways to regulatory reform. First, mobile-asset actors can use the credible threat that they will leave the country as a bargaining chip in negotiating
with policymakers. In this way, the threat of exit gives mobile-asset actors a
louder voice in the political marketplace and translates into more favorable
regulatory outcomes for these actors. But they do not even have to make
threats. Policymakers are well aware that important economic actors can
leave the country, so they may make preemptive regulatory concessions to
mobile actors in order to prevent an unwinnable political battle. Finally,
policymakers may be forced to make reactive regulatory reforms in order to
entice mobile-asset actors who have already left the country to return home.

In the category of indirect influence are those cases in which less-mobile-
asset actors, here the providers of financial services, lobby policymakers to
reform regulations in ways that will keep their mobile-asset customers from
deserting them. Paradoxically, this results in producer groups demanding
regulatory reforms that at first glance appear to be the exact opposite of
their interests. The Big Bang accord, whereby the LSE cartel agreed to dis-
mantle itself, is the most spectacular but by no means the only example of
such indirect influence. Logically, as with the category of direct influence,
producers' demands for reform can be both preemptive, for the purpose of
preserving business, and reactive, in an attempt to win it back. In the real
world, of course, it is more difficult to make such a distinction, since both
occur simultaneously.

There are several well-documented cases in which large-scale users of financial services, both borrowers and lenders, exploited the increased opportunities created by financial market openness either to escape unfavorable

domestic regulations or to pressure their governments into reform. The threat of exit by institutional investors in the United Kingdom sealed the fate of the LSE cartel and forced the pace of reform. The perceived need to improve investor-protection measures prompted the British Parliament to enact the Financial Services Act in 1986. The subsequent history of the act showed that the authorities took investor protection measures for institutions far more seriously than measures to protect individuals. In Japan, the threat of exit by corporate borrowers increased the pace of liberalization of the securities market. The need felt by Japanese authorities to attract foreign institutional investors and maintain a good international reputation also stimulated a new and wholly unprecedented concern for investor protection.

Promise of Entry

The second broad group of mechanisms by which internationalization affects political outcomes are the influences of foreign mobile-asset actors on domestic regulations. In a sense, this is the reverse of the previous group: instead of producers and regulators contending with the threat of exit of mobile-asset domestic actors, they are concerned with the promise of entry. This involves attracting the business of mobile foreign firms. The path of influence may go directly from the mobile-asset consumers to the regulators, as when policymakers decide to reform their markets so as to make them attractive to foreign businesses. The Bank of England's expressed desire to make London an international financial center was such a case. This desire had little, if anything, to do with specific direct pressure from British firms to attract foreign competition. Alternatively, the pathway might be indirect, as when domestic producers lobby for regulatory reforms that will bring in new business for them. The desire of Japanese financial institutions to attract American investors reinforced the pressure on the MOF to establish a new, improved supervisory agency modeled on America's well-respected SEC.

International Connections among Regulators

The third broad category of influence focuses on how internationalization prompts changes in relations among national regulators. Internationalization produces opportunities for firms to escape regulatory oversight, which therefore produces incentives for regulators to win back control. In addition, domestic constituents who feel put at a disadvantage by the regulatory structure of another country in which they wish to conduct business will lobby regulators and politicians. Such constituents may demand that their national governments support them in trying to bring about reform in these other countries. Regulators thus have multiple, sometimes conflicting incentives to pressure their opposite numbers in other countries. They can do so in two ways, either coercively or cooperatively. Instances of coercive pressure include British and American demands that Japan open its stock market to foreign membership and the liberalization of the euroyen market following the Yen–Dollar talks of 1984. Instances of cooperation include the increasing use of memoranda of understanding between national regulators to combat insider trading and other financial fraud cases.

Hostages and Divided Loyalties

The final category in which internationalization alters domestic politics concerns the shifts in private firms' political allegiances and regulatory preferences when they open branches or subsidiaries in foreign countries. First, these subsidiaries will typically be under the jurisdiction, and therefore the control, of a foreign government. This makes such subsidiaries prime targets as hostages in the event of a regulatory dispute between the host and home countries. The threat by the Bank of England and the U.S. Treasury that the subsidiaries of leading Japanese securities companies would not be granted dealers' privileges in the U.K. and U.S. government bond markets unless the Japanese authorities enacted reciprocal reforms for British and U.S. firms is one example. The harsh punishment meted out to Japan's Daiwa Bank and its U.S. subsidiary following the revelations that it had concealed trading losses in New York in 1996 is another such case.

Moreover, as firms expand overseas, their preferences change. Most obviously, firms that conduct business in many different markets would probably prefer broadly similar regulations and regulatory institutions in the various countries in which they do business. Such harmonization would presumably lower both the search costs of determining exactly what is or is not legal in a new country and the compliance costs of conforming with the various different regulations. For example, if accounting standards are not harmonized, then a firm must produce a different balance sheet for each country in which it wants to list shares. If there is one commonly accepted standard, then the firm needs to produce only one. In addition, firms planning to invest in new markets will seek assurances that their property rights will enjoy the same level of protection abroad that they have at home. Markets that provide such assurances will consequently be more attractive to them.

Winner and Losers in the Reform Process

Regulatory policies in both Britain and Japan have been shifting toward strengthening the power of mobile-asset holders, including institutional investors and corporate borrowers, at the expense of less-mobile-asset holders, including providers of financial services (banks, brokers, and securities companies) and small, relatively immobile-asset consumers of financial services such as individual investors. Mobile-asset holders have benefited in a number of ways from regulatory reform. First, they have benefited from increased market competition. Such competition has been encouraged by the lowering of intermarket and intramarket (or internal and external) barriers to entry among producers. Examples include the erosion of Article 65 in Japan, the abolition of single capacity through the Big Bang in the United Kingdom, and the entry of foreigners into both exchanges. Financial service intermediaries, both banks and investment banks/securities companies, now bear more of the costs and secure fewer of the rents of transactions. The second, closely related benefit to large investors and borrowers has been the vastly increased number and variety of available financial products. Such products, including futures, options, and other derivatives, have lowered transaction costs and given greater possibilities for diversification and speculative trading. The increase in such product diversity was achieved at the cost of a concurrent increase in the externalities of systemic risk and over-trading, but the risks and costs of both are born primarily by governments. Greater clarity in regulations has benefited large users of financial services. Finally, the move to a system of investor protection provided by govern-ment-administered regulation rather than by structure has been of direct benefit to institutional as opposed to private investors. One example of this trend has been fraud rules, which have vastly strengthened the property rights of shareholders vis-à-vis other groups. The logic of prohibitions on insider trading, for example, is that private corporate information should be the property of shareholders and not, for example, the managers or employ-ees of the corporation.

Smaller consumers of financial services, in contrast, have also lost out relative to big institutions. Small investors had in most cases been the beneficiaries of the old systems, benefiting both from cross-subsidization and from the structural regulatory protection given by functional seg-mentation and high entry barriers. In some instances, it is true, small in-vestors have also benefited from increased competition or from the im-provement in regulatory structures, but usually they have benefited relatively less than the big institutions. In other instances, notably over dealing costs on the LSE, they are worse off in absolute, not just relative, terms, since they are now paying more for the same services. The litany of financial scandals in both countries makes it clear that reregulation has not done an adequate job of replacing the structural protections of the old systems, which were done away with in the interests of lower transaction costs.

I should add some caveats. My argument is intended to explain the relative shift in regulatory outcomes that favor the more-mobile-asset players. It does not explain every aspect of the regulatory reform, nor does it offer a complete causal account of the reform process. In some instances, reforms were under-taken for reasons other than to benefit mobile asset holders. In both the Japanese and, to a lesser extent, the British cases, deregulation of the securi-ties markets was prompted by fiscal imperatives, specifically the need for a more efficient market for government bonds to help fund growing budget deficits. Populist outrage in reaction to financial scandals and malpractice also encouraged reform in both countries, most notably in the loss compen-sation scandals in Japan in 1991. Even there, public demands for reform dovetailed nicely with what institutional investors wanted anyway. In the Japanese case, pressure by the Group of Seven and the United States for the Japanese to liberalize their financial markets and recycle their trade surpluses acted as an important and independent agent for change, although I argue that the pressure was most effective when it coincided with the interests of the dissatisfied domestic actors who play the central role in my account.

Moreover, there are differences in the timing and content of the reforms and the process by which they were undertaken that my argument cannot explain, and these are best accounted for by unique domestic-level political variables. The power of the MOF in Japan and its strong desire to maintain control over the financial system stand in contrast to the relatively weak British regulators at the Bank of England who were more ideologically disposed to favor free markets.[41] These differences help account for the slower and less thorough-going deregulation in the Japanese case. Nonetheless, in highlighting the common mechanisms for change, my argument captures an important aspect of the relationship between globalization and reform that is not fully appreciated in the literature on international political economy.

III. Research Design

Examining the major regulatory changes in two dissimilar countries in the same issue area—securities-market regulations—provides a good test for my hypothesis on the effect of internationalization on domestic politics. Finance is one of the areas in which internationalization has been most advanced, and we therefore expect that it is in this area, if anywhere, that the effects of internationalization will be most clearly seen. This should be borne in mind when considering the findings. Financial regulations are something of an easy case for theories that predict that the effects of internationalization on domestic politics will be great. If international factors do not appear to have had any independent effect on domestic regulations, then this is powerful evidence for theories that assert the primacy of domestic political factors in explaining regulatory policies. However, the bias in my case selection against domestic explanations is mitigated by the fact that Britain and Japan are hard cases for international theories since they have been chosen to represent the opposite extremes of the issue of financial market regulation. It would truly be surprising and counterintuitive to find regulatory policy convergence between these two countries in this period.

Case Selection

Since the number and complexity of the reforms would be too long to list in detail, I will focus on a representative set of the most important reforms. In regulating financial markets, six broad issues must be addressed:

[41] This important difference is especially emphasized by Steven Vogel, *Freer Markets, More Rules.*

1. Access: Who or what type of firms are allowed into the market? (What external barriers to entry are desirable?)

2. Functional or intramarket competition: What services will these firms be allowed to provide, and what is the appropriate degree of competition within the market? (What internal barriers to entry are desirable?)

3. Price structure: How are prices to be determined, by the market mechanism or by some other method such as a system of government-administered prices?

4. Product diversity: What products can be offered and traded? What restrictions, if any, should be placed on who is allowed to buy or sell what particular product?

5. Consumer protection: What constitutes acceptable business practice and what constitutes fraud? Is there a need for more protection against fraud than the market dictum caveat emptor? What should this level of protection be?

6. Oversight: Which organization or organizations should be responsible for overseeing the markets and ensuring that the regulations are followed? Is such oversight best provided by self-regulation or by the government?

Finally, there is the separate but related issue of the degree to which national regulators should either compete or cooperate with regulators from other countries. When national economies are relatively isolated from one another, this issue is less important, but as the level of international business grows, questions of regulatory cooperation or cross-national harmonization become crucial.

For each of these issues I present representative cases to compare the regulatory solutions with each country. I examine how each country has historically addressed these questions, and how and whether their solutions have changed over time. The specific instances of reform are listed in table 1.1.

Each case of reform has different implications both for the type of regulatory changes in terms of who benefits and who loses. The dependent variable is regulatory reform. The independent variables are the interests of the major actors, of which the economic interests of large internationally mobile-asset consumers and producers of financial services, especially consumers, will be of primary importance; the exercise of power by the most powerful actor in the international system, the United States; and the initial distribution of political power in each country, which can be inferred by examining the beneficiaries of the original regulatory framework. Financial internationalization will be taken as an exogenous shock hitting both countries at more or less the same time in more or less the same way. Of course, this is somewhat oversimplified. To some extent the causal arrow points both ways, and, at least in part, domestic-level reforms prompt further internationalization. However, since financial internationalization was clearly under way before the major domestic-level reforms took place, it is reasonable to make the assumption that the most important influence was from the international level to the domestic.

IV. Outline of the Book

Chapter 2 looks more closely at earlier studies of regulation and discusses domestic theories of regulatory politics and their historical application to financial regulation in Britain and Japan. Chapter 3 discusses the effects of globalization on domestic politics and assesses the nature and extent of financial globalization in the postwar period.

Chapter 4, on Britain, and chapters 5 and 6, on Japan, present the evidence of regulatory reform. These chapters trace the passage of all of the major reforms of securities markets in both countries beginning in 1980, the year both countries abolished capital controls. For each reform I ask: What changed? Who wanted the change, and who opposed it? Who benefited, and who lost out? The data come from a variety of sources, of which over one hundred interviews with regulators, politicians, and practitioners have been the single most helpful source of information and guidance.[42]

Chapter 7 concludes by comparing the cases and indicating issues needing further research. It also discusses the wider applicability of my argument, both to other countries and to other issue areas. Finally, chapter 7 looks ahead to what may be in store for national and international financial regulation.

With financial markets in turmoil across the globe, with Japan still mired in recession, and with observers from U.S. President Bill Clinton on down calling for a new financial architecture, it is vital to understand the political and historical roots of the current financial system. The purpose of this book, if nothing else, is to shed some light on where the world may be heading by illuminating the path it has followed so far.

---

[42] Since many of the interviewees requested anonymity, I have in most cases avoided assigning specific views to specific individuals.

Chapter 2

Regulatory Politics and Financial Markets

For most of the postwar period, regulatory structures in Britain and Japan differed substantially as a result of numerous historical, political, and social factors. However, securities market regulations in both countries tended to be relatively favorable to the financial services providers—the banks, stockbrokers, and securities companies—at the expense of the consumers of financial services, both borrowers and investors. This outcome is exactly what would be predicted by the Stigler-Peltzman model of regulatory capture and is consistent with James Q. Wilson's theories about the politics of regulation. However, from the early 1980s, both countries have extensively reformed their financial markets. While the reforms have been a complex mixture of deregulation and increased regulation, the major beneficiaries of reform have been large consumers of financial services, notably institutional investors and multinational corporate borrowers. Service providers have lost many of their old privileges and have been exposed to greater competitive pressures and increased regulatory surveillance. Small consumers of financial services, when they have benefited from reform at all, have done less well relative to large consumers. In some instances small consumers of financial services are actually been worse off as a result of reform. The outcome of consumers benefiting at the expense of producers runs counter to currently prevailing theories of regulatory politics.

This chapter provides the reader with an understanding of both the economic rationale for financial regulation and the political influences on its provision. The first section discusses the major conceptual issues in financial market regulation, including the market-failure rationales for regulation and some of the regulatory solutions. The purpose of the section is to illustrate that different regulatory structures have different distributional consequences in terms of who bears more of the costs or receives more of the benefits. An understanding of these technicalities will help the reader to appreciate the distributional implications of the reforms described in later chapters. The second section shows how the provision of regulation is subject to political bargaining and discusses various models of regulatory politics. Finally, the third section argues that Stigler's capture theory of regulatory politics accurately explains the patterns of financial regulation in both Britain and Japan from 1945 until the early 1980s.

I. The Economics of Financial Regulation

Markets suffer distortions, and the extensive literature on market failure shows how regulation helps overcome these problems. Neoclassical economists believe that under conditions of perfect competition, the rule *caveat emptor* (let the buyer beware) is a sufficient safeguard against improper practice by the producers or sellers of goods or services. Producers of dangerous, substandard, or overly expensive goods will supposedly be shunned by their customers to the point where the most egregious offenders go bankrupt or are otherwise forced out of the marketplace. Perfect markets are thus, in the long run, self-policing. Most neoclassical economists recognize, however, that conditions of perfect competition rarely obtain in the real world and that there are conditions when regulations are required to maintain a healthy market.[1] These conditions include the existence of natural monopolies, the presence of externalities, and the problem of imperfect information. These sources of market failure provide the rationale for regulation. Public-interest theories of regulation hold that regulations are provided as public goods by a disinterested government in order to overcome these problems.

The market for financial services is a market like any other and is subject to many of the usual problems of market failure.[2] One distinguishing feature is that natural monopolies are extremely rare in finance.[3] Accordingly, the following focuses on the problems and regulatory solutions to the two other categories of market failure, externalities and information asymmetries.

Externalities

Externalities occur when some of the costs or benefits of producing a particular product are borne not by the producer but by society at large. Under such circumstances, resources will not be used in the most socially efficient way.[4] A producer who can keep all of the gains of production but escape

---

[1] See Joseph Stiglitz, *Economics of the Public Sector*, 2d ed. (New York: W. W. Norton, 1988); Kenneth J. Arrow, "Social Responsibility and Economic Efficiency," *Public Policy* 21, no. 3 (summer 1973): 303–317, or Ian Horowitz, "The Economic Foundations of Self-Regulating in the Professions," in *Regulating the Professions*, ed. Blair and Rubin (Lexington: Lexington Books, 1980).

[2] See Charles A. E. Goodhart, *Money, Information, and Uncertainty*, 2d ed. (London: Macmillan, 1989); T. Campbell, *Financial Institutions: Markets and Economic Activity* (New York: McGraw Hill, 1982), 365–386.

[3] Goodhart, *Money, Information, and Uncertainty*, 202. One case of monopoly recognized by Goodhart is that of a clearing house. He may be being too restrictive, however; there may be circumstances in which cartels, once formed, are able to exert monopolistic control over a particular market. Stock exchanges have that characteristic, for example.

[4] Put technically, producers will not produce on the Pareto-optimal frontier at which marginal costs equal marginal revenues.

some of the costs will rationally overproduce at a rate that maximizes profit, but for which society at large pays a greater than optimum price.[5]

In financial markets, the externality that poses the biggest problem is systemic risk. Banks and traders are so closely interconnected that the fortunes of all are inextricably linked. Failure by one small firm could bring down other, larger institutions and thus have disproportionately damaging effects on the entire market. This harms investors in other financial institutions, who have no responsibility for the original failure and who cannot be blamed for it under the caveat emptor doctrine that depositors bear the ultimate responsibility for ensuring the creditworthiness of their chosen bank. Moreover, a bank run may hurt even people who have no money invested in any financial institution. Thus, the discipline of the market may be insufficient to prevent socially suboptimal outcomes. The riots and social upheavals in Indonesia and Thailand in 1998–99 are striking evidence that financial mismanagement by even a few institutions can have very real and widespread costs. To overcome this problem, a 'lender-of-last-resort function, provided by a central bank, is an example of the sort of public good that the government can and arguably should provide.[6] The U.S. Savings and Loans crisis of the 1980s, the collapse of Baring Brothers in 1994, and the problems in Asia in the late 1990s clearly illustrate the extent and nature of the public good that a safety net provides.

Imperfect Information

Perfect competition requires perfect information. In the real world, however, large asymmetries exist between what various buyers and sellers know about the quality of the products in the market. This can lead to problems of adverse selection.[7] Regulations that lessen the information asymmetry or reduce the incentives of sellers to lie about quality should improve the functioning of the market.

The problem of information asymmetry is particularly acute in the financial services industry. In theory, a potential consumer of financial services should take the time and trouble to investigate the firm with which he or she

[5] One of the best and most often-cited examples of an externality is pollution. In a totally free market, a factory can emit toxic smog during production and have no incentive to curb its emission, even though the smog may harm the surrounding countryside and be extremely costly to society at large. The resulting situation is economically efficient for the producer but ultimately inefficient for society at large.

[6] The argument against providing this function is that a government guarantee to a bank or financial institution creates a moral-hazard problem. Investors in the bank have no incentive to check it for creditworthiness if their money is guaranteed. The officers of the bank have no incentive not to engage in high-risk, high-return activities if they reap all of the returns but have the risk limited by the government's guarantee to underwrite their mistakes.

[7] The problem of adverse selection is discussed in George Akerlof, "The Market for Lemons, Qualitative Uncertainty and the Market Mechanism," *Quarterly Journal of Economics* 84, no. 3 (August 1970): 488–500; and also in Charles Wilson, "The Nature of Equilibrium in Markets with Adverse Selection," *Bell Journal of Economics* 11 (1980): 108–130; and William Samuelson, "Bargaining under Asymmetric Information," *Econometrica* 52, no. 4 (1984): 995–1005.

is about to do business in order to establish that it is honest, reliable, and financially sound. In practice, it is prohibitively expensive in terms of transaction costs for most consumers to do this. It is very costly for an individual to gather sufficient information about, say, a potential counterparty to determine an appropriate price for that counterparty's services. Moreover, since the average individual transacts in financial markets infrequently but with a relatively high fraction of his or her disposable income, individuals are relatively more vulnerable to being exploited.[8]

Consumers usually do not have sufficient resources to distinguish between good and bad sellers of financial services, for example between banks that are well capitalized and those with hidden debts. The effect of this is to drive up prices for all consumers, with an overall loss of efficiency. Stiglitz and Andrew Weiss argue that the effects of information asymmetries in financial markets follow George Akerlof's analysis.[9] This suggests that consumers of financial services face a default risk (i.e., the possibility that the firm to which they entrust their money may go bust) and respond by demanding lower prices. Hayne Leland argues that to overcome the "lemons" problem of poor quality, governments should impose regulations mandating minimum standards of conduct by service providers.[10] The problem with such an approach is that it creates barriers to entry that tend to distort the market by encouraging the overproduction of high-quality goods or by facilitating rent-seeking by members of the regulated profession.[11]

Other problems occur when one party in an exchange uses superior information to exploit another.[12] The problems frequently occur as part of the agent-principal relationship, when an agent acting for someone else is able

---

[8] The intuition here is that it doesn't matter too much if we pay $1 for an undrinkable cup of coffee in a diner. We can punish the diner via the market mechanism of not going back. We have not lost much, and sooner or later the diner owner gets the message that no one ever comes back. He or she either improves the coffee or goes out of business. But if we invest $10,000 in a mutual fund that goes bust or gives us a poor return, it is difficult to punish the fund manager by taking our business elsewhere, since it is a lot less likely that we have any more business to give.

[9] Joseph E. Stiglitz and Andrew Weiss, "Credit Rationing in Markets with Imperfect Information," *American Economic Review* 71 (1981): 393–410.

[10] Hayne E. Leland, "Quacks, Lemons, and Licensing: A Theory of Minimum Quality Standards," *Journal of Political Economy* 87 (1979): 1328–1346.

[11] See, for example, Auner Shaked and John Sutton, "The Self-Regulating Professions," *Review of Economic Studies* 48 (1981): 217–234; or Carl Shapiro, "Investment, Moral Hazard, and Occupational Licensing," *Review of Economic Studies* 53 (1986): 843–862.

[12] See, for example, Ken Arrow, "The Economics of Agency," in *Principals and Agents: The Structure of Business*, ed. John Pratt and Richard Zeckhauser (Boston: Harvard Business School Press, 1985, 37–51); Edward Fama, "Agency Problems and the Theory of the Firm," *Journal of Political Economy* 88 (1980): 288–307; and Michael Jensen and William Meckling, "Theory of the Firm: Managerial Behavior, Agency Costs and Capital Structure," *Journal of Financial Economics* 3 (1976): 305–360; Richard Arnott and Joseph Stiglitz, "Labor Turnover, Wage Structures, and Moral Hazard: The Inefficiency of Competitive Markets," *Journal of Labor Economics* 3 (1985): 434–462.

to put his own interests ahead of those of the principal who is paying him. Principals often do not have the information to monitor their agents to prevent this.[13] Licensing regulations, enforced codes of conduct, or an enforced separation between the prescriber of a treatment and the provider are regulations that can ameliorate these types of market failure.

In financial markets, such problems can arise as variations of the principal-agent problem. Providers of financial services often act in a dual capacity as both the agent of the customer, in recommending the best course of action, and the principal, in carrying out that course of action for the customer. For example, a stockbroker is in a position both to recommend that an investor buy a particular stock and to earn a commission by carrying out the investor's trade. Accordingly, there are inherent conflicts of interest in the provision of the service. Financial services companies can act both as agents for their customers and separately as principals on their own account. For example, a broker may be asked to give investment advice about a particular stock by an investor. The investor may be unaware that the broker holds a large amount of the stock and wishes to get rid of it. Consumers of financial services, as principals, typically do not have the resources to monitor the financial services companies to determine if they, acting as their agents, will put their own interests first. Such conflicts of interest create problems that can damage the reputation of the entire market and therefore limit its long-term survival.

The opportunities for fraud are also ever present in financial markets, again facilitated by information asymmetry. A customer typically cannot tell whether he or she has the best deal, nor can he or she retaliate effectively through economic sanctions if he or she discovers that he or she has been exploited. Thus, there are few structural constraints on the perpetration of fraud by service providers. Insider trading is perhaps the most-cited example of this problem.[14] Unchecked, of course, fraud may ultimately destroy the reputation and hence the viability of the market.

Regulations to Mitigate Market Failure in Financial Markets

There is, therefore, a strong rationale for regulating financial markets. However, it is less clear what specific regulatory structure should be adopted to cope with each aspect of market failure, since each problem is susceptible to a variety of solutions, each one with its own distributional consequences and trade-offs.

Externalities: Systemic Risk

Systemic risk is perhaps the most significant negative externality facing the regulators of financial markets. The fact that financial firms are so closely

[13] As an analogy, a doctor could prescribe an expensive but unnecessary course of treatment to an unsuspecting patient, who lacked the medical skill to realize he or she was being exploited.

[14] See, for example, Frank Easterbrook, "Insider Trading as an Agency Problem," in *Principals and Agents*, ed. Pratt and Zeckhauser, 81–100.

interconnected makes them highly interdependent and creates the possibility that trouble at one institution will spread rapidly to all firms. If one financial firm makes a wrong bet on futures and goes bankrupt, it risks dragging other, healthy firms down with it. This might result in disproportionately damaging consequences to society. What form of regulation would help prevent these undesirable consequences? There are two basic approaches. One is to try to prevent financial collapses from happening. The other is to accept that some crashes will occur, but to provide some form of insurance to ameliorate the social and economic consequences. The two approaches—while similar in terms of their overall effectiveness—have very different distributional consequences.

The first approach, to attempt to prevent any (or any major) firms from collapsing, can be achieved in a number of ways. One way is with a system of functional segmentation between market sectors, which prevents the contagion problem of failure in one sector of the market spreading to others. Rules could stipulate that firms that invest in high-risk ventures not have ties to other firms that do not. The traditional American and Japanese practice of keeping commercial banks separate from investment banks has this separation effect. In contrast to commercial banks, which are controlled in terms of the areas in which they can do business, investment banks can engage in high-risk, high-reward activities. Investment banks are more likely to go bust, but the effects of their collapse are limited because of their insulation from the commercial banks. The downside is that such a system limits intramarket competition, and hence carries some efficiency costs in terms of making transaction costs higher than they would be with greater competition. Such a system of structural protection typically favors smaller borrowers and lenders, since the efficiency costs will be borne disproportionately by those who trade most actively in the market and therefore gain most from reduced transaction costs.

Another way to prevent firms from going bankrupt and causing systemic failure is to restrict product choice by limiting the availability of risky financial instruments such as futures, which can quickly lose value. Firms whose survival is important for the health of the overall financial system can be restricted in their use of such risky instruments. Such an approach ensures greater market stability at the expense of a loss of efficiency—again, market stability will be provided by higher prices for market users.[15]

A final way to prevent market collapse is by setting stringent standards for traders—in other words, by restricting market access to only those firms that the regulators are confident will not fail. Again, setting barriers to entry will restrict competition and hence impair price efficiency.

---

[15] The externality of overtrading, with problems stemming from increased volatility and misallocation of resources, can also be addressed by restrictions on the type and extent of products available. The Tobin tax, proposed as a small tax on all foreign-exchange transactions, is one such example. See Mahub ul Haq, Inge Kaul, and Isabelle Grunberg, eds., *The Tobin Tax: Coping with Financial Volatility* (Oxford: Oxford University Press, 1996).

Alternatively, regulations can be written with the aim of limiting or mitigating the consequences of collapse rather than the aim of preventing collapse. Governments can provide insurance or lender-of-last-resort facilities. Competition would be less fettered, which would lower transaction costs and benefit large-scale users of the financial markets. However, the costs of government-provided insurance are much more likely to be borne by a wider public. The costs of, say, bailing out a failed bank would be borne by all those who contribute to the bailout, which in the case of a government-financed operation, such as the MOF-inspired bailout of the Japanese *jusen* (housing loan) industry, means all taxpayers.

Comparing these two approaches, there is no reason to think that one is necessarily better than the other in providing safeguards against systemic risk. Each approach has its merits and demerits, and it is not at all clear that either is theoretically superior. Each can achieve the same end result, but by a different process with different distributional consequences and different side-effects. In the first solution, in which protection against collapse is structural in nature, all of the costs of providing market stability are borne by those who use the market. Thus, most of the costs are borne by large users of financial services, who pay in the form of higher user fees. Thus, the greatest marginal beneficiaries tend to be the smaller users of financial services. In the second solution, in which collapses are allowed to happen and the government agrees to help pick up the pieces, the chief beneficiaries of market stability are still the large-scale users of the markets, but the costs of protection are borne by a much wider group—the taxpayers. Hence, the marginal beneficiaries of this form of regulatory structure tend to be the larger users.

As discussed in later chapters, the governments of both Britain and Japan have been moving away from highly regulated systems of structural protection—in which the costs of financial stability are fully borne by consumers of financial services—toward a more laissez-faire system in which there is more financial instability and in which the costs of that instability are borne by the nation at large. In other words, the consumers of financial services have been systematically winning.

Information Asymmetries

Information asymmetries may also be tackled in a variety of ways, each with different distributional consequences. Here, too, regulations that embed structural protections into markets tend to reduce competition and so result in higher prices, which benefit producers but hurt consumers. For small consumers, these higher prices are offset by the gains they make in terms of having information imbalances reduced. Large-scale consumers—for whom information asymmetries are typically much less of a problem—are at a relative disadvantage in such an approach. In contrast, more market-based approaches, such as enforcing transparency, tend to take the cost of reducing information imbalances off the shoulders of consumers and put it on the shoulders of the producers. And as discussed later, financial reforms in the past two decades or so have tended overwhelmingly to be toward the second kind.

Problems of adverse selection can be addressed by restricting the number of sellers (or producers) in the market and/or ensuring their high moral and professional standards. This can be achieved by maintaining a formal cartel over which the authorities can exercise a high degree of influence. Another approach is for governments to maintain a licensing system for the vendors of services or to require rigorous standards for industry professionals to ensure high individual standards of competence and moral integrity. Such a licensing system could ameliorate adverse-selection problems by providing customers with a low-cost way of knowing if the firm they are dealing with is sound and reputable. Requiring functional separation, such as barring brokers or investment advisors from trading, eliminates problems caused by conflicts of interest. The system of dual capacity on the LSE is one such example of the effective structural separation of responsibilities, ensuring that the agent who prescribed a course of action for a principal was not the individual who provided the service.[16] Alternatively, specific laws may address specific problems by outlining what practices are acceptable. Under this approach, a system of oversight must be put in place to ensure compliance with these laws.[17] All these approaches restrict competition in the industry and drive prices up. However, all also provide high levels of protection against fraud.

A more market-based solution that does not erect either internal or external barriers to entry into the market is to enforce transparency—in other words, to let anyone sell services as long as buyers know what sort of firm they are dealing with. Rigorous disclosure requirements for the vendors of financial services can thus decrease information asymmetries between the buyers and sellers of financial services. This was a key part of the philosophy underpinning the U.S. Securities Laws of 1933 and 1934. The purpose of the Securities Act of 1933, according to one of its sponsors, Democratic Congressman Sam Rayburn, was to provide "all information that is pertinent that would put him on notice and guard, and then let him beware."[18] The act, according to Senator Carl Mapes "will not prevent anybody from putting his money into rat holes or into highly speculative ventures if he sees fit to do so."[19]

The distributional effects of the two approaches are different. As with the

---

[16] The analogy here is to the problems that arise when a doctor both diagnoses ailments and benefits economically from the sale and administration of the drugs needed to cure them. He or she would face perverse incentives to prescribe treatments based on how much each would earn, not on how efficacious each was to the patient's condition.

[17] For example, practices such as insider trading or selling very risky derivatives to unsophisticated first-time investors with not much money can be outlawed, despite the presumption of caveat emptor.

[18] Quoted in Bernard Schwartz, ed., *The Economic Regulation of Business and Industry: A Legislative History of U.S. Regulatory Agencies*, vol. 4 (New York: R. R. Bowker, 1973), 2549.

[19] Quoted in ibid., 2606.

discussion of systemic risk, structural protections tend to favor smaller users since they face larger problems of information asymmetry and are hence in greater need of structural protection. In contrast, structural protections inhibit competition and tend to create inefficiencies and raise transaction costs. Once again, higher transaction costs disproportionately hurt those who trade more in uncompetitive markets where they are unable to dictate fair market prices.

In summary, there are a variety of possible regulatory solutions to each instance of market failure. So far, the literature on regulation has not established that one regulation or set of regulations is better than the others. This point is well made by David Vogel, who compared the different approaches Britain and the United States took to regulating financial services. Whereas the United States had a "rule-oriented, legalistic, and strictly regulated" regulatory culture, Britain relied on the "extensive use of self-regulation" and informal social control.[20] However, despite these considerable differences in regulatory style, the regulatory outcomes were not so very different: "The far stricter legal controls exercised by American regulatory authorities appear to have been no more successful in preventing periodic scandal and fraud. Such episodes continue to occur in both societies. On balance, British holders of insurance policies, bank depositors, and investors appear to be no better or worse protected than their counterparts in the United States."[21] However, even though it is difficult and perhaps impossible to establish whether the various styles of regulation are better or worse overall for each country, it is clear that the styles of regulations have observable distributional consequences that can be identified.

II. The Politics of Financial Regulation

As the preceding discussion indicated, there are various rationales for regulating financial markets. Even if we accept market-failure problems as reason enough to regulate markets, there are many different regulatory structures that can address these problems. These structures are not distributionally neutral, and they will therefore be subject to political bargaining. Accordingly, it is time to consider how the provision of financial market regulation may be influenced by political rather than economic factors.

There are two schools of thought explaining how social institutions such as market regulations come into being: collective goods and distributional conflict.[22] The collective goods school, as discussed, is concerned with identifying the benefits that institutions bring: the gains from exchange. This literature

[20] David Vogel, *National Styles of Regulation: Environmental Policy in Great Britain and the United States* (Ithaca: Cornell University Press, 1986), 217.

[21] Ibid., 219–220.

[22] Knight, *Institutions and Social Conflict.*

shows how institutional structures such as markets can increase these gains for all actors. Markets lower the costs of exchange, and the more efficient the market, the higher the welfare gains for all.[23] According to this school, institutions arise out of cooperation among actors to capture gains from exchange.

The distributional conflict school argues that such a view is unrealistic for two reasons. First, the collective-action problem is endemic to the provision of public goods; thus, the collective goods school cannot explain how the institutions come to be established in the first place. Second, there are many institutional solutions possible for any given problem, and the collective goods school is unable to predict which specific institutional form will be adopted. In short, while the collective goods school does a good job of explaining the demand for a particular institution, it is unable to explain its supply—either how it came into being or the form it took. Jack Knight argues, "The ongoing development of social institutions is not best explained as a Pareto-superior response to collective goals or benefits but, rather, as a by-product of conflicts over distributional gains by private, self-interested rational actors.[24]

Regulations are one such set of social institutions, and so, according to Sam Peltzman, "what is basically at stake in the regulatory process is a transfer of wealth."[25] Accordingly, there should be political fights over these distributional costs or benefits, and in this book I assume that regulations are the result of political battles for the redistribution of wealth. The task, then, is to understand who wins and who loses these battles.

Several models of regulatory reform can be found in the literature on domestic politics.[26] Most agree that in order to explain a particular regulatory policy, the key is to identify the relevant actors, their interests, the political resources they can use, and the impact of institutional structure on the decision-making process. From these variables we can determine the differences in the abilities of the actors to influence the regulatory process.

The Economic Theory of Regulation

In this section I examine one of the models of regulatory reform: the economic theory of regulation (sometimes known as the theory of regulatory capture, or the Stigler-Peltzman model).

Stigler's basic idea is that producer groups will beat consumer groups in any political battle to capture bureaucratic agents and obtain favorable regulations. According to Stigler and others, regulations can confer economic benefits or costs on an industry, and the producer groups in that industry are better able to secure those benefits than are their consumers. Specifically, Stigler argued that producer groups want three types of regulation: barriers to entry, restrictions on substitute products and encouragement of complementary products, and the

---

[23] Ronald Coase, "The Problem of Social Cost," *Journal of Law and Economics* 3 (1960): 1–44.

[24] Knight, *Institutions and Social Conflict*, 19.

[25] Peltzman, "Growth of Government," 213.

[26] Roger Noll and Bruce Owen, *The Political Economy of Deregulation* (Washington, D.C.: American Enterprise Institute, 1983); Martha Derthick and Paul Quick, *The Politics of Deregulation* (Washington, D.C.: Brookings Institution, 1985).

ability to engage in price-fixing.[27] Such regulations entail efficiency costs usually borne by others, such as the consumers of the product; consumers pay higher prices than they would in a world of perfect competition without regulation.

Thus, it is in the economic self-interest of industry groups to lobby for favorable regulation and in the interest of those who will bear the costs, the consumers, to lobby against such regulation and in favor of rules that benefit them. The political battle is unequal, however, since different groups face different barriers to the goal of organizing effectively to lobby for change. Small groups with high per capita stakes in the outcome, who are typically but not necessarily producer groups, are generally more capable of overcoming the collective-action problem and lobbying effectively than are large, diffuse groups with low per capita stakes such as consumer groups.[28] According to Stigler, therefore, "regulation is acquired by the industry and is designed and operated primarily for its benefit."[29]

Peltzman adds that although the odds are high that policy outcomes will be biased in favor of producer groups because of their greater ability to lobby successfully, there are limits to the power of special interests. This is because large, diffuse groups of consumers have at least some political power in the form of votes and because politicians who lean too heavily in support of special interests at the expense of general interests ultimately alienate a sufficient number of voters to damage their chances of reelection. There is, in other words, a trade-off that politicians face between satisfying special interests and the public good.

Stephen McGee, William Brock, and Leslie Young have modeled this approach formally.[30] They argue that "wealth comes from two sources: production and predation."[31] Regulatory or other policies that redistribute income are a form of predation, and since rationally self-interested individuals do not care from which source their wealth derives, they will invest in both production and in the political lobbying that constitutes predation.[32] McGee, Brock, and Young argue that there is a trade-off between economic efficiency and political efficiency, and that rent-seeking by special interests results in economically inefficient outcomes—"the invisible foot," to contrast with Adam Smith's "invisible hand," which supposedly allocates resources efficiently as a result of self-interested productive behavior.[33]

[27] Stigler, "Theory of Economic Regulation," 5–7. He notes that a fourth type of beneficial state action, direct cash subsidies to the industry, is less appealing to producer groups because subsidies attract new rivals who will dilute the benefits per firm.

[28] See Olson, *Logic of Collective Action* for a full discussion of the free-rider problem, and why small groups can organize more easily.

[29] Stigler, "Theory of Economic Regulation," 3.

[30] Stephen McGee, William Brock, and Leslie Young, *Black Hole Tariffs and Endogenous Policy Theory* (Cambridge: Cambridge University Press, 1989).

[31] Ibid., 1.

[32] Technically, "until the marginal returns from each are identical. At this point, a redistributive equilibrium exists." Ibid.

[33] Adam Smith, *An Inquiry into the Nature and Causes of the Wealth of Nations* (Chicago: University of Chicago Press, 1976).

The Politics of Regulation

Wilson challenges the economic theory of regulation more fundamentally and develops another facet of the argument about regulatory politics.[34] He notes that the prediction of the economic theory of regulation that regulations will favor producers does not always hold true in practice. Wilson explains this phenomenon in part by attacking the assumption that politicians and bureaucrats do not have independent interests and that in the battle between special interest groups with money and the voting public at large the politicians will usually go with the money. Wilson argues that sometimes politicians benefit more by courting voters than by courting special interests. For many regulatory issues, of which environmental standards are one example, public-interest concerns can be manipulated by political entrepreneurs to gain regulation that hurts the industry involved. Wilson looks at whether the costs and/or benefits of a proposed regulation are spread widely or concentrated narrowly to predict what sort of politics result. Widely dispersed costs and widely dispersed benefits, for example from tax policies, result in majoritarian politics fought chiefly between political parties. On issues for which both costs and benefits are narrowly concentrated, such as from the allocation of industrial policies, the political battle is fought between rival interest groups. When the costs of regulation are narrowly concentrated but the benefits dispersed widely, such as from environmental regulation, then the issue becomes subject to entrepreneurial politics, with an elected politician using the power of ideas to mobilize electoral support for a particular issue. When the costs of regulation are widely dispersed but the benefits are narrow, for example from the regulation of cartels, then the political battles will resemble the Stigler-Peltzman model of producer group capture. This typology is summarized in table 2.1. For three of the four possible outcomes, then, Wilson disagrees with Stigler. Both agree, however, that for the fourth outcome, in which the costs of regulation are widespread but the benefits are concentrated, the result will be clientelistic politics characterized by producer-group capture. Financial regulation falls squarely into this last category.

The literature on structural choice refines Wilson's argument that politicians and bureaucrats have independent interests by recognizing that institutional decision making takes place under uncertainty. Terry Moe notes that institutional reforms such as the establishment of new regulatory agencies may result from legislators' or special-interest groups' attempting to embed their own agendas into the legislative process because they fear that they will soon be voted out of office and replaced by ideological opponents.[35] Under such circumstances, special-interest groups have a strong motivation to create institutional designs that systematically favor their own interests and that can reasonably be expected to last somewhat longer than the tenure in office of a majority of sympathetic politicians. The rationale is that it is easier and

---

[34] Wilson, *Politics of Regulation*.

[35] Terry Moe, "Interests, Institutions and Positive Political Theory," *Studies in American Political Development* 2 (1987): 237–299.

Table 2.1. Wilson's typology of regulatory politics

Dispersion Costs	Dispersion Benefits	Type of Politics	Example
Wide	Wide	Majoritarian politics	Tax policy
Narrow	Narrow	Interest-group politics	Industrial subsidies
Narrow	Wide	Entrepreneurial politics	Environment
Wide	Narrow	Client politics (small-group capture)	Financial regulation

Source: Adapted from James Q. Wilson, *The Politics of Regulation* (New York: Basic Books, 1974).

quicker to vote a party out of office than it is to reform or replace an existing bureaucratic institution, and that such institutions are therefore "stickier" and more likely to operate in the long term. In other words, regulatory agency design may not simply reflect the interests of current power-holders. It may also reflect the desire of those in power to protect their interests in the future.

The thrust of much of the regulatory politics literature, then, is that regulations are mechanisms by which the politically powerful can capture rents. Regulatory politics are about the redistribution of resources from the politically weak to the politically strong. The key to understanding regulatory outcomes under these circumstances is to identify the relevant actors, their interests, and their political power. Political power comes both in the form of resources, such as votes, money, or ideas, and in the organizational ability to overcome collective-action problems and mobilize politically. This ability to organize is, in turn, a function of the size and concentration of the group and of the relative incentive of its members to organize. Finally, access to the decision-making arena may vary from group to group, and this also mediates how much political power each group wields.

III. The Politics of Regulation in Postwar Britain and Japan

Both Stigler's and Wilson's theories of regulation do a good job of predicting the winners and losers of financial regulation in Britain and Japan for much of the postwar period.[36] The private actors who benefited most from regulation were the service providers (the producers)—the financial service intermediaries, who were allowed to indulge in a variety of protected, rent-creating ac-

[36] This is a Rosenbluth's central argument. She notes that Japan, in contrast to the United States, has "centralized state authority, rigid political parties, and concentrated producer interests [that] tend to exclude unorganized interests. . . . these are the conditions under which [Stigler's] theory of regulation predicts outcomes most accurately" (Rosenbluth, *Financial Politics in Contemporary Japan,* 211).

Table 2.2. Securities market regulation, 1947–1980

Issue Area	Description	Example	Britain	Japan
Market access	Who is allowed to trade in the market?	Stock exchange membership	Ban on foreign ownership	Ban on foreign ownership
Intramarket competition	In which business areas can different firms participate?	Segregation of commercial and investment banking	Ban on bank ownership of brokerages (single capacity)	Banks banned from securities business; may own 5% of brokerage (Article 65)
Product diversity	What financial instruments may be traded and by whom?	Trading of futures, options and other derivatives	Futures banned on LSE (may be traded on other U.K. markets)	Futures and options banned throughout markets
Price controls	Are prices set by regulation or by the market?	Fixed vs. negotiated brokerage commissions on stock trades	Fixed commissions	Fixed commissions
Consumer protection	What constitutes fraud, and what is acceptable business practice?	Permissibility of insider trading	Some restrictions on insider trading	Few restrictions on insider trading
Regulatory oversight	Who oversees the market?	Which regulatory agency is responsible for enforcing laws?	Self-regulation, with informal guidance from Bank of England, and DTI	Informal guidance from MOF

Note: Abbreviations: DTI, Department of Trade and Industry; LSE, London Stock Exchange; MOF, Ministry of Finance; TSE, Tokyo Stock Exchange.

tivities. The regulations themselves were exactly those predicted by Stigler: barriers to entry, restrictions on substitute products, and price-fixing arrangements. In both Britain and Japan, the barriers to entry took various forms. The members of local stock exchanges were protected from international competition by regulations banning foreigners from competing in the market. The brokers were also protected by a series of intramarket barriers to entry that inhibited competition from other domestic financial institutions such as banks. Substitute products were also suppressed; the restrictions on most forms of futures trading in both countries for most of the postwar period are an example. Finally, in both countries, prices in the form of brokerage commissions were fixed. Consumers were poorly served by the lack of competition and higher prices that these regulations entailed. Large customers, who would have benefited more from the lower transaction costs associated with greater competition and economies of scale, were especially poorly served. The key features of regulatory policies in Britain and Japan are summarized in table 2.2.

There was, however, one important political difference between the two countries that explains the relatively greater concern for the protection of individual consumers in Britain. In Japan, power resided with an interventionist bureaucracy and the system of financial regulation was tightly controlled.[37] However, the bureaucrats needed the cooperation of the banks and brokers to carry out the regulatory policy and were therefore unwilling to enforce particularly strict oversight of the activities of the banks and brokers, especially in their dealings with individual customers. In Britain, in contrast, the power of politicians over the bureaucrats was considerably stronger, making financial regulation more susceptible to a certain degree of populist influence.

This difference in the distribution of political power shows up in the different ways in which regulatory oversight and investor protection were handled. In Japan, oversight was handled by the MOF, but the close ties between the MOF and the securities industry meant that the laws concerning investor protection, where they existed at all, were vague and loosely enforced. In Britain, in contrast, although regulatory oversight was fragmented among many agencies, there was a relatively higher degree of concern for investor protection of private individuals. This protection was provided by both structural features (discussed later) and by an ethic of self-regulation by the industry itself. Yet producer dominance was undermined in both countries in the 1980s and 1990s.

The most obvious cause for this shift appears to be the integration of the world's financial markets. In chapter 3, I present competing perspectives on the effects of globalization on domestic politics and assess whether finance is truly "global" yet.

[37] See Johnson, *MITI and the Japanese Economic Miracle* for the definitive statement on bureaucratic dominance in Japan; and Zysman, *Governments, Markets and Growth*, for how the bureaucracy used financial regulation to control the economy.

Globalization
and National Politics

This chapter explores financial internationalization in theory and practice. The first section discusses how internationalization has affected domestic politics and, more specifically, how greater international capital mobility has affected domestic financial regulations. The literature on this subject falls into two main camps: those who argue for and those who argue against the proposition that globalization has caused a convergence in the previously diverse regulatory institutions of different countries. The evidence presented in this book challenges both camps. For those who deny that global economic integration has had much effect on domestic politics, the evidence of the convergence of regulatory policies in two very different countries presents a real puzzle. At the same time, the evidence refutes those convergence theorists who argue that globalization is followed by a competition in laxity as regulatory policies in different countries converge to the lowest common standard. This, I argue, has not happened. Indeed, the evidence suggests that the opposite is happening. Moreover, I show how proponents of the convergence school often differ on the mechanisms by which globalization is translated into national policy outcomes, and I suggest ways that these causal mechanisms can be better understood.

The second section of this chapter defines the internationalization of finance and the degree to which it really exists. The section demonstrates that, although there are important qualifications to the notion of a single, integrated world capital market, the opportunities for financial service users to "exit" their home markets and to raise or invest funds in other national or international markets have increased dramatically since the mid- to late 1970s. This section therefore acts as an introduction to the empirical case studies that follow.

I. Theories of Internationalization and Domestic Politics

Much of the recent work in comparative and international political economy has focused on the relationship between international economic change and domestic politics. A growing subfield of that literature has examined the extent to which increases in the international mobility of financial capital have influenced the domestic policies of sovereign states. This debate encompasses a wide range of opinions, from those who argue that international capital mobility has completely undermined national autonomies to those who claim that international changes have had little or no discernible effect on domestic policies. This section reviews this debate, beginning with the proponents of the capital-mobility hypothesis, who argue that financial globalization has had a significant effect on domestic policy in many countries, and followed by the opponents of this view. I conclude that while many agree that capital mobility affects domestic politics, there is less agreement about why, how, and under what circumstances. Some of the theories advanced about the precise effects of internationalization on domestic politics are then considered, focusing on the so-called competition in laxity, the "race to the top," U.S. hegemony, and international cooperation. I conclude that none of the existing theories adequately explains the policy outcomes observed in Britain and Japan.

The Capital-Mobility Hypothesis

In the 1990s there has been an outpouring of research that argues that the internationalization of the world economy has had an enormous impact upon the ability of sovereign countries to control their economies. Conventional wisdom, at least in the popular press, is that the internationalization of financial markets has dramatically undermined the national sovereignty of all countries. Works with titles such as *The End of Geography* or *The Borderless World* attest to the popularity of this view.[1] The academic literature is usually less sensationalist, but many scholars of international political economy assert that the internationalization of finance has exercised a new and powerful influence on domestic policymaking.[2]

Michael Webb examines changes in the patterns of international coordination of macroeconomic adjustment policies under the impact of international capital market integration. He identifies a common pattern of policy shifts from the mid-1960s to the early 1980s and cites Kenneth Waltz's view that "if different states act similarly in response to similar phenomena, we are justified in thinking that there may be some kind of structural effect at

---

[1] At least this appears to be true in the business sections of airport bookstores. See Richard O'Brien, *Global Financial Integration: The End of Geography* (London: Royal Institute for International Affairs, 1992); and Kenichi Ohmae, *The Borderless World: Power and Strategy in an Interdependent Economy* (New York: Harper Business, 1990). See also Gregory Millman, *The Vandals' Crown: How Rebel Currency Traders Overthrew the World's Central Banks* (New York: Free Press, 1995). The news media also seem to subscribe to this view: Thomas Friedman claims that the world now has two superpowers—the United States and Moody's rating agency (Thomas Friedman, "Don't Mess with Moody's," *New York Times*, 22 February 1991, A15). Martin Walker writes that "Conventional concepts of state power are simply dwarfed by the awesome might of the new global financial markets. . . . Like the medieval popes [the global markets] embody a power that transcends frontiers, commands an alternative allegiance from the citizens of individual states and can humble governments and leaders" (Martin Walker, "A Power Second to None," *Japan Times*, 21 June 1995, 17).

[2] The debate has been excellently reviewed by Benjamin Cohen, "Phoenix Risen: The Resurrection of Global Finance," *World Politics* 48, no. 1 (1996): 268–296.

work."[3] Accordingly, he argues that "we are justified in considering it [international capital mobility] an element of the international economic structure and studying the effects of the structure on the policies of individual governments."[4]

John Goodman and Louis Pauly share this view. They examine the liberalization of capital markets in advanced industrial democracies and conclude that "the fundamental convergence in the direction of [capital market liberalization] noted in all of our case studies suggests that systemic forces are now dominant in the financial area."[5] They go on to argue that economic liberalization "has been driven by fundamental changes in the structures of international production and financial intermediation, which made it easier and more urgent for private firms—specifically corporations and financial institutions whose aspirations had become increasingly global—effectively to pursue strategies of evasion and exit."[6]

Paulette Kurzer comes to a similar conclusion based on her study of the decline of social democratic welfare policies in western European countries. She argues that "high capital mobility and deepening financial integration prompt governments to remove or alter institutions and practices objectionable to business and finance."[7] Similar to Goodman and Pauly, she identifies a shift in power toward private actors with internationally mobile assets and away from governments and actors with relatively immobile assets such as labor: "As business and finance became more mobile, their power resources increased and those of labor decreased . . . governments have lost the ability to carve out national economic strategies."[8] David Andrews, in his study of monetary relations among the United States, Japan, and Europe, also argues in favor of the international capital mobility hypothesis, in which capital mobility represents a structural constraint on domestic policy autonomy.[9] He writes that "the nature of international capital mobility sys-

---

[3] Webb, "International Economic Structures," 312; see also his *Political Economy of Policy Coordination.*

[4] Webb, "International Economic Structures," 313. See Kenneth Waltz, *Theory of International Politics* (Reading, Mass.: Addison-Wesley, 1979), 69–73.

[5] John Goodman and Louis Pauly, "The Obsolescence of Capital Controls," *World Politics* (October 1993): 46, 79. Notice that these authors and Webb infer the power of mobile capital from the evidence of cross-national policy convergence. See also Louis Pauly, "National Financial Structures, Capital Mobility, and International Economic Rules: The Normative Consequences of East Asian, European and American Distinctiveness," *Policy Sciences* 27, no. 4 (1994).

[6] Goodman and Pauly, *Obsolescence of Capital Controls,* 51.

[7] Kurzer, *Business and Banking,* 245.

[8] Ibid., viii. Cohen attributes the view that business has been systematically favored by capital mobility to Jonathan Moses, "Abdication from National Policy Autonomy: What's Left to Leave?" *Politics and Society* 22, no. 2 (1994): 125–148; and Stephen Gill and David Law, "Global Hegemony and the Structural Power of Capital," *International Studies Quarterly* 33, no. 4 (1989): 475–99. Both quoted in Cohen, "Phoenix Risen," 28, 29.

[9] Andrews, "Capital Mobility and State Autonomy."

tematically constrains state behavior by rewarding some actions and punishing others."[10]

Finally, much of the economic literature and almost all of the practitioner-focused work on the subject lend support for the international capital-mobility hypothesis.[11] Understandably, such accounts are often more concerned with the when and what of reform than the why or even the how. Nonetheless, many stress the similarities of response of different countries to common pressures. They often share the assumption that regulatory reform was an inevitable outcome of internationalization, in which domestic political concerns played only a small role in determining the final outcomes.

Objections to the International Capital-Mobility Hypothesis

The international capital-mobility argument has come under attack from a variety of quarters, beginning with those who dispute that capital really is more mobile today. There are two variants of this attack. First, there are those who point out that capital is not more mobile now than it was in certain previous eras, such as the late nineteenth and early twentieth centuries.[12] Therefore, they argue, any effects attributed to contemporary mobility should also have been witnessed in these earlier periods. In fact, however, there is little historical evidence to suggest that high levels of capital mobility in previous eras had the sorts of domestic-level effects we now see. Second, there are those who look for the observable implications of capital mobility, such as the complete cross-national convergence of real interest rates. This second camp argues that in fact these implications are not observed.[13] I discuss the proposition that capital is not, in fact, internationally mobile in greater detail later in this chapter. For the time being, I accept that, at least since the mid-1970s, there has been a significant increase in the ease with which portfolio capital can move across national borders, even though this increase in mobility does not amount to a wholly integrated borderless world.

---

[10] Ibid, 197.

[11] See, among others, Meerschwam, *Breaking Financial Boundaries;* Hayes and Hubbard, *Investment Banking;* and Ralph Bryant, *International Financial Intermediation* (Washington, D.C.: Brookings Institution, 1987). George Stigler writes in one such account that in Britain "the changing shape of financial markets appears to be dictating regulatory developments rather than vice-versa." George Stigler, "The Context of Regulation," in *Financial Deregulation,* ed. Richard Dale (Cambridge: Woodhead Faulkner, 1986), 2.

[12] See Robert Zevin, "Are Financial Markets More Open?" in *Financial Openness and National Autonomy,* ed. Tariq Banuri and Juliet Schor (Oxford: Clarendon Press, 1992), 51–52. This criticism is leveled at Webb by Helen Milner in her review of *Political Economy of Policy Coordination,* by Michael Webb (*American Political Science Review* 90, no. 2 (1996): 473.

[13] Work here has been reviewed by Robert Wade, "Globalization and Its Limits," in *Convergence or Diversity?* ed. Suzanne Berger and Ron Dore (Ithaca: Cornell University Press, 1996), 60–88. He concludes that the current level of global integration is far from complete and that "national economic borders still define the boundaries of systems of capital accumulations" (39). He cites the debate among economists such as Kasman and Piggott, who argue that no cross-national convergence in real interest rates has been observed; Martin Feldstein and Charles Horioka, who point to the overwhelmingly domestic determinants of investment levels; and Jeffrey Frankel, who refutes both of these views.

A second objection to the capital-mobility hypothesis is that it implies that states are powerless to stem or reverse the trend of increasing capital-market integration. Yet the history of financial developments since World War II shows that the conscious decisions of states have driven the development of the markets.[14] According to this view, what states have given, states can ultimately take away.[15] While this view is accurate in its assessment that international markets do not exist wholly in the absence of national governments, it does not follow that national governments are not strongly influenced by market pressures.[16]

The third and most telling attack on the international capital-mobility hypothesis comes from those who argue that even though states are subject to the pressures of a changing international environment, domestic variables such as coalitions of interest groups or the nature of political institutions mediate the influence of capital mobility to such a degree that internationalization may be regarded as a secondary or even irrelevant influence on domestic politics. This argument is supported by evidence that, despite facing the common systemic-level pressure of international capital mobility, different states have nonetheless responded in different ways.

This third viewpoint is most popular, perhaps not surprisingly, among political scientists who look at the domestic processes of change in specific countries and who often conclude that policy change may be best explained by reference to domestic political concerns. Geoff Garret examines the hypothesis that international financial integration leads to an erosion of the Keynesian welfare policies of western European states and concludes that, although increased capital integration since the 1980s has exerted "powerful pressures for convergence of economic policies," such convergence has not actually happened. He states that "the evidence of fiscal policy conflicts sharply with the convergence thesis."[17] Michael Loriaux argues that regulatory reform in the 1980s in France was "the strategic choice of a rational state actor: liberalization was an attempt by state elites to regain control over its monetary authority and not . . . to surrender the future evolution of the French political economy to the laws of the marketplace."[18] Sofia Perez explicitly rejects the convergence thesis in her study of credit regulation in

[14] See, for example, Helleiner, *States and the Reemergence of Global Finance*, or Strange, *Casino Capitalism*.

[15] Susan Strange uses the term "non-decisions" to describe the various points at which states could have hampered the progress of financial internationalization but chose not to do so. Strange, *Casino Capitalism*, 2.

[16] This point is made strongly by Andrews, "Capital Mobility and State Autonomy."

[17] Geoff Garret, "Capital Mobility, Trade and the Domestic Politics of Economic Policy," *International Organization* 49 (Fall 1995): 659. A similar view is expressed in Geoff Garret and Peter Lange, "Internationalization, Institutions and Political Change," *International Organization* 49 (1995): 627–656, which argues against the functionalist reasoning of Frieden, Rogowski, Milner, and others, who assume that changes in actor preferences caused by international economic changes hardly ever map cleanly onto domestic political outcomes.

[18] Michael Loriaux, *France after Hegemony: International Change and Financial Reform* (Ithaca: Cornell University Press, 1991), 14.

Europe in the 1970s and 1980s. The fact that some countries adopted selective credit regulation while others did not prompts her to argue that "domestic and politically motivated macroeconomic policy choices by government officials play a much greater role in driving change and determining regulatory outcomes than is generally recognized."[19]

The accounts of deregulation in Japan can be grouped into two main groups: those that stress international pressures, and those that stress internal pressures.[20] Each group can be further subdivided into those that stress economic and market forces, and those that stress political forces. Accounts that stress the role of international economic forces include those of David Meerschwam and of Samuel Hayes and Philip Hubbard.[21] While enlightening on the important role of international market pressures, these accounts typically overlook the political processes by which internationalization is mediated in policy outcomes. They cannot explain, for example, why the British deregulated quickly and suddenly while the Japanese adopted a slow and piecemeal approach. Other accounts stress the importance of *gaiatsu* (outside pressure), and argue that Japan deregulated because it was forced to do so by the United States and other foreign governments.[22] Such accounts lack two vital ingredients. First, they cannot explain why foreign pressure was sometimes immediately successful, such as in response to demands to allow foreigners onto the TSE, and was at other times unsuccessful for long periods, such as in response to demands that Japan liberalize its rules governing the management of public pension funds. Second, these accounts cannot explain why the reforms in Japan closely resembled the reforms in Britain when there is no evidence that foreign-governmental pressure played a role in the deregulation of British markets. If foreign-governmental pressure was not necessary in the British case—and no one suggests that it was—then why should it have been necessary in the Japanese case?

Several recent accounts stress the domestic origins of Japanese deregulation, explicitly rejecting the role of international factors and denying that Japanese and other countries' regulatory policies have been converging. Ulrike Schaede claims that in the Japanese regulatory framework "there is no indication whatsoever of convergence" with the United States "or any

[19] Sofia Perez, "Macroeconomic Choices and Institutional Change: The Politics of Financial Interventionism and Its Abandonment in Post-War Europe" (paper presented at the annual meeting of the American Political Science Association, Chicago, September 1995), 2.

[20] This typology is similar to that used by Rosenbluth, who offers a three-fold categorization of international pressure, MOF-led reform, and Liberal Democratic Party–led reform. Rosenbluth, *Financial Politics in Contemporary Japan*, 2–3. My characterization follows the second-image and second-image reversed typologies first discussed by Kenneth Waltz, *Man, the State, and War* (New York: Columbia University Press, 1959); and Peter Gourevitch, *Politics in Hard Times* (Ithaca: Cornell University Press, 1986).

[21] Meerschwam, *Breaking Financial Boundaries*; and Hayes and Hubbard, *Investment Banking*.

[22] See Jeffrey A. Frankel, *The Yen/Dollar Agreement: Liberalizing Japanese Capital Markets* (Washington, D.C.: Institute for International Economics, 1984). For a more general version of this argument, see Kent Calder, "Japanese Foreign Economic Policy: Explaining the Reactive State," *World Politics* 40 (1988): 517–541.

other system of capitalism."[23] Changes in regulations were, she writes, "a pragmatic adaptation to the ways in which the world is turning on Japan," revealing no underlying change in the way the Japanese public or bureaucracy conceives of regulation.[24] Steven Vogel argues that there are still nationally distinct patterns of regulatory change and distinguishes between the centralized, methodical, controlled bureaucrat-led reregulation in Japan and the more fragmentary, speedy, and marketized reform process in the United Kingdom.[25] In the case of Japan, he argues that bureaucrats in the MOF "have still managed to run their financial revolution their way" and that "the evidence from the financial system reform case strongly supports my contention that MOF officials have followed their own priorities—and not those of financial institutions or party politicians."[26] Finally, Andrew Sobel writes concerning changes in global financial markets that "the international outcome [financial integration] is solidly rooted in domestic policy dilemmas and distributional debates,"[27] and that "[financial] markets remained distinctively national."[28]

The weakness of these arguments lies in the degree to which they ignore or fail to explain the degree to which market structures have converged. Vogel, for example, notes that although the regulatory processes by which Britain and Japan undertook reform are quite distinct, the market outcome of liberalization is essentially the same in both cases. He maintains, however, that there is an important distinction to be drawn between market outcomes, which refer to changes in the nature of competition, and regulatory outcomes, which refer to the nature of the regulatory structure. Vogel argues that even though market outcomes are converging between Britain and Japan, regulatory outcomes are not. Although I concede that the distinction is a valid one, I suggest that, in terms of economic and distributional consequences, market outcomes are far more important than regulatory ones.

The problem with Schaede's view is that despite a uniquely Japanese view of regulation, Japan's policymakers are arriving at regulatory decisions that are producing a Japanese capital market that is much more similar to those of the United States and Britain than was the case twenty years ago. I suggest that if policy outcomes are similar from country to country, then the questions of how the Japanese went about producing those outcomes or what guiding philosophy they used to rationalize their decisions are of secondary importance.

Frances McCall Rosenbluth's important 1989 study of deregulation in the Japanese banking industry offers evidence for the importance of both

---

[23] Ulricke Schaede, *Change and Continuity in Japanese Regulation*, Haas School of Business Working Paper 66 (Berkeley: Haas School of Business, 1994), 1–2.

[24] Ibid, 1.

[25] Steven Vogel, "The Bureaucratic Approach to the Financial Revolution," *Governance* 7 no. 3 (1994): 23; see also Vogel, *Freer Markets, More Rules*.

[26] Vogel, "Bureaucratic Approach," 237.

[27] Sobel, *Domestic Choices, International Markets*, 19.

[28] Ibid., 143.

international and domestic influences on regulatory reform. My explanation for the deregulation of the Japanese securities market is consistent with hers, although I examine different cases. She recognizes "that financial institutions and practices in Tokyo bear a growing resemblance to those of New York and London testifies to strong international market pressures."[29] On the other hand, she argues that the process of change is inherently political. Rosenbluth demonstrates that regulatory outcomes were the immediate result of domestic political maneuverings within and between the Liberal Democracy Party, the MOF, and the special-interest groups, which in her cases were the banks. She uses Stigler's theory of economic regulation to account for the relative power of producer groups. The importance of financial globalization, in particular in the form of the euromarkets, lies in its influence on shifting the preferences of the financial institutions.[30] Finally, Rosenbluth discusses the importance of internationalization in providing exit options for the customers of financial services. She argues: "Once national boundaries are penetrated and domestic firms must compete against foreign firms operating under different rules, domestic production may become impossible to sustain. We should expect the domestic firms to seek changes in domestic regulation that will allow them to retain competitiveness under the changed circumstances."[31] Concretely, then, she argues that "deregulation has been propelled by financial institutions, acting in cooperation with the Ministry of Finance and sometimes politicians, to construct a new set of rules they need to compete in a changing economic environment."[32]

To summarize this debate: the literature arguing for the primacy of domestic politics in explaining regulatory reform correctly captures the extent to which systemic-level pressures must be filtered through domestic political structures. By definition, national regulatory outcomes must be rooted in national decisions. This camp is also correct in noting that despite the popular rhetoric of a global twenty-four-hour-a-day capital market, differences in structure and regulation remain among even the most internationalized

---

[29] Rosenbluth, *Financial Politics in Contemporary Japan*, 1.

[30] See especially chapter 5, "Coping with the Euromarket," in Rosenbluth, *Financial Politics in Contemporary Japan*, 137–166. This evenhandedness in assessing the importance of international factors on Japanese politics is also evident in her other work. Of the effect of internationalization on Japan in general she writes: "Japan's case does not negate the importance of internationalization, but rather underscores the importance of domestic political institutions in channeling international forces. . . . It is not enough to understand domestic politics in isolation of the world environment, for much domestic change would remain mysterious. At the same time, evaluation of international forces alone could lead observers far from the mark. In Japan today . . . one cannot understand one without the other." Frances McCall Rosenbluth, "Internationalization and Electoral Politics in Japan," in *Internationalization and Domestic Politics*, ed. Robert Keohane and Helen Milner (Cambridge: Cambridge University Press, 1990), 138–139.

[31] Rosenbluth, *Financial Politics in Contemporary Japan*, 11.

[32] Ibid., 5.

markets. The weakness of domestic-politics explanations for reform, however, is that they give no reason to expect that the pattern of reforms in one country will be similar to the pattern of reforms in another. Evidence of policy convergence between countries, in other words, damages the credibility of purely domestic-level explanations. However, as I suggest here and demonstrate in later chapters, there has been considerable policy convergence on the issue of financial regulation—certainly more than could be explained by mere coincidence. To put it simply: If domestic politics are such important determinants of change, why do different countries all do more or less the same thing?

The theories that stress that international-level pressures create policy convergence correctly capture the importance of common systemic pressures on diverse countries. On the other hand, many of these theories fail to predict what sorts of policies will be converged on. Nor do they often account for variations in the degree to which convergence has occurred. Policies on some issues converge to near unanimity, while on other issues nations remain stubbornly distinct. On which issues do policies converge? Why? On which issues do policies not converge? These questions often go unanswered.

Clearly, both sides of the debate have some merit. Moreover, as Benjamin Cohen puts it, "The interesting question . . . is not whether financial globalization imposes a constraint on sovereign states; it clearly does. Rather, we should now be asking *how* the discipline works and *under what conditions.*"[33]

Financial Globalization and Domestic Regulatory Structures
In this section I review some of the ways in which financial globalization has been thought to influence domestic regulatory structures. Four of the main strands of thinking on this topic may be summarized as competition in laxity, race to the top, U.S. hegemony, and international cooperation.

Competition in Laxity
According to classical economics, almost all forms of regulation are burdensome and costly to private enterprise. Therefore, businesses will, whenever possible, migrate to the jurisdiction with the lowest level of regulations, the lowest transaction costs, and maximum flexibility. In a world of isolated markets this exit option is not possible, but economic integration has the effect of opening the floodgates. As soon as consumers of financial services are able to make transactions in foreign markets, runs this argument, they will flock to the country (or market) with the lowest level of regulation. This idea is not new. As Adam Smith put it:

> The proprietor of stock is properly a citizen of the world, and is not necessarily attached to any particular county. He would be apt to abandon the country in which he was exposed to a vexatious inquisition, in order to be as-

---

[33] Cohen, "Phoenix Risen," 24.

sessed to a burdensome tax, and would remove his stock to some other country where he could carry on his business, or enjoy his fortune more at ease.[34]

The corollary is that once consumers of financial services have a choice of markets, policymakers in all countries will be forced to deregulate or witness the mass exit of all their domestic financial transactions to more lax climes. While few argue that such competitive deregulation is a good thing, the belief that it is likely to occur is surprisingly popular, due in part to the clarity and logical consistency of its predictions.[35] Ralph Bryant, for example, argues that because

> financial intermediation is more "footloose" than most other economic activities . . . the scope exists for an individual locality or nation to try to lure financial activity within its borders by imposing less stringent regulation, taxation, and supervision than that prevailing elsewhere . . . [which] can be described —provocatively—as a "competition in laxity."[36]

Charles Kindleberger describes the same phenomenon in more colorful terms:

> Internationally, the pressure to deregulate becomes strong, as equity demands that banks and firms in one country should be as free to engage in profitable activities as those in another. Like small boys wanting to break away from apron strings, the first to get his mother's permission, say, to camp out overnight, leads through competitive pressure to all getting it.[37]

Of particular interest in light of subsequent events is Kindleberger's wholly inaccurate prediction that "deregulation may induce the discarding of safeguards that were considered important in ensuring the protection of the ordinary investor: . . . prohibitions against insider trading and the like."[38] Philip Cerny discusses the same possibility: "Governments, international regimes and regulatory authorities within governments will increasingly come to be 'whipsawed' between different sectors and firms in the financial services industry seeking the most amenable regulators and the most permissive rules—what is called 'regulatory arbitrage' or 'competition in laxity.'"[39]
According to Richard Mackenzie and Dwight Lee:

> The increased mobility of capital, coupled with the growing economic integration of national economies, has dramatically expanded the scope and in-

---

[34] Smith, *Wealth of Nations*, 848.

[35] Exceptions include proponents of the free-banking school, who make a case for the greater stability of unregulated markets.

[36] Bryant, *International Financial Intermediation*, 139.

[37] Charles Kindleberger, *International Capital Movements* (Cambridge: Cambridge University Press, 1985), 72.

[38] Ibid.

[39] Cerny, *Finance and World Politics*, 15.

tensity of competitive markets. This growth in business competitiveness has necessarily forced governments into a competitive struggle for the world's human and physical capital base. As a consequence, governments have lost much of the monopoly power that undergirded their growth in earlier decades. World governments have had to compete against one another to lure and retain the physical and human capital that is now so crucial to modern production processes and to the tax bases on which governments depend.[40]

Adherents of the competition-in-laxity view, then, expect that the increased internationalization of finance will be accompanied by a race to the bottom, in which states compete for financial business by lowering regulatory standards.[41] Yet such a race to the bottom has not happened. On the contrary, although internationalization has been followed by deregulation on some issues, there has also been a shift to higher standards of regulation in certain other critical issue areas. This gives at least some credence to the mirror-image of competition in laxity, which is the race to the top.[42]

Race to the Top

The hypothesis that nations in an open world economy will engage in competitive reregulation follows much the same logic as does competition in laxity. The only difference is in the preferences of the mobile-asset actors, who according to this model will migrate to the state with the strictest rather than the laxest set of regulations. Barry Weingast, for example, accounts for the rapid growth of the U.S. economy in the 1880s using the facts that there were few barriers to capital movement across state boundaries and that the states competed with each other to attract capital by making promises to create secure property rights.[43]

David Vogel presents a compelling case for this view. He argues that increased levels of international trade have been accompanied by an upward shift in regulatory standards for consumer protection and the environment:

---

[40] Mackenzie and Lee, *Quicksilver Capital* (New York: Free Press, 1991), xi.

[41] A very striking example of the desire of certain types of business to migrate to lax regulatory climes was revealed by the recently revealed copper-trading losses incurred by the Sumitomo Corporation on the London Metal Exchange (LME). The LME had much laxer rules than its rival, the New York Commodities Exchange (Comex), regarding issues of disclosure of trading positions, off-exchange trading, credit arrangements, price reporting, punishment for the infringement of regulations, and ability of regulators to trade on the exchange. Perhaps as a result of this laxity, the trading volume of copper on the LME is nearly twenty times the volume it is on Comex. It will be interesting to see whether the revelation of Sumitomo's market manipulation will result in any strengthening of regulations on the LME. See Stephanie Strom, "A Market Ripe for Manipulation," *New York Times*, 12 July 1996, D.1.

[42] See Edward Kane, "Competitive Financial Reregulation: An International Perspective," in *Threats to International Stability*, ed. R. Portes and Alexander Swobsa (Cambridge: Cambridge University Press, 1987), 111–147. I am grateful to Steven Vogel for this reference.

[43] Barry Weingast, "Constitutions as Governance Structures: The Political Foundations of Secure Markets," *Journal of Institutional and Theoretical Economics* 146, no. 1 (1993): 286–301.

in his words, the "California effect" has outweighed the "Delaware effect."[44] Vogel accounts for this shift with reference to the strength of the consumer and environmental movements in the most economically powerful states, most notably the United States and Germany. Citizens in these countries were able, in effect, to use their superior market power to force economically weaker countries to improve their regulatory standards. For example, the U.S. consumer boycott of dolphin-unfriendly tuna was a key element in the decision by other countries to improve their regulations governing tuna fishing.[45]

Yet the evidence for a race to the top is as ambiguous as for a race to the bottom. Strengthened regulations for some issues have been accompanied by deregulation for others. This suggests that we must look further for an explanation—perhaps drawing from realist thinking and looking at the interests of the global hegemon.

U.S. Hegemony

An implicit assumption of the competition-in-laxity view is that nations have roughly equal powers. Therefore, a state faced with a neighbors who adopt strategies of competitive deregulation has no choice but to follow suit. However, if one state is more powerful than another, it has a second option: to coerce its weaker neighbors into adopting policies more in line with its own interests. Hence, although all states are faced with a common challenge in the form of financial market integration, their choice of response might vary according to their market powers.

However, only integrated markets provide a strong state with the incentive to influence the domestic regulations of its neighbors, since it is only in an open world that private economic actors can exploit the differences in regulatory standards between two countries. Moreover, the strong state will only feel the need to intervene if, by chance, its regulations are more burdensome or business-unfriendly than those of its rivals, causing domestic firms to move abroad and escape to less-onerous regulatory climes.[46] Therefore,

---

[44] Vogel, *Trading Up*. Delaware has the least demanding state laws covering incorporation, so historically companies that wanted to avoid excessive state regulation set up their headquarters there. In contrast, California sets relatively high regulatory standards for companies that incorporate there.

[45] At issue was the mesh size of the nets used by fishermen to catch tuna. Smaller-mesh nets caught more tuna, which was therefore cheaper, but they also snared and killed dolphins. Larger-mesh nets, mandatory for American fishermen, were dolphin friendly but made the catch more expensive. The United States was able to dictate the use of larger-mesh nets to other countries. Note, however, that there may be a difference between higher regulatory standards and better ones. Extremely high standards of environmental protection may come with their own costs in other areas.

[46] Proponents of strong regulation could argue, of course, that the presence of strong regulations in economically powerful countries is not coincidental, but causally related. Although this may very well be true in the very long run, it may not be true for specific regulations or sets of regulations at specific times.

coercion is a rational strategy for a state that has an interest in maintaining a particular type of regulatory regime under the following circumstances:

1. The state in question is more powerful than the others.
2. The economies of these states are integrated.
3. The regulatory regime of the more powerful state is more stringent than those of the others.

International finance during the 1970s and 1980s met these conditions. The United States was the dominant international actor, both in terms of conventional military power and in terms of market power. A combination of historical factors stretching back to the populist backlash against Wall Street in the aftermath of the 1929 Stock Market Crash and the subsequent enactment of a raft of banking and securities laws meant that the United States had one of the toughest regimes of financial market regulation in the world. Moreover, as global financial markets became more integrated it became easier and easier for American firms and, to a lesser extent, American individuals to circumvent strict U.S. regulations by dealing abroad.

Consequently, the United States did not have to respond to internationalization passively by deregulating. Instead, the United States had the means and motivation to force other countries to adopt American standards on issues in which its regulatory authority was being undermined. Many commentators argue that the United States did indeed exert significant influence over regulatory reforms in other countries. Some note that the pressure was direct and coercive. David Haddock and Jonathan Macey describe the crusade by the SEC to eradicate insider trading globally.[47] Jeffrey Frankel attributes the liberalization of Japan's financial markets to U.S. pressure during the Yen-Dollar talks of 1984.[48] Others believe that while U.S. influence over other countries was important, it was indirect rather than coercive. Michael Moran, for example, writes that "the Americanization of regulation is . . . deep and pervasive."[49] He borrows Susan Strange's concept of American structural power to account for the systemic diffusion of American influence. Pauly, too, uses the image of the United States as "bellwether" to describe American influence over financial regulation.[50]

This hypothesis predicts that cross-national regulatory reform results from American pressure on other countries, which in turn results in regulatory reforms that systematically favor American interests.

Yet there is only patchy evidence of the United States applying direct pressure on other countries to reform. The United States made direct threats to other countries over some issues, such as access to the Japanese stock market, and it negotiated strongly for the liberalization of Japan's

[47] Haddock and Macey, "Controlling Insider Trading in Europe and America."
[48] Frankel, *The Yen/Dollar Agreement.* This is discussed further in chapter 5.
[49] Moran, *The Politics of the Financial Services Revolution,* 132–134.
[50] Pauly, *Opening Financial Markets,* 179.

financial markets during the Yen-Dollar talks of 1984. Yet there is scant evidence that the United States wanted to dictate the passage of most reforms. There is more evidence of indirect U.S. influence, although this is much harder to measure or evaluate. Certainly some U.S. regulatory structures were adopted elsewhere, but by no means all of them. The shift away from functional segmentation of markets and toward universal forms of financial intermediation is the most important shift away from American standards. There is, in short, not enough evidence to support the claim that the United States systematically determined the regulatory outcomes, either directly or indirectly, in either Britain or Japan.

International Cooperation

A fourth alternative possibility for national regulators in an integrated world economy is to develop patterns of cooperation in order to win back at the international level what might be lost at the domestic level. To the extent that regulators have common interests separate from those of their national constituents, we might expect to see increased efforts at international cooperation or coordination following periods of capital internationalization. Whether such cooperation is observed depends not just on the assumption that regulators have separate interests, but also on such variables as the existing institutional structures for cooperation, the presence of cross-national epistemic communities, and the particular nature of the regulatory problems concerned.[51] In general, however, we expect such efforts in international cooperation to be accompanied by a degree of harmonization of regulatory standards. Moreover, such harmonization would tend toward higher rather than lower standards of regulation, leaving regulators in all countries with at least as much control over their markets as they had had before financial globalization required them to coordinate their activities on an international basis. Unfortunately, while it might be comforting to believe that regulators are indeed working cooperatively to retain control over financial markets, there is not very much evidence that they are doing so in any systematic fashion.

In summary, then, the debate over the causes of financial market reform is unresolved and divided between those who believe that financial globalization has led to policy convergence, and those who believe that there has been very little policy convergence. I conclude that there is simply too much evidence of policy convergence to ignore, and therefore I accept that financial globalization is a cause of domestic policy reform. However, it remains

[51] See Ethan Kapstein, *Governing the Global Economy* (Cambridge: Harvard University Press, 1994), for the view that nation-states have been able to recapture at the international level the regulatory control they had lost at the domestic level by means of cooperation. The resulting system of "international cooperation based on home country control" leaves states able to "enjoy the benefits of interdependence while maintaining national responsibility for the sector in question" (180). See also Kapstein, "Resolving the Regulator's Dilemma" *International Organization* 43 (spring 1989): 323–347, for an argument about the role of epistemic communities in the area of capital-adequacy requirements for internationally active banks.

unclear how globalization has affected domestic politics. None of the four hypotheses discussed adequately explains the observed pattern of regulatory reforms in Britain and Japan.

I suggest that the argument presented in chapter 1 helps to bridge the gap between the international and domestic levels of analysis. It captures both the systemic-level demand-side for reform and the domestic-level supply-side in a single model. My argument identifies the interests and strategies of the most economically mobile actors, who are best able to exploit opportunities of increased openness. The argument draws on the logic of the competition-in-laxity school in its recognition that international openness benefits actors with internationally mobile assets, and that this creates systematically similar effects upon domestic policymakers. Unlike most variants of this view, however, mine specifies more distinctly the interests of the actors with internationally mobile assets. Moreover, the argument recognizes that even though openness benefits certain actors, the benefit does not always or necessarily translate uniformly into similar policy choices. The preferences of mobile-asset actors must still be filtered through the lens of domestic politics, and existing domestic political institutions and alliances therefore cannot be ignored. Finally, I recognize that openness affects different categories of mobile actors in different ways and that this has an effect on the mechanisms through which their political leverage is exercised.

II. The Internationalization of Finance

So far in this chapter and in chapter 2, I have suggested that the Stigler-Peltzman model of regulatory capture does a good job of explaining regulatory policies toward finance in both Britain and Japan until about 1980, but is unable to explain the shift in policies toward consumer interests that occurred in the decade and a half after that time. I argue that the key change was the internationalization of finance, which gave an exit option to certain consumers and thereby altered the nature of political competition in this area. The next step of the argument, then, is to demonstrate that the exit option did indeed become real in the 1970s and 1980s.

However, before examining the patterns of market regulation and deregulation in Britain and Japan, this section first provides some historical background on international finance. The 1970s and 1980s saw a dramatic increase in the volume of international (cross-border) flows of financial capital.[52] This structural change in the world economy had a dramatic effect on the regulation of international securities transactions and on the regula-

[52] The current era of high international financial activity is not the first in world history. According to economist Robert Zevin, although the degree of integration of capital markets in the 1990s is unprecedented by the standards of the postwar era, it is not at all unusual by historical standards. Indeed, he argues, the period roughly from 1870 to 1970, when national governments had the upper hand over private actors in their struggle to control money, was the historic aberration. Zevin, "Are Financial Markets More Open?"

tion of domestic financial markets, as well. This section surveys the nature and causes of this trend and examines the question of the extent to which financial markets really became more international in these two decades.

The Bretton Woods System and the Era of Capital Controls

The sharp expansion in international banking in the 1920s was brought to an abrupt end by the U.S. Stock Market Crash of 1929. Many blamed speculative finance for the crash and hence for the Depression, as the Pecora Senate hearings in the U.S. Senate make clear.[53] John Maynard Keynes was one among many in the 1930s who warned against letting financial speculation spiral out of control into a casino. British and American leaders therefore planned a new gold-standard system of fixed exchange rates even before the end of World War II. This view underlies the Bretton Woods agreement on fixed exchange rates. U.S. Treasury Secretary Henry Morgenthau announced that the new system would "drive the usurious money lenders from the temple of international finance."[54] The Bretton Woods agreement endorsed the principle of free trade but specifically rejected the principle of free capital movement. Keynes is quoted as saying, "Not merely as a feature of the transition, but as a permanent arrangement, the plan accords to every member government the explicit right to control all capital movements."[55] The Bretton Woods system aimed to restore stability to the international payments system by making the dollar fully convertible to gold. The exchange rates of all other currencies were then pegged to the dollar at fixed rates that could be renegotiated if they appeared to be fundamentally wrong.[56] While the stability of the system may have encouraged trade, fixed exchange rates, however, were inimical to international financial flows.[57]

Growth of the Euromarkets

The fixed-exchange-rate system ultimately proved unsustainable. The major reason was the development of the eurocurrency markets in the 1950s

[53] And hence, at least to some people, speculation was ultimately responsible for World War II.

[54] Quoted in "Capital of Capital," *The Economist*, 7 October 1995, 5.

[55] John M. Keynes, *The Collected Writings of J. M. Keynes*, vol. 26, *Activities 1941–46: Shaping the Post-War World, Bretton Woods and Reparations*, ed. Donald Moggeridge (Cambridge: Cambridge University Press, 1980), 17; quoted in Helleiner, *States and the Reemergence of Global Finance*, 25.

[56] The British, for instance, devalued the pound against the dollar in 1967. The United States could not devalue because in order for the system to work at least one currency, the dollar, had to be fixed. This was not a problem as long as the United States kept its external accounts in surplus or at least close to surplus. The system was therefore vulnerable to a change in the U.S. trade position.

[57] Helleiner, *States and the Reemergence of Global Finance*. See also Armand Van Dormael, *Bretton Woods: Birth of a Monetary System* (London: Macmillan, 1978); Richard Gardner, *Sterling-Dollar Diplomacy in Current Perspective: The Origins and the Prospects of Our International Economic Order* (New York: Columbia University Press, 1980); and Alfred Eckes, *A Search for Solvency: Bretton Woods and the International Monetary System 1941–71* (Austin: University of Texas Press, 1975) for detailed discussions of the Bretton Woods Agreement.

and 1960s. "Eurocurrency" is any currency that is held outside its country of origin: the most common form is the eurodollar, a dollar held outside the United States by either an American or a foreigner.[58] The development of these markets was facilitated by a series of policy choices by both Britain, which allowed the markets to operate in London, and the United States, whose decisions to impose capital controls provided a crucial economic boost.

The euromarket originated in the late 1950s when British bankers in London used the dollar deposits they were holding for overseas residents to make dollar loans. They were able, by doing so, to continue to provide an international financing business despite capital controls on sterling and a relative decline in demand for services from British traders. As such, the business was very popular with the Bank of England, which saw the euromarkets as a means for Britain to retain its position as a center for international finance without compromising its domestic economic policy. The Bank of England accordingly did its best to encourage the development of the markets. For example, in 1962 it permitted the issuance, in London, of foreign securities denominated in foreign currencies.[59] The experience and skill in international financing of British investment banks such as S. G. Warburg also played a key role in developing the markets. Warburg acted as lead manager for the first eurobond, an issue for the Italian state highway authority Eurostrada in 1963.

The decision of the United States to impose capital controls to curtail the capital outflows that it had sustained since 1960 unwittingly helped Britain develop the euromarkets. Capital outflows from the United States resulted from the declining confidence of investors in the dollar's convertibility to gold. The Kennedy administration did not curb the attacks on the dollar by raising interest rates. Instead, it adopted a series of capital control measures, including the Interest Equalization Tax (IET) in 1963, the Voluntary Foreign Credit Restraint Program in 1965, and the Foreign Direct Investment Program. The IET imposed taxes on all new issues of foreign securities sold in the United States. The result was that American borrowers and investors in bonds simply shifted offshore to London in ever-increasing numbers in order to avoid the tax.[60] As a result, the market for all eurosecurities grew rapidly and was boosted by improvements in telecommunications and information technology, which assisted trading in the absence of a single trading exchange. The Association of International Bond Dealers

[58] Hence, a eurobond is a bond denominated in one currency, but issued outside that country. A eurodollar bond is denominated in dollars and issued outside the United States, say in London. It would be bought by holders of eurodollar deposits. The prevalence of dollars was partially a result of Federal Reserve Board Regulation Q, which limited the rate of interest that U.S. banks could pay depositors. The result of this regulation was that many U.S. depositors held their dollars offshore, where interest rates were unregulated and often higher.

[59] Helleiner, *States and the Reemergence of Global Finance*, 84.

[60] Meerschwam writes that "The adoption of the IET in 1963 created the Eurosecurities market." Meerschwam, *Breaking Financial Boundaries*, 28.

(AIBD), a private self-regulatory organization, was founded in 1969. New financial instruments were continually being added to the available stock, including adjustable-coupon retractable bonds, multiple-tranche issues, floating-rate certificates of deposit, and floating-rate notes (FRNs).[61] The market grew from $150 million in 1963 to $175 billion in 1986.[62]

The Collapse of Bretton Woods and the Advent of Floating Exchange Rates

The development of the eurocurrency markets was one factor that undermined the Bretton Woods system. More fundamental economic pressures, including persistent trade imbalances among the United States, Germany, and Japan, also eroded the system. A sharp deterioration in the U.S. current account in the late 1960s was accompanied by a sharp increase in long-term capital outflows from the United States, as private citizens sold dollars and bought foreign assets in the euromarkets in anticipation of a downward revision of the dollar's (fixed) exchange rate. The capital-account deficit was $12.9 billion in 1970 and plunged to $19.3 billion in 1971. The 1971 U.S. *Economic Report of the President* reported that:

> The large capital movements occurring . . . in response to changes in relative interest rates and monetary conditions are the outgrowth of the increasing internationalization of capital markets, especially the development of the Euro-dollar market. The increasing mobility of capital is a reflection of the growing flexibility and responsiveness of capital markets, which contribute to the efficient international allocation of investment and production.[63]

The U.S. government's first response was "to close the gold window" in 1971.[64] From that point onward, the United States would not be obliged to convert dollars to gold for other central banks at the fixed rate of $35 per ounce. Then, at the Smithsonian Conference in December 1971, the United States and its major trading partners agreed to reset exchange rates. Bilateral exchange-rate adjustments between the dollar and other currencies were replaced with multilateral adjustments. Speculative capital flows continued, however, and the efforts of countries outside the United States to control them with unilateral capital controls proved fruitless. The International Monetary Fund (IMF) reported that:

> The rapid growth in the size of international markets in short-term funds in the late 1960s, mainly in the form of "Euro" markets in bank deposits denominated in foreign currency, induced a number of major countries to impose or extend regulatory measures. . . . [However,] comprehensive and ef-

---

[61] See Hayes and Hubbard, *Investment Banking*, 54–55.

[62] *Euromoney Magazine*, March 1987, 435.

[63] *Economic Report of the President* (Washington, D.C.: U.S. Government Printing Office, 1971), 126.

[64] The political aspects of this decision are discussed in Joanne Gowa, *Closing the Gold Window: Domestic Politics and the End of Bretton Woods* (Ithaca: Cornell University Press, 1983).

fective restrictive controls on international capital movements were widely considered neither feasible nor, at least in their entirety, desirable. . . . At the same time . . . the actual movements have become very large.[65]

For two years, countries struggled to keep the fixed-exchange-rate system intact, but to no avail. Meanwhile, attitudes toward the desirability of maintaining the system changed radically. Within the U.S. private-sector financial community, floating exchange rates began to seem not just inevitable but attractive. Henry Wallich, an economist and central banker, remarked that some people seemed to believe that floating exchange rates would cure cancer.[66] One by one, countries adopted floating exchange rates, and in 1973 a global system of floating exchange rates had replaced the Bretton Woods order.

A profound consequence of the collapse of Bretton Woods was a vast increase in the ease with which capital could now move around the world. The increasing rapidity of capital flows was due at least in part to underlying economic factors. One particularly important event was the 1973–74 Oil Shock, which sent oil prices skyrocketing five times higher almost overnight. This ushered in a period of massive trade imbalances between oil-rich and oil-poor countries, along with spiraling and volatile inflation. This combination caused exchange rates, as well as the prices of all financial assets, to fluctuate dramatically, leading to greatly increased international financial activity by speculators and by those who wished to hedge either interest rates or exchange-rate risks. Between 1964 and 1985 international banking grew at a compound rate of 26 percent per year, far outstripping growth in world trade, which grew at 12.5 percent, and world output, which grew at 10.5 percent during the same period.[67]

Are Financial Markets More Integrated?

This book assumes that financial markets increasingly opened to foreign borrowers and lenders after the mid-1970s. In other words, there was an increase in international capital mobility in this period. However, economists debate what constitutes international capital mobility and the extent to which and by what definition capital actually is more mobile now than, say, in the 1960s.

For the purposes of my argument, there are two distinct dimensions of financial integration that affect an individual country, each with two facets. The

[65] IMF, *The Role of the Exchange Rate in the Adjustment of International Payments* (Washington, D.C.: International Monetary Fund, 1970), 25.

[66] Quoted in Kit McMahon, "Market Forces and Official Responses," *Midland Bank Review* (spring 1987): 4–8. A former official at the Bank of England, McMahon notes that the only people who appeared to have any doubts about the end of Bretton Woods were the central bankers, who in 1974 toasted fixed exchange rates "like so many disheartened Jacobites" (4).

[67] Bryant, *International Financial Intermediation.* The data for international banking are derived from the Morgan Guaranty Trust Company's "Bank Lending Trends," *World Financial Markets,* July 1985, 1–11.

first dimension concerns the availability of an exit option for domestic borrowers. First, is there a pool of capital or investment funds that exists outside that country and out of the reach of that country's regulations? If so, how easy and/or costly is it for domestic borrowers to tap into it and so bypass domestic sources of investment funds? Second, is there a class of foreign borrowers able to raise funds in the domestic market? This second fact may be of concern to policymakers who wish to attract capital into their countries, in other words who are concerned with the entry of international investors.

The second dimension concerns lenders. First, do markets exist abroad that are sufficiently deep and liquid to allow domestic lenders to invest in them, and so bypass domestic institutional arrangements? What, in other words, are the exit options for domestic lenders?[68] Second, is there a class of international borrowers who are able to borrow in local markets? This facet covers the possibilities of entry into the domestic market.

Each facet has different policy implications, and integration along one dimension need not necessarily entail integration along another. Indeed, I hold that focusing on the wrong type of integration can lead to the wrong conclusions. A crucial point is that a country can be highly internationalized in that domestic borrowers can easily borrow abroad, and investors can easily invest abroad, but the same country can be relatively poorly "internationalized" in the sense that foreigners are impeded from either lending or borrowing within its borders.

The ability of foreign financial intermediaries to operate in a country adds another dimension to the problem. A country can have a closed capital market, in the sense that its domestic financial intermediaries are relatively protected from foreign competition, but remain open in important ways if that country's own borrowers and lenders can operate offshore. In other words, there can be an asymmetry between the access that a country's firms have to foreign markets and the access that foreign firms have to that country's market. Moreover, firms here can refer either to consumers of financial services—including borrowers, lenders, or both—or to financial intermediaries who are the producers of financial services.

This illustrates an important point about the term "internationalization"—it has several dimensions, and each dimension has different implications. Hence, care must be taken to specify which precise aspect of internationalization is being discussed. Another equally important point is that internationalization is a continuum, not an either/or proposition. The tendency to generalize about markets being either open or closed masks a more complex underlying reality. What is important is changes in the relative ease of overcoming barriers between domestic and foreign markets.

---

[68] The two dimensions are similar to those suggested by Stephan Haggard and Sylvia Maxfield, who identify restrictions on inflows and outflows of capital as the key dimensions of financial internationalization. Stephan Haggard and Sylvia Maxfield, "The Political Economy of Financial Internationalization in the Developing World," *International Organization* 50, no. 1 (1996): 36.

Evidence of Internationalization

Along the first dimension, there is ample evidence of a sharp increase in the international investment-fund pool that borrowers can tap when they wish to exit their home market. The stock of international loans grew from $175 billion (5 percent of the total GNP of all industrialized countries) to $2.5 trillion (or 17 percent of the total GNP of all industrialized countries) between 1973 and 1989.[69] In 1973 the daily volume of foreign-exchange trading was $10–20 billion. In 1983 it was $60 billion. In 1992 it was $900 billion.[70] The ratio of foreign-exchange transactions to world trade rose from 10:1 in 1983 to 60:1 in 1992. In 1980 the total stock of financial assets traded in the global capital markets was $5 trillion. In 1992 it was $35 trillion, or about twice the GDP of all OECD countries.[71] As for the ability of foreigners to invest in home markets, the evidence also shows growing integration. The share of American pension-fund assets held in foreign securities rose from 0.7 percent in 1980 to 6 percent in 1993. The share of British pension fund assets held in foreign securities rose from 10 percent to 20 percent.

Along the second dimension, the existence of large international markets in which portfolio investors can invest, the evidence again supports internationalization. The stock of eurocurrency and foreign bonds rose from $259 billion (3 percent of the total GNP of industrialized countries) to $1,085 (8 percent of the total GNP) between 1982 and 1988, and to approximately $2 trillion by 1994.[72] The volume of international equity transactions grew at an average rate of 18 percent per year from 1979 to 1988, when the annual volume totaled $1.2 trillion.[73] The U.S. treasury market, one of the largest and most open of all financial markets, became a popular haven for international investors. Foreigners held 7 percent of U.S. Federal Government debt in 1970, and 17 percent in 1988.[74] In other ways, too, the United States became a market for foreigners wishing to lend abroad. In 1970 there were fifty foreign banking offices in the United States. In 1985 there were 780.[75] The average correlation of U.S. stocks to those of other major markets was 0.35 in the period 1975–79. It rose to 0.62 in 1985–88.[76] Dealing spreads (bid-ask spreads) on deposits of eurocurrencies declined sharply throughout the 1980s, implying that there was a much higher demand for such deposits and greater competition in international lending, which caused a paring of

[69] IMF, *Determinants and Systemic Consequences*, 5.

[70] Bank for International Settlements, quoted in "Survey of the World Economy," *The Economist*, 7 October 1995, 10.

[71] McKinsey Consulting Group, *The Global Capital Market: Supply, Demand, Pricing and Allocation* (Global Institute, 1994), quoted in *The Economist*, 7 October 1995, 11.

[72] Bank for International Settlements, quoted in "Survey of the World Economy," 10.

[73] IMF, *Determinants and Systemic Consequences*, 6, 7.

[74] Ibid., 10.

[75] Ibid.

[76] Salomon Brothers 1989, quoted in ibid., 5.

profit margins for lenders.[77] A dramatic fall in bid-ask spreads on eurosterling and euroyen provides evidence of vastly increased use of these currencies in international markets during the 1980s.

Evidence against Internationalization

Several economists have noted that many aspects of cross-national economic convergence do not square with the thesis that financial markets are fully integrated. Martin Feldstein and Charles Horioka argue that in a world of perfect capital mobility, domestic investors can just as easily borrow abroad as at home. Therefore, domestic savings rates need not be correlated with domestic investment rates. In fact, Feldstein and Horioka discover that in practice there was a high correlation between the ratios of investment to income and savings to income. Changes in the levels of domestic savings had very large effects on levels of domestic investments—implying that capital mobility across national borders was low, at least at the time of their study in 1980.[78] Robert Wade makes a related point.[79] Substantial differences remain in the price of borrowed funds—the real interest rate—in different countries. While some economists, such as Frankel, argue that these differences are declining, others, including Bruce Kasman and Charles Piggott, find no evidence of convergence.[80]

Thus, there is a dispute over how far the internationalization of finance has progressed, and the caveats presented by Feldstein and Horioka show that there is as yet no such thing as a single capital market. Nonetheless, there is little disagreement among economists over the trend toward internationalization since the 1970s. Moreover, there is general agreement that integration in markets for short-term financial instruments has progressed far faster for, say, foreign direct investment. Wade writes that "there is no doubt that the world market for standardized financial assets like currencies, government bonds and commodities, currency and interest futures has become highly integrated over the 1980s."[81] Frankel rejects the conclusion of Feldstein and Horioka, arguing that:

> The barriers to cross-border flows are sufficiently low that, by 1989, financial markets can be said to be virtually completely integrated among the large industrial countries . . . But this is a different proposition from saying that real

[77] The spread is the difference between the bid (the interest rate at which an institution will take a deposit) and the "ask" (the slightly higher rate at which an institution will lend the money out). The spread therefore represents a profit margin for the institution. As elsewhere, profit margins shrink under increased competition.

[78] Martin Feldstein and Charles Horioka, "Domestic Saving and International Capital Flows," *Economic Journal* 90 (June 1980): 314–329.

[79] Robert Wade, "Globalization and Its Limits: Reports of the Death of the National Economy Are Greatly Exaggerated," in *National Diversity and Global Capitalism*, ed. Suzanne Berger and Ronald Dore (Ithaca: Cornell University Press, 1996).

[80] Bruce Kasman and Charles Piggott, "Interest Rate Divergence among the Major Industrial Countries," *Federal Reserve Bank of New York Quarterly Review* (fall 1988): 28–44.

[81] Wade, "Globalization and Its Limits," 21.

interest rates are equalized across countries, which is still different from say-ing that investment projects in a country are unaffected by a shortfall in na-tional saving.[82]

Martin Feldstein and Philippe Bacchetta argue that the high correlation between domestic savings and investments had begun to break down by the late 1980s.[83] An IMF review in 1991 concluded that:

Recent studies of interest rate differentials suggest that integration in major financial markets has proceeded quite far for short-term instruments. In contrast, the presence of exchange risk still limits the degree of financial integration for longer-term markets—although returns on longer-term debt and equity instruments have recently shown a greater tendency to move to-gether—especially during periods of turbulence such as October 1987.[84]

This assessment is shared by Robert Zevin, who also finds that both closed and covered interest parity measures show a steady path toward greater effi-ciency (i.e., higher integration) from the 1960s until the 1980s, with the trend being especially marked after 1974.[85] In other words, there is little serious dis-pute that, along the dimensions I have outlined, financial markets were more international and more integrated in the mid-1990s than in 1970 or even 1980.

This section shows that the degree to which a genuinely international finan-cial market operating outside the regulatory jurisdictions of both Britain and Japan changed significantly between the mid-1970s and the 1990s. It is difficult to be too precise, but it makes sense to talk about the pre-1973 pe-riod as one in which domestic borrowers and lenders were largely confined to their local financial institutions. By the late 1980s, the option of exiting the home country and raising money or investing abroad increased signifi-cantly. It was this fact, perhaps more than any other, that influenced the subsequent development of domestic regulation in both countries.

[82] Jeffrey Frankel, "Quantifying International Capital Mobility in the 1980s," in *National Savings and Economic Performance*, ed. Douglas Bernheim and John Shonen (Chicago: Univer-sity of Chicago Press, 1991), 228. Frankel offers four definitions of perfect (international) cap-ital mobility: (1) the Feldstein and Horioka definition: domestic savings rates are uncorrelated with domestic investment because in a world of perfect capital mobility, domestic investors can just as easily borrow from abroad as at home; (2) real interest-rate parity: international capital flows should equalize real interest rates across countries; (3) uncovered interest parity: capital flows equalize expected rates of return on countries' bonds despite exposure to foreign-exchange risk; and (4) closed interest parity: capital flows equalize interest rates across countries when contracted in a common currency. The fourth definition is closely related to covered interest-rate parity, in which the interest rates on instruments issued by comparable borrowers but in different currencies are equal once the cost of cover in foreign-exchange for-ward markets has been adjusted for.

[83] Feldstein and Bacchetta, *National Savings and International Investment* (Washington, D.C.: National Bureau of Economic Reserves).

[84] IMF, *Determinants and Systemic Consequences*, 10.

[85] Robert Zevin, "Are Financial Markets More Open?"

In this chapter I examine ways in which an increase in international economic integration may influence regulatory outcomes across national borders. I suggest that explanations for regulatory reform that do not take into account both international and domestic factors are inadequate in explaining the policy outcomes in Britain and Japan. I argue that the crucial effect of internationalization on domestic politics lies in the shift of political power toward mobile-asset-holding private-sector economic actors. Such actors are able to exploit on the domestic level the exit opportunities provided by increased openness on the international level. In chapter 1, I outline a set of policy preferences that internationally mobile consumers of financial services might hold. If the mobility hypothesis is correct, then the regulatory reforms undertaken by national governments in response to internationalization should match these preferences. The next three chapters examine the extent to which they do.

Chapter 4

Financial Reform
in the United Kingdom

The British financial landscape changed drastically over the course of a few years in the 1980s. This chapter considers the major reforms. The key events were the Big Bang deregulation of the Stock Exchange and the new regulatory structure imposed by the U.K. Financial Services Act. Both reforms occurred in 1986. A key aspect of the latter reform was the establishment of the Securities and Investments Board (SIB), which can be compared with the U.S.'s SEC and Japan's SESC, established in 1991. In addition, a series of lesser reforms cumulatively brought big changes to London's financial landscape. The development of the London International Financial Futures Market (LIFFE) and the ban on insider trading are two representative cases chosen for discussion.

The Big Bang reform was about greater market competition, involving issues of market access, intramarket competition, and price controls. The development of LIFFE greatly expanded product diversity. The issue of regulatory oversight is dealt with under the section on the SIB, and questions of investor protection, acceptable business practice, and fraud are covered by the sections on the FSA and the regulation of insider trading. This chapter examines the reforms on a case-by-case basis rather than chronologically, since this allows for a more focused consideration of the various issues pertaining to each case. In each case we see how the financial services industry acquiesced to reforms in the face of competitive pressures and how these reforms turned out to serve the interests of large investors in internationally mobile financial services.

I. Background: The City before 1986

In the postwar period until the mid-1970s, British financial services were divided into three broad categories.[1] The first was what is traditionally thought of as the city establishment. The city included the official cartels, notably the LSE and the insurance giant Lloyds of London, and also the largest financial firms, including the big four clearing banks, which conducted High Street or retail banking,[2] and the merchant banks, which con-

---

[1] Background may be found in A. G. Ellinger and I. H. Stewart, *A Post-War History of the Stock Market* (Cambridge: Woodhead-Faulkner, 1980).
[2] Barclays, National Westminster, Lloyds, and the Midland.

ducted investment banking. The most prestigious of the merchant banks belonged to the Merchant Bank Acceptance Committee and were therefore known as accepting houses. Also included in this category were the big life insurance companies, led by Prudential Assurance. These firms were informally regulated. Oversight was typically a mixture of self-regulation and informal guidance by the regulatory authorities, with whom the city kept close ties. These authorities included the Bank of England, the Treasury, and the Department of Trade and Industry. Made up of a series of relatively small and well-defined cartels, the industry had both the means and the incentive to behave ethically and honestly toward customers and one another. The geographic closeness of the British financial community, working in the confines of the square mile of the city of London and drinking in the same pubs, facilitated effective self-regulation. In addition, close social ties in financial circles tended to facilitate effective self-governance. Many practitioners and regulators came from similar backgrounds: public school,[3] followed by college at Oxford or Cambridge, or occasionally a stint in the military.[4] They were in close touch with regulators at the Bank of England or the Treasury. A code of honor provided investor protection. The motto *Dictum meum pactum* (My word is my bond) was an article of faith in the city, and it appeared to work reasonably well in the pre-Big Bang years.[5]

The second broad category of financial institutions in Britain comprised firms that dealt with British retail clients but were outside the cartels. This group included licensed securities dealers and commodities and futures brokers. The markets in which these firms operated were described by one judge as a jungle.[6] The formal structure of regulatory oversight was almost, but not quite, as weak as in the city. A series of statutes stemming from the 1939 Prevention of Fraud (Investments) Act required all dealers in securities to be licensed and provided a limited degree of investor protection. A series of scandals in the 1970s and early 1980s demonstrated that this law was growing decreasingly effective.[7] The firms involved were too small and numerous to allow effective self-regulation. Furthermore,

[3] In Britain, the public schools are the most elite private schools.

[4] The social ties in the city are analyzed in Tom Lupton and Shirley Wilson, "The Social Background and Connections of Top Decision Makers," *Manchester School* 27, no. 1 (1959): 30–51. Michael Lisle-Williams explores the role of the upper classes in the discount houses in "Beyond the Market: The Survival of Family Capitalism in the English Merchant Banks" (*British Journal of Sociology* 35, no. 2 [1984]: 241–71). A lighter account is found in Joseph Wechsberg, *The Merchant Bankers* (New York: Simon and Schuster, 1966).

[5] To go back in time a bit, it was noted that "The want of a written contract between members had in practice no evil results, and out of the millions of contracts made on the Stock Exchange, such a thing was hardly known as a dispute as to the existence of a contract or as to its terms." *Report of the Commissioners of the London Stock Exchange Commission*, 1878, quoted in Colin Chapman, *How the Stock Market Works* (London: Century Hutchinson, 1988), 31.

[6] John Plender and Paul Wallace, *The Square Mile* (London: Hutchinson, 1985), 155.

[7] A full account is given in Julian Franks and Colin Mayer, *Risk, Regulation, and Investor Protection* (Oxford: Clarendon Press, 1989).

the Department of Trade and the Fraud Squad did not always exercise effective oversight.

The final category of financial institutions was the international offshore or euromarkets, which were regulated by the government very lightly. This had been a long-standing deliberate policy choice of successive governments and Bank of England officials, who wished to maintain London's status as a major international financial center.[8] Because the euromarkets were separated from the retail financial needs of the domestic public and because both the financial intermediaries and their customers tended to be overwhelmingly foreign (whose protection was therefore of less-pressing political importance) there were relatively few political pressures to regulate them closely. Moreover, since both market participants and customers were big investment institutions that could take care of themselves, there was less need for regulatory protection. Two private self-regulatory organizations, the Association of International Bond Dealers (AIBD), founded in 1969, and the International Primary Market Association (IPMA), founded in 1984, governed the euromarkets. The rule of caveat emptor applied. A common joke among traders, after saddling one another with worthless securities, was "My word is *your* bond."

The 1984 Gower Report on Investor Protection devoted less than two pages to euromarkets, a telling comment on the indifference of regulators to investor protection in these markets. The fact that these offshore markets existed in close geographic proximity to the insular and domestically oriented LSE did not mean that the markets were closely connected. U.K. firms raised their funds overwhelmingly in the domestic marketplace. U.K. investors, especially retail investors, put their money in the Stock Exchange rather than the euromarkets. Nonetheless, the euromarkets overtook the domestic markets in terms of both size and growth. Between 1970 and 1984 the number of foreign banks operating in London in the euromarkets grew from 163 to 403, while turnover in eurocurrency grew from $35 billion to $460 billion in the same period. This increase in turnover was three times the rate on the LSE in the same period, which went from £44 billion in 1970 to £173 billion in 1984.[9]

Responsibility for regulating the domestic markets was loose and, by Japanese standards, fragmented. The Stock Exchange Council was the self-regulatory organization responsible for overseeing the LSE, while the Department of Trade and Industry (DTI) was in charge of licensing off-LSE transactions. The enforcement of laws was the responsibility of the Crown Prosecution Service and the city of London police, since most investment business took place in their geographic district. Within the police, the Fraud Squad had special responsibility for white-collar crime. The Bank of England had responsibility for the banking sector and for the overall health

---

[8] See Eric Helleiner, *States and the Future of Global Finance* (Ithaca: Cornell University Press, 1994), 83–100.

[9] Chapman, *How the Stock Market Works*, 15; Janet Rutterford, *Introduction to Stock Exchange Investment* (London: Macmillan, 1983), 20.

of the industry.[10] The Bank of England traditionally had a strong preference for informal guidance–in the words of Monty Python, "A nod's as good as a wink to a blind bat." However, the bank's reputation for effective supervision took the first of several severe knocks following the secondary banking crisis of 1973–74 and, as we see later, it ultimately lost the right to exercise supervision at all.[11] The fact that in the 1980s the chairman of the LSE and the governor of the Bank of England met formally just once a year, at the invariably festive LSE Christmas luncheon, is an indication of how loose the ties used to be between the regulatory jurisdictions.

The political power of the city was, and still is, a contentious issue. The social and ideological ties between the Conservative Party and the city were obvious, and many assumed that an identity of backgrounds implied an identity of interests. The Labour Party was deeply suspicious of the arch-capitalist bankers, especially in its socialist heyday in the 1970s and early 1980s, and it was an article of Labour Party faith that the city was politically powerful and that its interests were in direct opposition to those of the working classes and to the health of the British economy more generally.[12] As Neil Kinnock, then Labour leader, put it in 1986: "The contempt expressed for 'the City' by a wide spectrum of opinion ranging from working managers and pressurized entrepreneurs to me and my fellow socialists is entirely justified."[13]

Actually, socialist fears about both the power of the city and its friendly relationship with the Conservative Party were shown to be exaggerated by events in the 1980s. Many observers have commented on the political power of financial interests over issues of macroeconomic policy, but this is a separate issue from that of the structure of finance itself.[14] The truth was that, aside from the few occasions when some scandal broke, the regulation of fi-

---

[10] See Steven Fay, *Portrait of an Old Lady* (London: Viking, 1987) for an account of the internal politics at the Bank of England. The title refers to the bank's revealing nickname, "The Old Lady of Threadneedle Street"; in bygone days bankers clearly regarded the bank as being as fussy, inquisitive, and harmless as the stereotypical British little old lady.

[11] See Michael Moran, *The Politics of Banking: The Strange Case of Competition and Credit Control*, 2d ed. (London: Macmillan, 1984), and Margaret Reid, *The Secondary Banking Crisis, 1973–75: Its Causes and Course* (London: Macmillan, 1982).

[12] Sidney Pollard writes that "it is clear that the constitutional authority of the government over the Bank, which is there to fulfill certain technical duties on behalf of the Treasury, has never been fully or even approximately implemented." Moreover, he continues, "industry has every time to be sacrificed on the altar of the City's and the financial system's primacy" (*The Wasting of the British Economy* [New York: St. Martin's Press, 1982], 85, 87). Jerry Cloakley and Laurence Harris write that "The impression for left-wing politicians is that . . . the City competes with the state for the power to govern in one important area, the governance of the economy, and that when the conflicts become acute, the City wins" (*The City of Capital* [Oxford: Blackwell, 1983], 234). In Nicolas Costello, Jonathan Mimie, and Sevmas Milne, *Beyond the Casino Economy* (London: Vergo, 1989), the title says it all.

[13] Neil Kinnock, *Making Our Way* (Oxford: Blackwell, 1986), 111.

[14] See, for example, Frank Longstreth, "The City, Industry, and the State" in *State and Society in Contemporary Capitalism*, ed. Colin Crouch (New York: St. Martin's Press, 1979), 157–190.

nancial services did not loom large on the political agenda of either party. Governments of any political stripe had strong incentives to keep London as an internationally competitive financial center, since financial services have always represented a huge percentage of employment and invisible earnings. Even in 1985, before the boom that followed deregulation, financial services, excluding net interest receipts, accounted for 10.6 percent of the GDP. In 1984 the sector accounted directly for 10 percent of all U.K. employment, excluding significant second-order employment effects in related professions such as law, telecommunications, and information technology, let alone gourmet sandwich shops and wine bars.[15]

According to Anthony Part, permanent secretary to the Treasury in the early 1980s, "We saw the City of London in good shape . . . preeminent internationally and contributing invaluably to invisible exports and so (usually) making the country's overall balance of payments tolerable. . . . Ministers were not much preoccupied by relations with the City, except when a large takeover and jobs were involved."[16] Given this laissez-faire view, it is not surprising that one of the most important developments in augmenting London's position as an international financial center, the founding of LIFFE, was a result of pure market forces.

II. The London International Financial Futures Exchange

LIFFE was founded in 1982 as an act of private entrepreneurship.[17] The successful Chicago Board of Trade and Options Exchange, founded in 1975, was a model for brokers such as John Barkshire of the British merchant bank Mercantile House. He recognized the attractiveness to institutional investors of highly liquid financial instruments that could be leveraged by margin trading and could be used either to hedge positions or for pure speculation. Barkshire developed the idea of a British equivalent and made his case to the Bank of England, which was at first very reluctant to support the idea.[18] Moreover, many British financial firms were somewhat skeptical both that such a venture would be profitable and that the bank would ever agree to it. Brian Williamson, the first chairman of LIFFE, is reported as saying that the establishment of the exchange involved a long fight between "the establishment and the newcomers."[19] The LSE was suspicious that such an exchange would pose a direct competitive threat to it. This suspicion was soon confirmed, as both exchanges introduced almost identical rival contracts for traded options on currencies. The Conservative Party did not appear to take much interest in the discussions, in part because the Falk-

[15] "London as a Financial Center," *Bank of England Quarterly Bulletin* 29, no. 4 (November 1989): 516–528.

[16] Anthony Part, *The Making of a Mandarin* (London: Andre Deutsch, 1990), 143.

[17] LIFFE is pronounced to rhyme with "knife."

[18] Plender and Wallace, *The Square Mile*, 69.

[19] Anthony Hilton, *City within a State* (London: I. B. Tauris, 1987), 75.

lands War demanded a great deal of attention in the spring and summer of 1992, and it was apparently content to let the market take its own course.[20] Eventually, a mixed collection of some 370 private brokers, banks, and commodities dealers agreed to become members, and the LIFFE opened for business in September 1992.[21]

The LIFFE was clearly intended to appeal to institutional investors rather than private individuals. The exchange was highly automated for both quotation (price-setting) and settlement, although it borrowed the open-outcry system and blazingly colorful jackets from Chicago. The instruments on which it offered futures were those that most appealed to international and institutional investors: eurodollar deposits, U.S. Treasury Bonds, and gilts, which quickly achieved the highest trading volumes. The appeal of the exchange to institutional investors was in both hedging and trading. For U.K. institutional investors who typically invested heavily in gilts, the market was particularly welcome. According to one leading institutional investor "We take the LIFFE long gilt contract as the purest price of long gilts."[22]

Yet while LIFFE was established relatively easily and soon turned into a resounding success for all concerned, the battle for the soul of the LSE was a longer and more difficult one for the institutional investors to win, although, as we see later, win they surely did.

III. The Big Bang: Deregulating the London Stock Exchange

The LSE was the main market for the securities, both stocks and bonds, of British and several foreign companies.[23] Most important, it also served as the market for British government bonds (gilts), which accounted for around half of all turnover. In order to provide a reliable system of investor protection, the LSE maintained a strict system of functional segregation in the market. This system was known as single capacity and divided the market into brokers and jobbers. Brokers, akin to retailers, took orders from outside clients to buy and sell stock. However, they were prohibited from owning stock themselves. Thus, they executed the order by dealing with the jobbers, who acted as wholesalers. For this, the brokers charged a fixed commission. The amount of commission varied somewhat with size of order, but was set by rule.[24] Price competition among brokers was there-

---

[20] LIFFE is not mentioned once in Chancellor Lawson's thousand–page biography. Nigel Lawson, *The View from Number Eleven: Memoirs of a Tory Radical* (London: Bantam, 1992).

[21] John Carson-Parker, *LIFFE* (London: Euromoney Publications, 1986).

[22] Margaret Reid, *All-Change at the City* (London: Macmillan, 1988), 117. Gilts are British government bonds, commonly referred to as gilt-edged stocks.

[23] There were also a few regional stock exchanges (e.g., in Manchester, Liverpool, and Edinburgh), but transaction volumes on these exchanges were dwarfed by that in London.

[24] The system of single capacity had been present since the LSE's Deed of Settlement was signed in 1802. The 1847 Rule Book specifically banned partnerships between brokers and jobbers, although it was not until 1908 that individual members were banned from acting in

fore impossible. The jobbers held stock, traded it among themselves, and took positions.[25] They were, however, prohibited from dealing directly with the investing public. They made their money on their own positions, and on the spread between the price at which they bought stock and the slightly higher price at which they sold it. Profits were therefore somewhat risky.

The purpose of the broker-jobber distinction was investor protection. Because of the huge information asymmetries between a broker and a private investor, the former was in a position to exploit the latter by offering bad advice or bad prices. For example, if a stockbroker had been allowed to own a large amount of a particular stock, he or she may want to keep the price of that stock high. Thus, he or she might be tempted to advise a client to buy it, whether or not it would be in his interest. If the investor is unaware of the broker's self-interest in the deal, he may unsuspectingly follow the bad advice. One solution to this problem is to try to prevent the sales staff and traders from knowing what open positions of securities their company owns. This is the rationale behind the fire walls in American securities firms, which separate stockbrokering, fund management, underwriting, and other activities. The single-capacity system was a more elegant and watertight solution. If brokers had no other business than dealing for clients, there could be no conflicts of interest. The same rationale worked for the exclusion of other financial firms from the LSE. The LSE authorities believed that only independent members could act truly impartially. Dealing on the LSE was therefore limited to members, and strict measures were taken to insure that these members were independent. Until 1969, members could only be partnerships. Even when they were allowed to form limited companies, no outside institution such as a clearing bank or a foreign securities company was allowed more than a minority shareholding. The limit of outside ownership was 10 percent of the LSE membership until 1982, and 29.9 percent from 1982 until the Big Bang abolished the restriction entirely.

In other words, the structure of the LSE provided a high degree of investor protection. This protection was of particular benefit to smaller investors, who typically faced much greater problems of information asymmetry *vis-à-vis* their brokers than did institutional investors. However, as with any system of financial regulation that limits internal competition, there were costs involved in terms of price distortions and market inefficiencies. Thus, the structure eroded the competitiveness of both the LSE and its individual members.

There were two primary problems with the old LSE. First, the ban on outside ownership of brokerages meant that member firms remained small and undercapitalized by international standards, especially in comparison

---

both capacities. Fixed minimum commissions had been introduced in 1912 to strengthen the system of single capacity as it had been reformulated in 1908. Plender and Wallace, *The Square Mile*, 82.

[25] Their status was analogous to the U.S. market makers for Treasury bonds.

with American or Japanese securities firms. Brokers and jobbers therefore could not generate economies of scale. Their customers paid unnecessarily high prices as a result. Second, the single-capacity system relied on fixed commissions. This was known as the link argument.[26] The LSE regarded fixed commissions as necessary for the survival of single capacity because such commissions insured the financial health of both brokers and jobbers. In practice, this meant that the brokers were guaranteed income and did not have to compete with each other on price. If fixed commissions were abandoned, the argument went, the result would be a price war in which the brokers' revenues would collapse. This would increase the temptation for them to bypass the jobbers by surreptitiously matching buy and sell orders, and to start trading on their own account. Had they done so, they could have assured their own profits but destroyed the jobbers, whose livelihood depended on the volume of deals the brokers brought them. In addition, the impartiality of the brokers' relationships with the clients would be compromised. Consequently, price competition on the LSE was expressly forbidden, which again increased prices for LSE customers. The relationship between single capacity, fixed commissions, and investor protection proved the most contentious issue in the reform debate. The 1970s, however, saw the cozy world of the LSE come under increasing pressure from within and without.

Pressures to Reform the London Stock Exchange

It would be tempting to think that the Big Bang was made possible only by the election of Thatcher's Conservative Party in 1979. Certainly the reform has all the hallmarks of a classic piece of Thatcherite deregulation—a protected cartel swept away by a doctrinally laissez-faire government. But, in fact, the pressures for reform had been building for several years before Thatcher came to power. Competitive economic pressures to deregulate the LSE came from both international and domestic levels and had become acute by the late 1970s. Then, in 1979, during the last days of James Callaghan's Labour government, the LSE came under domestic political attack from the Office of Fair Trading. All these factors played a role in the reform process, but it was not until the biggest customers of the LSE—the institutional investors—were able to exercise a highly credible threat to abandon the London market that the fate of the old LSE was sealed. The new Conservative administration was certainly ideologically sympathetic to the notion of encouraging competition on the Exchange, but in fact played the role of follower rather than leader in the events that were to unfold.

Financial Globalization and the Impetus to Reform

Global financial integration first threatened the old LSE in the mid-1970s. The two most significant aspects of the globalization of finance, as far as the LSE was concerned, were the 1975 May Day deregulation of the

---

[26] Reid, *All-Change in the City*, 29.

New York Stock Exchange, and the 1979 abolition of LSE controls in the United Kingdom. May Day deregulation led to a dramatic reduction in average commission rates in the United States and a major restructuring and consolidation of U.S. securities firms. This undermined the competitive position of the LSE in two ways. First, British investors who wished to invest in the United States did so almost exclusively through the cheaper, better U.S. brokers. Second, and more of a direct threat, the shares of British companies began to be traded in New York rather than in London. This was done using shares in American Depository Receipt (ADR) form, which escaped the fixed commissions and stamp duty of the LSE. Dealing costs were therefore significantly lower. One estimate puts commission rates for the largest transactions at around 0.4 percent in London versus 0.15 percent or lower in the United States.[27] (See table 4.1.) These problems were exacerbated by the lifting of the exchange controls, one of the first acts of Geoffrey Howe as Conservative Chancellor of the Exchequer.[28] British capital flooded out of the country, via American firms or to ADRs in New York.

By 1983 ADRs accounted for approximately 7 percent of trading in U.K. equities, a very significant proportion of such a small-margin business and one that was rising fast.[29] ADR trading was concentrated in the stocks of the big internationally renowned companies, which had the reputations and resources to tap foreign markets. In 1984, 62 percent of the trading in Imperial Chemical Industries (ICI), one of Britain's largest capitalization stocks, was being conducted outside London, mostly in New York. Trading in the United States also accounted for 48 percent of turnover in Glaxo shares, 28 percent of British Telecom, and 20 percent of British Petroleum. The most active traders were the British institutional investors, who showed no national loyalty to British brokers if they could get a better price in another market or from a foreign broker. As Mick Newmarch of British insurance giant Prudential Assurance remarked, "When we have a significant buying programme on we check all available markets. We take the attitude that we deal wherever we can get the best price."[30] It is estimated that 95 percent of the investments made by the top twenty British pension funds were handled by foreign firms.[31] The LSE was keenly aware of the threat to its existence. Sir Nicholas Goodison, the chairman of the LSE, continually monitored the competitive threat from New York, commenting in 1985 that "This threat is made more serious by the growing practice of trading U.K. stocks in ADR form. . . . in the last twelve months there has been a significant increase in the amount of U.K. stock traded in that form. This severely

[27] George Webb, *The Bigger Bang* (London: Waterlow, 1987), 18.

[28] His decision, apparently, was taken despite the doubts of many, including Thatcher, who warned him that he would have to take full responsibility if things went wrong. See J. Hillman and P. Clarke, *Geoffrey Howe: A Quiet Revolutionary* (London: Wiedenfeld and Nicholson, 1988), 149.

[29] *Bank of England Quarterly Bulletin* 33, no. 1 (1993).

[30] Figures and quotation from Chapman, *How the Stock Market Works*, 17.

[31] Plender and Wallace, *The Square Mile*, 48.

Table 4.1. Transactions costs in major markets, 1982

Center	Commission Rates (%)		
	£500	£50,000	£500,000
London	2.0	0.6	0.4
Tokyo	1.25	0.85	0.6
New York	2.8	0.5	0.3

Note: Commission charges applied to purchases only.

Source: "London Stock Exchange Evidence to the Wilson Committee, 1980," updated in Janette Rutterford, *Introduction to Stock Exchange Investment* (London: Macmillan, 1983), 15.

threatens London's competitiveness."[32] The same point was not lost on others in the City. The Midland Bank Review noted in 1985, "Without reform the Stock Exchange is threatened by massive transfer of business to other centers, particularly New York, stemming from the rapid expansion of international dealings, while undercapitalized Stock Exchange firms also appear ill-equipped to compete with the giant U.S. and Japanese securities houses."[33]

It was becoming clear by the early 1980s that the LSE was in danger of becoming internationally irrelevant. Fixed commissions made it uncompetitive as a market, while independence and the single-capacity system ensured that its members remained financially tiny compared to U.S. or Japanese brokerages. The combined capital of all LSE members was less than that of Merrill Lynch, which was in turn dwarfed by Japan's Nomura Securities.[34]

A final nail in the old LSE's coffin was the introduction in the early 1980s of a new eurocurrency instrument, the equity-convertible eurobond. This ten-year bond gave holders the option of receiving their capital in the form of shares in the company rather than cash. In effect this allowed British and foreign companies to issue shares, and investors to trade them, without ever going through the LSE.[35] The Stock Exchange Council was well aware of the dangers and were actively considering reform. In other words, this case fits the prediction that global financial integration, by bringing competition to previously insulated domestic markets, was the primary impetus for

[32] Nicholas Goodison, "London in the International Marketplace," *Stock Exchange Quarterly* (December 1985), 16.
[33] *Midland Bank Review* (spring 1985), 21.
[34] Reid, *All-Change in the City*, 44.
[35] Chapman, *How the Stock Market Works*, 15.

deregulatory reform. This view is shared by, among others, the chairman of the Bank of England.[36]

Domestic Pressures for Reform

In addition, there were at least three domestic factors that contributed to the Big Bang, two economic and one political. These are the rise of institutional investors, the collapse of the jobbers, and the court case brought against the LSE by the Office of Fair Trading.

The Rise of Institutional Investors   The most striking trends in the postwar history of the LSE were the declining importance of private investors and the concurrent increase in prominence of institutional investors. Figures for the percentage ownership of U.K. shares are illustrative. In 1963, individuals owned 54 percent of U.K. shares, while institutional investors owned 30 percent. By 1981, individual ownership had dropped to 28 percent, and institutional ownership jumped to 58 percent.[37] This had a major effect on stock market business. As we have seen, the LSE was structured to provide a high degree of investor protection, at the cost of relatively high fixed commissions. This structure was appropriate with a large private client base, and, as table 4.1 illustrates, in comparision with the United States, private clients actually paid relatively low commission rates compared to institutional investors. But big institutions did not need the protection of single capacity. They had the resources to determine if they were being cheated and the market power to retaliate. They dealt frequently and in large quantities, and preferred cheap dealing, which fixed commissions didn't permit. They became increasingly frustrated with the old system.[38] The largest single investor in U.K. stocks was the Prudential Assurance Company. Newmarch, Prudential's head of investments, later commented: "For too long, we felt, those whose affairs we are employed to manage had been denied the benefit which would flow ... from the introduction of serious competition into the affairs of the Stock Exchange."[39]

In the 1970s, the LSE's biggest customers went so far as to set up their own exchange, ARIEL, in an attempt to bypass the official LSE and its too-high commissions.[40] The computerized system matched large buy and sell

[36] Sir Robin Leigh-Pemberton, "Changing Boundaries in Financial Services," *Bank of England Quarterly Bulletin* 24, no. 1 (March 1984): 40–44.

[37] *Stock Exchange Quarterly* (June 1985): 7.

[38] Interview, official from Prudential Insurance, Reading, June 1993.

[39] Reid, *All-Change in the City*, 90. Newmarch is strikingly rotund, and it was with glee that some commentators referred to him as "the largest single investor in the market."

[40] The system was set up by the Merchant Bankers Accepting Houses Committee and actively supported by the men from Prudential. It was abandoned after the agreement to scrap fixed commissions in 1983. ARIEL stood (or rather, didn't stand) for Automated Real-Time Investment Ltd. Rutterford, *Introduction to Stock Exchange Investment*, 12, 352. Goodhart, "The Economics of the Big Bang," *Midland Bank Review* (summer 1987): 6–15; Reid, *All-Change in the City*, 44.

orders at a fraction of the LSE's commission. It prompted the LSE to reduce commission charges on large transactions on at least three occasions, but the Bank of England refused to use it for their gilt business, and it never took off. Its presence, however, dramatically underscored that big customers regarded the LSE's rules on fixed commissions as unacceptable. The larger and more competitive brokers chafed too, wanting to compete on price for the rich institutional business, but forbidden by LSE rules from doing so.[41] An unfortunate consequence of the inability of brokers to compete directly on price was the brokers' widespread practice of competing for business with an array of nonmonetary incentives. Some incentives, such as the offer of good market research, served some economic good. Other practices, such as offering clients bribes in the form of expensive meals, trips to exotic locations, lavish presents, and so on, were wasteful and created price distortions.[42]

The Decline of the Jobbers   The second problem facing the LSE was the increasing strain on the jobbers. This had two causes. First, the total volume of shares being traded increased throughout the 1970s. Second, thanks to the rise of institutional investors, the average transaction size was increasing. Both of these trends entailed that the jobbers, as wholesalers to the system, were forced to take open positions in larger and larger volumes. This increased their risk and required increasing amounts of capital in order to fund trading positions. But the jobbers were small, since the restrictions on ownership meant that capital was very difficult to raise. Many went bankrupt or merged. In 1958 there were 108 jobbers, but by 1980 there were only fourteen, of which only five were of any significance. An internal report in 1976 revealed serious profit losses among the jobbers and concluded that the loss of any of the big five jobbers "would put an intolerable strain on the single capacity dealing system."[43] It was in response to this problem that the LSE began to relax the membership rules, first allowing partnerships to become limited companies in 1969 and then increasing the amount of permissible outside ownership of a member firm to 29.9 percent in 1982.

In short, by the late 1970s, the old LSE rules were becoming increasingly outdated, even for domestic market conditions. The reluctance to liberalize stemmed from a reluctance to abandon the single capacity system, which itself prevented more radical reform. In addition, until the lifting of exchange controls in 1979, international competition was not acute and there was no alternative for the LSE's customers but to bite the bullet and accept the costs of market inefficiencies. However, the LSE was attempting to deal with some of the efficiency problems by cutting commission rates on large

---

[41] Interviews, officials at S. G Warburg, London, July 1990.

[42] Interviews with market participants, London, 1992.

[43] Sir Nicholas Goodison, "The Stock Exchange at the Turning Point," *Stock Exchange Quarterly* (March 1985):8–16.

deals and relaxing membership rules. Under consideration in the early 1980s was a proposal to allow outside ownership of jobbers but not brokers. This would have had the effect of allowing the jobbers to expand, giving them a vital injection of capital, which would have allowed them to better serve the large investors but would have preserved the independence of the brokerage and therefore maintained structural protection for small investors. It is possible that such a reform would have been accepted by the Stock Exchange Council.[44] But paradoxically, a blow was to fall only months prior to this action, which was to hamstring reform from 1979 until 1983, in the form of a court case brought against the LSE by the Office of Fair Trading.

The Office of Fair Trading Court Case   In 1976, the Labour government had extended the authority of the Office of Fair Trading (OFT) to investigate cartelistic practices in service industries under an amendment to the 1956 Restrictive Trade Practices Act. In February 1979, as the last chill winds of Prime Minister Jim Callaghan's "Winter of Discontent" blew out, the OFT referred 173 of the LSE's rules—virtually the whole book—to the Restrictive Practices Court. The main targets of the case were the exclusion of outsiders, the broker-jobber division, and fixed commissions: all were cited as cartelistic and anti-competitive.

The LSE had appealed unsuccessfully to the Labour Minister for Trade in 1976 to gain exemption from the new terms of the act and continued to appeal for exemption—always unsuccessfully—to every minister for trade, both Labour and Conservative, from 1976 until 1983. It is perhaps understandable that both Labour ministers, Shirley Williams and Roy Hattersley, were deaf to the pleas of an institution that their party regarded with such suspicion. But it was a bitter and unexpected blow that after the Conservative victory of May 1979 two more ministers should reject their appeal. Their refusal to help can perhaps be explained in part by the prevailing Thatcherite belief in free market competition and also by a reluctance by the Conservatives to be caught doing favors for their traditional friends in the city. It also demonstrates how the LSE's accustomed political power was being eroded.[45]

The OFT case threatened the LSE two ways. First, a successful legal defense would take considerable time and expense, especially since the OFT case was, prima facie, extremely strong: the market was indeed a price-fixing cartel. Second, and more fundamentally, the Stock Exchange Council believed that the only possible defense was one that encompassed the entire system, arguing that individual restrictive practices such as fixed commissions were a necessary part of a system that ultimately worked for the public

---

[44] Interview with a member of the Stock Exchange Council, December 1992.

[45] The case also supports the tart observation of Conservative backbencher Julian Critchley that Mrs. Thatcher was unable to look at a great British institution without hitting it with her handbag.

good. This meant, as the LSE was later to argue, that while the case was in progress, any reform of any part of the rules was impossible. Goodison wrote that the restrictive practices case "potentially attacked every rule and regulation laid down by the Stock Exchange. Each was assumed to be against the public interest unless proved otherwise. Any rule against the public interest would have to be abandoned. This would have been disastrous to the fabric of investor protection."[46]

Institutional Pressures

In other words, by the early 1980s, pressures on the LSE from all sides were becoming overwhelming. At this point, it is worth considering what interests each of the major players had in the reform process.

The London Stock Exchange Member Firms   The members of the LSE, as expected, were divided, but not hopelessly so. As we have seen, the members of the council were acutely aware of the competitive threats that they faced, both from New York and from the hostility of their large clients. They had begun to undertake reform on their own account, and there is no reason to suppose that they would not have continued to do so, had it not been for the OFT case. In truth, the real division was between those who were determined to save single capacity and those who eventually came to believe that its demise was inevitable. This division was based not only on international competitiveness or, more accurately, on self-perceptions of international competitiveness, but on more philosophical differences about who the LSE should be serving and how. Note that the small size of all the LSE member firms made it unlikely that any but the largest would be internationally competitive. Rather this is a case of a local cartel more or less unanimously accepting the inevitability of liberalization.[47] The bigger and better of the brokers and jobbers were somewhat more upbeat about their prospects in the brave new world. But the bloodletting in New York after the May Day reform served as a grim reminder that a sudden increase in competition would be painful for all competitors.[48] Against that, the prospect of being bought out at an exorbitant price by a well-heeled and ill-informed clearing bank or foreign institution sweetened the pill for most brokers and helped undermine resistance to deregulation.

[46] Goodison, "Stock Exchange at the Turning Point," 16. To recapitulate the link argument: single capacity was desirable because of its built-in investor protection. Fixed commissions were essential to the viability of single capacity because by guaranteeing the brokers' income, they ensured that brokers would deal impartially, through the jobbers. Therefore, single capacity and fixed commissions were desirable even though they were anticompetition.

[47] Moran disagrees, referring to the stockbroking community as backward and lazy and inefficient and insisting that the LSE was deadlocked on the issue of reform. Moran, *Politics of the Financial Services Revolution*, 55–87, 139. This view ignores the series of reforms that the LSE had already undertaken to improve competitiveness before 1983.

[48] Interviews with staff of LSE member firms, 1992.

Investors Predictably, the biggest customers—institutional investors—were becoming increasingly impatient with the old rules, especially fixed commissions. As customers do, they put pressure on the LSE not by lobbying, but by taking their business elsewhere. As such, the financial integration represented by the lifting of exchange controls in 1979 greatly increased the leverage they had over reform.

The smaller customers, individual investors, benefited from the old rules in two ways: investor protection and, because rates were fixed, low commissions, which, in effect, were subsidized by the relatively high rates paid by the big institutions. Yet there is little evidence that they mounted serious opposition to reform. One explanation for this is that they faced a collective-action problem, compounded by the fact that the LSE was not a democracy, and it was hard for them to get representation. Another explanation might involve linkage. In the early and mid-1980s there was considerable optimism about the beneficial effects of privatization and Thatcher's bid to expand the number of shareholders. Deregulation was viewed as part of this movement, and the adverse effects on commission rates were lost in the euphoria and hype put out by the brokers and the government.

The Office of Fair Trading The OFT's interest in the case was crystal clear. It wanted to get rid of cartels, which it did by bringing them to court. It didn't care about broader issues of the best ways to achieve market reform nor was it supposed to. Hence, although it rapidly became clear that its case was damaging to London as a financial center by delaying the reform process, it persisted in bringing the case to court.

One result of the OFT case, paradoxically, was that between 1976 and 1983, when the case was abandoned, any reform became impossible. There is, therefore, considerable controversy over the role of the OFT in bringing about reform of the LSE. Some hail the body and Sir Gordon Borrie, its head, as crucial to the deregulatory process. Moran calls Borrie "a formidable and skilled inquisitor"[49] and writes that:

> private interests could not independently organize effective reforming coalitions. The interests of firms were so divided that change either ground to a halt, or happened with agonizing slowness. The resulting stalemates had to be broken by the intervention of state agencies: . . . the Office of Fair Trading and then the Bank of England after the interests on the Stock Exchange argued themselves into immobility in the early 1980s.[50]

Some, however, argue that the case held up reform rather than "broke the log-jam," to use Moran's phrase. Goodison, chairman of the LSE, was understandably critical of the OFT, but more impartial observers included Robin

[49] Moran, *Politics of the Financial Services Revolution*, 129.
[50] Ibid., 124.

Leigh-Pemberton, the governor of the Bank of England, who wrote, "Innovation and development in our securities industry were severely hampered during the period of the restrictive practices case against the Stock Exchange; this coincided with a phase of exceptional change in the shape of the international securities industry to which the British response started relatively late."[51]

Eddie George, executive director and subsequent governor of the Bank of England said of the Big Bang:

> The proximate cause was the OFT's reference to the Restrictive Practices Court and the Government/Stock Exchange agreement . . . but although the timing might have been different, commercial pressure of competition would have made changes necessary in any event, and likely to be similar in nature. . . . [T]he main conclusion I draw is that we must for the future avoid getting into a situation where pressure for change is held back and allowed to build up behind a restriction, so that it breaks out with unnecessary disruptive force once the restriction is removed.[52]

Nor were they alone. Jim Gower, author of the Financial Services Act, commented that as a way to undertake important reforms, the court case was "dotty." Harold Wilson, former Labour Prime Minister, agreed.[53]

The Bank of England   The bank's main interest is best summed up by the bank's governor: "our goal . . . [is] keeping London as one of the three major international markets in financial services."[54] The bank was, if anything, indifferent to the fate of individual British financial firms. In the same speech, the governor remarked: "When losses come, and they will come, they should be construed not as a failure of the new City but rather as evidence of market forces at work in a competitive environment."[55]

Eddie George, executive director, was also frank about the prospects of firms in the new markets: "All the participants have made their own assessments in full knowledge—or perhaps, more appropriately, full ignorance, of the facts. . . . Our aim will be to ensure that it is their own money that they lose rather than that of their customers or other counterparties."[56]

[51] Leigh-Pemberton, "Changing Boundaries," 41.

[52] Edward A. J. George, "The City Revolution," *Bank of England Quarterly Bulletin* 25, no. 3 (September 1985): 422.

[53] "Goodison and the Government to Settle out of Court," *The Economist*, 23 July 1983, 67. City opinion about Borrie ranged from a diplomatic "He's a very tough nut" to a delicately reasoned "He's a nasty, bitter, vindictive old bastard." Interviews, summer 1990 and winter 1992.

[54] *Bank of England Quarterly Bulletin* 25, no. 4 (December 1985): 535.

[55] Ibid.

[56] *Bank of England Quarterly Bulletin* 25, no. 3 (September 1985): 422. Eddie George was later to become the governor of the bank, where he would attract vitriolic criticism for his decision in 1994 to allow Barings Bank to go bankrupt rather than use public money to bail it out after it lost over $1 billion in unauthorized futures trading in Singapore. This incident revealed starkly his (and the bank's) commitment to a laissez-faire approach to regulation, which puts market efficiency ahead of considerations of distributional fairness or the inadequacies of caveat emptor as a mechanism for investor protection.

The Conservative Party   The Conservatives faced conflicting pressures, but the balance in 1979 should have been overwhelmingly in favor of reform. They had always been seen as friends of the city. The LSE was lobbying hard to get the OFT case dropped, promising that it would reform itself. It was clear to Chancellor of the Exchequer Nigel Lawson, at least, that reforms were "urgently needed" to improve the LSE's international prospects, which were an important part of the economically vital financial services industry.[57] Deregulation and more competition were mainstays of Thatcherism. Yet from 1979 until 1983, the Tories refused to act. When they did, the bargain they struck was just what the OFT wanted anyway—an end to fixed commissions.

So why did it take them so long? Part of the answer seems to be the desire not to be caught doing favors for the city. To have cut a deal with the LSE sooner would have been to invite charges of hypocrisy and favoritism, as indeed it eventually did. Even the traditionally pro-Conservative journal *The Economist* was critical of the accord: "This retreat is a political mistake. . . . It is not only the left wing of the Labour party that will see something odd in Mr. Norman Tebbit, the employment secretary, at full gallop against trade union practices that act against the public interest while the reins are pulled on an inquiry into such practices in the City."[58]

It is significant that the deal was struck immediately after the 1983 election, when the party was less politically vulnerable. The OFT's case was due to come up in January 1984, which lent urgency to the decision and helps explain the promptness with which the Tories acted after the election. The personal influence of Nigel Lawson may also be a factor. Ordinarily, the minister for trade would have been more involved in the issue, but Cecil Parkinson, minister at that time, was tied up in a scandal involving an illegitimate child, and it was up to Lawson to persuade Thatcher that dropping the OFT case would be a good idea. Thatcher herself does not appear to have been much interested in the issue, although she expressed misgivings about the unseemliness of appearing to do the city a favor. Lawson reminded her that they were at the start of a new term of office and that by the time the next election came around "it would have become clear that the reforms on which we were insisting were genuine."[59] But in the final analysis, liberalization of the LSE was something that the Conservatives acquiesced to rather than initiated. The Goodison–Parkinson deal was seen as a triumph for the LSE—but it proved a pyhrric victory for the member firms.

---

[57] Lawson, *The View from Number Eleven*, 398–402.

[58] "Doing the City a Favor," *The Economist*, 23 July 1983, 16.

[59] Lawson, *The View from Number Eleven*, 400. Thatcher's lack of visibility on the issue of financial reform is tellingly illustrated by the fact that a major survey of the economic policies of her first two administrations, from 1979 to 1987, does not even mention the Big Bang. See Peter Jenkins, *Mrs. Thatcher's Revolution: The Ending of the Social Era* (Cambridge: Harvard University Press, 1988).

The Big Bang

Shortly after the 1983 Conservative election victory, Parkinson, the new trade and industry secretary, agreed to drop the OFT case. In return, Goodison, the LSE chairman, agreed to abandon fixed commissions, allow outsiders into the council, and also allow them to buy member firms or to apply directly for their own seats on the LSE. The single-capacity system was not formally surrendered, but the link argument proved correct: once fixed commissions were dropped, single capacity made no sense and was abandoned in a few months. October 27, 1986, was set as the date when all the restrictions would be scrapped in one fell swoop—hence, the name Big Bang.

At the same time, the LSE decided to introduce a new automated dealing system to cope with the changed structure. SEAQ (Stock Exchange Automated Quotation) was designed to maintain a quote-driven market in which market makers (as the jobbers were now called) continuously published buying and selling prices for stocks. The model the LSE used was the highly successful U.S. National Association of Securities Dealers Automated Quotation system (NASDAQ). The alternative to a quote-driven market is an order-driven one, in which brokers match actual buying and selling orders for stock. The NYSE, for example, is order-driven. The decision to continue with a quote-driven system, although seemingly technical, is important to understand. A quote-driven market, in which an investor can trade regardless of whether there is a counterparty, is usually more liquid. Big investors can be assured of being able to deal immediately in large volumes of shares. However, such a system relies absolutely on the presence of well-capitalized market makers and is accordingly more expensive. An order-driven market is typically less expensive, especially for small investors, but it is less able to handle very large trades. Thus, the LSE's decision to maintain the quote-driven system was one that consciously favored large investors over small ones.

A minor but poignant result of automation was that the traditional system of personal trading on the historic old trading floor was abandoned in 1986. This was after the LSE, unaware of how successful SEAQ would be, had just spent £3 million on upgrading the floor.

Hence, the main features of Big Bang were the abolition of fixed commission rates, the end of the broker-jobber distinction (single capacity), the abolition of entry barriers (banks and foreign institutions could become LSE members), and the introduction of SEAQ.

Fallout from the Explosion

Who were the winners and who were the losers from Big Bang? Commentators are virtually unanimous that the big winners were the big investors holding internationally mobile assets and that the losers included brokers and the small investors. A survey of financial practitioners conducted one year after Big Bang clearly identified the winners and losers of the reform. In answer to the question, "Who are the major beneficiaries of the 'Big Bang'?" respondents drawn from private industry and the city answered:

first, institutional investors (32 percent); second, stockbrokers (27 percent); third, industry (19 percent); and, last, private shareholders (2 percent).[60] The big customers—the institutional investors, insurance companies, and pension funds—benefited most from reduced costs. Increased competition and the abolition of fixed commissions caused dealing costs for large trades to fall dramatically, by an average of 30 percent from 1986 to 1987.[61] Moreover, these cost savings were sustained over time. Five years later, in 1991, *The Economist* calculated that average transaction costs (including the spread, stamp duty, and average commission) had fallen from just under 2 percent to just over 1 percent for wholesale trades of over £500,000.[62] The SEAQ trading system, although it had considerable teething troubles, turned out to be well suited to the needs of the large investors.

Next to benefit was London as a financial center. The turnover and value of U.K. equity-share dealing rose almost fourfold between 1986 and 1987, and stabilized at the higher level.[63] In 1986, the average daily turnover of U.K. equities was worth approximately £500 million, and, in 1995, it was over £2 billion. But the real success was the ability of the newly efficient LSE to attract equity trading business from abroad, especially from Europe. By 1991 over half the trading in large French shares and a quarter of the trading in big German shares were being conducted in London—thanks to London's lower costs and also to the fact that most rival exchanges used order-driven systems, which international investors prefer less. Average daily value of trading in foreign equities in London, often in the form of Global Depository Receipts, rose from less than £500 million in 1986 to over £3 billion in 1995.[64] In 1993, the trading volume of foreign equities in London surpassed the trading volume of domestic shares for the first time. Indeed, just as New York's May Day had provoked change in London, so the Big Bang provoked a series of deregulatory measures by the major European exchanges. With the increase in turnover came employment benefits and tax receipts for the country as a whole: the financial services sector grew by 59 percent between 1985 and 1987.[65]

The fortunes of the LSE's old member firms were mixed. Increased competition from a flood of American, Japanese, and European firms more than offset the increase in turnover volumes. The cut in commission rates hurt the brokers badly. Brokers' collective income from trading commissions on domestic equities fell by almost 40 percent in the months following liberalization.[66] The costs of the necessary new technology were high, and, in a

---

[60] Business Opinions Ltd., *The Big Bang One Year On* (London: Business Opinions Ltd., 1987).

[61] International Stock Exchange, *Quality of Market Quarterly Review* (summer 1990): 19–21.

[62] "Five Years since Big Bang," *The Economist*, 26 October 1991, 23–26.

[63] Ibid.

[64] "London's Market Misfit," *The Economist*, 23 September 1995, 61–66.

[65] *Bank of England Quarterly Bulletin* 29, no. 3 (November 1989).

[66] *The Economist*, 13 December 1986, 92. Income fell from £653 million (annualized) in the three months prior to Big Bang to £400 million (annualized) in the three months afterwards. This decline matches almost exactly the average 40 percent cut in commission rates.

herd-like rush to provide one-stop financial shopping, many banks, brokers, and investment houses spent millions of pounds on mergers and joint ventures that generally did not pay off. According to one estimate, the industry lost a collective £2 billion in the four years after 1986.[67] A later estimate puts the costs of technology, office, and trading losses attributable to Big Bang at £4 billion by 1991.[68]

Offsetting the corporate misery, however, were the personal fortunes made by many members of the old LSE who sold their businesses at inflated prices to the outsiders who were rushing headlong to buy into the new market. These outsiders—British commercial banks and foreign investment houses—competed fiercely for the local talent in what one observer called "the greatest sting of the century."[69]

The clearest losers were private investors. Minimum commissions rose sharply, from about £7–10 in the pre-1986 days to £20–25 and even up to £50 as brokers fought for the institutional business and abandoned the small fry.[70] Average rates of commission for individuals rose from about 0.9 percent to 1.1 percent. Even this figure masked the true extent of the rise in commissions for small investors, since many brokerages maintained a minimum commission of up to £50, which dramatically increased the effective commission rate.[71] Dealing spreads on the largest stocks narrowed, but by 1990 spreads on the smaller stocks typically favored by small investors had more than doubled.[72] In addition, of course, individual investors no longer enjoyed built-in protection against the sort of moral hazards that are inherent in a dual-capacity system, where one's broker is also one's competitor in stock trading.

Indeed, the difficulties and expenses for small investors quickly grew so bad that in four years the Conservative government, anxious to promote its idea of a share-owning democracy, openly called for the LSE to do more for small investors.[73] John Redwood,[74] the corporate affairs minister, announced in 1990 that "I would like them [the Exchange] to put more emphasis on the retail business."[75] In this, he was unsuccessful. Five years later, the LSE was still serving individual investors so poorly that an alternative computer-based share market known as Tradepoint was established. Small investors welcomed it even though it was actually designed primarily to

[67] Richard Melcher, "Big Bang, Big Bust, Big Lessons," *Business Week*, 6 March 1989, 38–39.

[68] "London's Market Misfit."

[69] Interview, fund manager, London, June 1993.

[70] S. G. Warburg Equity Trading Department, "Commission Rates" (internal memo), and interviews, London, August 1992.

[71] International Stock Exchange, *Quality of Markets Quarterly Review* (Oct. 1987).

[72] International Stock Exchange, *Quality of Markets Quarterly Review* (1990).

[73] "Redwood Proposes New Stock Market for Private Investors," *Financial Times*, 14 August 1990, 14.

[74] The same Redwood who failed to dislodge John Major for leadership of the Conservative party in the summer of 1995.

[75] Clare Dobie, "Redwood Calls on ISE [International Stock Exchange] to Do More for Small Investors," *The Independent*, 14 August 1990, 6.

serve institutional traders. The reason for its appeal to small investors was that it opened the door to more competition and, hence, they believed, to lower costs. Moreover, the fact that the LSE monopoly on share trading was lost opened the door to other rival trading systems that could be more specifically tailored to individuals. ESI, another private company, announced on the eve of Tradepoint's inauguration that it would develop a screen-based trading system specifically for private investors on the Internet, starting with small company shares. Donald Butcher, chairman of the U.K. Shareholders Association, a lobby group for private investors, said of Tradepoint, "Low-cost alternatives to the Stock Exchange's system must be welcomed. Though market makers do make prices in smaller company stocks, the spread between buy and sell is often wide."[76]

Many assumed that the new Labour government, elected in 1997, would undo, or at least significantly alter, the Conservatives' liberalizing reforms. But, in fact, the Third Way did not include any plans to undo the Big Bang or even to tinker with the financial market. Tony Blair, Labour leader, and Chancellor Gordon Brown had touted the value of a stakeholder as compared to a shareholder economy when they were in opposition. Once in power, they began echoing their Conservative predecessors' belief in the importance of open competitive financial markets. Voicing a sentiment that contrasts strikingly with that of Neil Kinnock, quoted earlier, Brown wrote: "Financial services lie at the heart of a modern, dynamic economy. The effectiveness and competitiveness of all our industries depends on the availability and efficiency of the increasingly wide array of financial products and services. The standard of living of all of us depends on them."[77]

IV. The Financial Services Act of 1986

Turning back now to the 1980s, we find it ironic that at the same time that the government was sanctioning reforms that would hurt private investors in order to help big financial institutions, it was also approving legislation that would have exactly the opposite effect.

While the LSE was struggling with its reforms, financial services outside the organized exchanges were also coming under increasing government scrutiny. But whereas the stimulus for reform of the LSE had been in large measure economic, necessitated by the demands of domestic and international competition, the stimulus for reform of these other services was very largely political.

---

[76] Donald Butcher, quoted in Catherine Barron, "Tradepoint: Beginning of the End," *Investors Chronicle*, 18 August 1995, 15.

[77] Gordon Brown, quoted in Tim Herrington and George Staple, "U.K. Plans New Super-SIB," *International Financial Law Review* (August 1997): 26.

The city suffered periodic scandals, and regulatory reforms often followed in their wake.[78] A striking example is the passage of the 1979 Banking Act, a belated but direct response to the Secondary Banking Crisis of 1973.[79] In the late 1970s and early 1980s, a series of well-publicized scandals involving investment firms outside the LSE proved politically embarrassing.[80] Slater-Walker, in 1975—77, was probably the best-known one. In 1981, Norton-Warburg, a supposedly mainstream investment management group, went bankrupt, losing £4.5 million of client funds. Its director was jailed on fraud charges. These and other cases rarely involved large sums of money in absolute terms, but often involved a few individuals losing their entire life savings. As such, they made good headlines and great copy. As we have seen, the Conservatives were "not insensitive" to charges of city favoritism.[81] So, in July 1981, Gower was commissioned by the Conservative minister of trade to conduct a report on investor protection. His report was the basis for a white paper in January 1985, which in turn became law in November 1986 as the Financial Services Act.

The act had to tread the narrow line between stifling competition and protecting investors. Too much regulation would drive business away, being cumbersome and expensive, both to administer and to operate under. Too little would not solve the problems of fraud that it was designed to prevent. Gower's report had stressed that the level of regulation and supervision should not "seek to achieve the impossible task of protecting fools from their own folly," but that it should be "no greater than is necessary to protect reasonable people from being made fools of."[82] Unfortunately, the definition of what was necessary to protect people and what constituted reasonable were not made clear. Moreover, Gower was not required to, nor did he, consider the financial costs of the new regulations.

The bill came down heavily on the safe side of more regulation rather than less. Lawson writes, "What eventually emerged was something far more cumbersome and bureaucratic than I, or, I believe any of us in government had ever envisaged."[83] The original bill contained 212 sections, 300

[78] For a fuller exploration of this topic, see Michael Clarke, *Fallen Idols: Elites and the Search for the Acceptable Face of Capitalism* (London: Junction Books, 1981).

[79] See Moran, *The Politics of Banking.*

[80] These are listed in Julian Franks and Colin Mayer, *Risk, Regulation and Investor Protection: The Case of Investment Management* (Oxford: Clarendon, 1990).

[81] To quote Jock Bruce-Gardyne, *Mrs. Thatcher's First Administration* (London: Macmillan, 1984), 84.

[82] Quoted in Lawson, *The View from Number Eleven*, 401. It is interesting to compare this sentiment with those given in the United States as the Securities Act of 1933 was being drawn up. Senator Rayburn, sponsor of the bill, wanted legislation that would ensure that the investor could obtain "all information that is pertinent that would put him on notice and on guard, and then let him beware." Senator Mapes pointed out that the bill "will not prevent anybody from putting his money into rat holes . . . if he sees fit to do so." Quoted in Bernard Schwartz, ed., *The Economic Regulation of Business and Industry: A Legislative History of U.S. Regulatory Agencies* 4 (New York: R. R. Bowker, 1973), 2549, 2606.

[83] Lawson, *The View from Number Eleven*, 401.

pages, and 600 amendments. It had been drafted by lawyers and bureaucrats, and practitioners found it a nightmare even to understand, let alone implement.[84]

The centerpiece of the bill was the establishment of a new regulatory structure. At the top was the SIB, a quasi-governmental body accountable directly to the secretary of trade and industry, composed of both practitioners and bureaucrats. All investment firms had to be authorized and were organized into one of the self-regulatory organizations (SROs). Initially there were five SROs: (1) the LSE and the International Securities Regulatory Organization merged to form the Securities Association (SA); (2) The Investment Management Regulatory Organisation (IMRO) represented all of the larger and some of the smaller but more prestigious fund managers; (3) The Association of Futures Brokers and Dealers (AFBD) represented futures brokers and dealers; (4) The Financial Intermediaries, Managers and Brokers Regulatory Association (FIMBRA) represented the small operators, typically those serving retail clients; and (5) LAUTRO, the Life Assurance and Unit Trust Regulatory Organisation, represented the insurers and unit trusts (the U.K. equivalent of U.S. mutual funds). The act required that any firm wishing to conduct financial services had to register with one of the SROs or with the SIB directly. The SROs were responsible for drawing up and overseeing rules concerning business practices in their fields. It was their responsibility to ensure compliance with their rules, and with those of the higher authority, the SIB. This they did by requiring the firms in their bailiwicks to provide personnel to act as practitioner-regulators. The SROs were manned chiefly by private employees on secondment, and each individual firm was required to hire at least one in-house compliance officer.

In short, the new system of practitioner-based regulation in a statutory framework was fragmented and cumbersome. The costs of the new structure were to be borne by the financial services industry, most directly by the payment of fees to the SROs. The act went a long way toward codifying and formalizing regulatory practices in the city, but the two-tier nature of the system, with both the SIB and an SRO exercising supervision, maintained a degree of fragmentation that still contrasted with Japan's centralized authority. The problems of this fragmentation soon became apparent, and, over the next decade and a half, the two-tier structure was streamlined to the point of extinction.

The new rules concerning investment business seemed excessive to many industry professionals. The act attempted to codify what constituted good business practice for an exhaustive list of investment business activities, from listing a eurobond to selling life insurance to private individuals over the phone. "Chinese walls"—legal barriers between separate departments

---

[84] Interviews, London, July 1993. The title of Claire Makin's "First Big Bang, Now Big Brother" (*Institutional Investor* [May 1988]: 58–67) gives a sense of how the industry viewed the new regime.

such as trading and fund management—were required of all firms that conducted more than one line of business. Most contentiously, the act allowed customers to bring civil suits against financial intermediaries for misconduct. As already discussed, individual customers of financial services were more in need of regulatory protection than institutions, but the act did not make this distinction and erred on the side of caution. For example, a broker making a share transaction for a client was required to prove that he or she had secured the best available price at the time of the order. To this end, it was required that the broker make public the price and volume of the deal as soon as it was executed. This is appropriate if the deal is a small one for a private client who cannot check for himself or herself what the broker is up to. For a large institutional investor seeking to deal in a big volume of shares in a thin market without upsetting the price, the requirement was not only unnecessary but damaging. Some rules were widely regarded as simply petty, such as the requirement that all fund managers file records of where and when brokers treated them to lunch.[85]

Problems with the Financial Services Act

The SIB, a constitutional novelty, was financed by levies on the private financial firms it regulated, but was not accountable to either them or Parliament. Its unusual hybrid nature owes much to the uneasy compromise from which it was born. On the one hand, Gower was known to favor a strong and central regulator modeled along the lines of America's SEC.[86] On the other hand, the Conservative government was known to be ideologically hostile to any extension of government that could be avoided; certainly the creation of a big new bureaucratic agency was unlikely to go down well with the Thatcherites. Those in the city generally preferred self-regulation where possible, but there is also evidence that some were in favor of a greater degree of regulatory oversight. The Governor's Group, a think tank appointed by the governor of the Bank of England and consisting of ten prominent city figures including Goodison, the LSE chief, were asked to look into the feasibility of continued self-regulation. They are reported to have concluded that self-regulation would work, but only with beefed-up statutory underpinning. There was even a minority suggestion that the Bank of England take over the role of stock market regulation.[87]

The bank, however, was ambivalent. It was reluctant to see an SEC-type body established that would clearly undercut its preeminence as the chief overseer of London's markets.[88] Nevertheless, it was reeling under a series of criticisms stemming from its failure to prevent the collapse of the Johnson-Matthey Bank. An example of the type of rhetoric employed

---

[85] A point repeated at numerous interviews, London, May–June 1990.
[86] Gower had himself lost money in one of the financial collapses that prompted his report, which may have partially colored his judgment.
[87] Reid, *All-Change in the City*, 246.
[88] Hilton, *City within a State*, 31.

against the bank is provided by the following salubrious exchange in the Mother of Parliaments. Brian Sedgemore, a Labour party MP, argued that the Johnson-Matthey banking scandal had arisen from "the wanton and negligent behaviour of [Governor of the Bank of England] Mr. Robin Leigh-Pemberton. . . . How can anyone trust a system of supervision organized by that appalling deadbeat?" To this, Lawson, the Conservative chancellor of the exchequer, replied, "To call Mr. Sedgemore a pest would be an insult to pests"; this remark prompted Sedgemore to call Lawson a "sniveling little git."[89]

Many in the bank believed that future collapses and scandals were inevitable, and that, moreover, as bankers they did not necessarily have the expertise to prevent them from occurring in securities markets. Creating a new regulatory body with specific responsibility for oversight, but deliberately kept less powerful than the bank, would have been an ideal way to divert political criticism from the bank in the years ahead without compromising its position. Leigh-Pemberton therefore reportedly accepted the idea of the SIB and, calling in turn on the heads of all of the major banks, he "ordered the City to do likewise."[90]

Yet the nature of the SIB was not the only problem with the Financial Services Act. City firms soon complained bitterly about the costs of the new rules it imposed. Obviously the real losers from the act were the unscrupulous or the incompetent, and equally obviously they faced considerable difficulties in mobilizing politically. But all financial intermediaries were potentially hurt, not just by the direct costs of compliance, but in terms of lost business, reduced competition, and stifled innovation as the onerous new requirements scared new participants, especially foreign ones, away. David Lomax, economic advisor to the NatWest Bank, wrote that, "the only major threat to the future health of the financial services industry in the UK is that of excessive or inappropriate legislation." He calculated that the direct costs to the city of the Financial Services Act were in the order of £100 million, a figure that *The Independent* newspaper argued was actually too low.[91] Charles Goodhart of the London School of Economics wrote that the act resulted in overregulation as a response to "a series of minor but well-publicized scandals." Arguing that since the regulators did not have to bear the burden of costs, but did have to face political flak in the event of scandals, "the lengthy and detailed SIB rule book seems not to have left reasonable investor protection at a minimum."[92] Moreover, there was little concern with limiting the costs of regulation; indeed, costs had been deliberately excluded from Gower's terms of reference.

[89] Parliamentary debate, 17 December 1985, quoted in *Institutional Investor*, June 1986, 76. "Git" is a relatively modern British term of abuse approximately equivalent to the American expression "jerk."

[90] Hilton, *City within a State*, 31.

[91] Charles Lomax, *London Markets after Big Bang* (London: Butterworth's, 1987).

[92] Charles Goodhart, "The Costs of Regulation," in *Financial Regulation, or Overregulation?* ed. Arthur Seldon (London: Institute for Economic Affairs, 1988), 18–29.

Once the act became law, the dangers of overregulation soon became apparent, even to the regulators themselves. The governor of the Bank of England remarked in 1989:

> I am very conscious of the costs that have been, and continue to be, involved in regulation and therefore welcome not only the SIB's simplified rulebook but also the Secretary of State's acknowledgment of these costs and his intention to amend legislation accordingly. We shall need to remain vigilant in striking the balance between the protection of investors and the costs imposed on the activities of financial firms if London's competitiveness is not to be eroded and 'regulatory arbitrage' . . . is not to become a criterion in decisions on where to conduct business.[93]

Such apparent disregard for London's competitive position or for the preferences of the biggest brokers and investors scarcely accords with the explanation of Big Bang that stresses that competition was the driving force and that institutional investors were the agents for radical change. But, in fact, the terms of the act have been continuously and dramatically amended to the point where, not much more than a decade later, the regulatory structure imposed in 1986 is almost unrecognizable. So why was it passed in its original form, against the interests of the big investors?

The answer is that there is little evidence that institutional investors were greatly involved in the drafting of the act. Later on, they threw their weight behind the efforts of the intermediaries to rewrite the act to allow far greater freedom of action in trades between professionals.[94] Small investors were the intended beneficiaries of the act, but there does not appear to have been any large or well-coordinated campaign by small investors to get more protection.[95] The pressure from them appears to have worked indirectly, if at all. Is this, then, a case of political entrepreneurship on behalf of the Conservative Party? This certainly seems to be part of the explanation. They were anxious to avoid the stigma of being "soft on the city," and it is significant that the city, too, recognized the political dangers of being given favors. The big firms waited until after the 1987 election before launching their big lobbying campaign against the 1986 act.[96] Yet this is not the whole story. As seen from Lawson's comments, the original act did not meet with the approval of many Conservatives, and its history has been one of constant amendment to the point of virtual extinction. Another part of the explanation for why the act was so unfriendly to big city interests is that the drafters of the bill, Treasury bureaucrats and lawyers, were insulated from the lobbying efforts of the city and, indeed, of the Conservative Party, and drew up an act with reference exclusively to prudential problems as they perceived

[93] The Governor of the Bank of England, "Monetary Policy, Equity Markets and the City's Infrastructure," *Bank of England Quarterly Bulletin* 29, no. 4 (1989): 530.

[94] Interviews with regulators and market professionals, May—June 1990.

[95] Charles Goodhart, *Money, Information, and Uncertainty* (1989), 208.

[96] Reid, *All-Change in the City*, 251.

them. It was in this form that it went before Parliament, and it has been amended to better suit the larger investors ever since.

The first blow struck by the city against the original act was the prompt dismissal of the unpopular first head of the SIB, Sir Kenneth Berrill. Berrill, described by Lawson as somewhat peripatetic, was held responsible for the SIB's overly bureaucratic approach.[97] He was not reappointed in 1988, and David Gowland writes that he "was effectively sacked. His replacement, David Walker of the Bank of England, was a popular City choice, one that heralded "a move to a less onerous system of regulation."[98] According to Lawson,

"While the regulatory system ushered in by the FSA still suffers from a number of its early defects, there has been a considerable improvement and simplification since the Government and the Bank replaced Berrill as SIB chairman in 1988 with the Bank's David Walker."[99] The trend of appointing chief regulators more sympathetic to the needs of the large city institutions was continued in 1992 when Walker was replaced by Andrew Large, a former euromarket practitioner who shared his predecessor's concern with keeping regulatory costs low.

Yet even as the large institutions were pushing successfully for more amenable chief regulators, more fundamental flaws in the new structure were becoming apparent. One major problem was the fragmented and confused nature of the two-tier system, with supervisory authority divided among the SIB and the five SROs. Another problem was that the act made no distinction between the protection of retail investors—who require extensive and elaborate regulatory protection—and institutional investors, who do not. The result was regulatory compromise that satisfied no one. It was too strong and expensive for the institutions. On the other hand, it was too weak for the individuals. As one banker put it: "The Financial Services Act was like trying to dam a river with 3 bricks . . . wherever you put them, the water will just go somewhere else."[100] What followed was a decade of seemingly endless financial scandals—erupting at the rate of about one major scandal every year— that suggested that far from ending fraud in the City, the Financial Services Act had actually made things worse for smaller investors.

Financial Scandals in the Aftermath of the Financial Services Act
Guinness, 1986–1993

In 1986, Guinness, the brewing company, launched a hostile takeover of Distillers, another drinks company. The takeover pitched Guinness into a bidding battle with Argyll, a supermarket group. To bolster its bid, Guinness engaged in an illegal operation to artificially support its own share

---

[97] Lawson, *The View from Number Eleven*, 399.
[98] David Gowland, *Regulation of Financial Markets in the 1980s* (Aldershot: Edward Elgar, 1990), 242.
[99] Lawson, *The View from Number Eleven*, 402.
[100] Interview with merchant banker, London.

price. The aftermath was a succession of three long, complex, and expensive court cases that lasted until 1993, when the final defendant, a nonexecutive director, was acquitted. Earnest Saunders, the chairman of Guinness, was sentenced to five years in prison but was freed after ten months on the grounds that he .was suffering from Alzheimer's disease—from which he made a swift and medically miraculous recovery shortly after his release. The cost to the taxpayer of the cases was estimated at £70 million.[101]

Barlow Clowes, 1988–1989

Barlow Clowes was licensed in 1985 to manage approximately £200 million in offshore funds for some 1,500 retail clients: most of the money came from the pensions, life savings, or redundancy (retirement) payments of the elderly or retired. In May 1988, the company collapsed with less than £2 million in assets, and Chairman Peter Clowes admitted to having spent about $100 million of his clients' money on, among other things, jet planes, a luxury yacht, and a chateau in France. Two government inquiries and a 113–day trial later, two of the seven people charged in the case—Clowes and his deputy chairman—were imprisoned. The case cost the government £50 million in court costs and £155 million in compensation to the cheated investors. Blair, then opposition spokesman on trade and industry, accused the DTI of "years of incompetence and gullibility" in allowing the firm to operate.[102]

Blue Arrow, 1987–92

In September 1987, the highly prestigious investment bank County NatWest underwrote a rights issue of £800 million for Blue Arrow, an employment agency. The issue was a flop, attracting less than a 40 percent take-up. County then pressured Philips and Drew—the stockbrokers to Blue Arrow, owned by the giant Union Bank of Switzerland (UBS)—and County NatWest Securities secretly to buy up more of the shares in order to make the offering appear more attractive to investors. Several investors, including many large institutions, were taken in by the ruse and bought shares. The bogus share-buying resulted in County NatWest Securities holding a 9.5 percent stake in Blue Arrow in a secret account that even their own traders did not know about, in breach of the U.K. Companies Act, which requires disclosure of more than a 5 percent stake in another company. Three months later, in December 1987, County announced the Blue Arrow stake, and the DTI began inquiries.

The DTI report was issued in 1989. Several NatWest executives resigned and the Serious Fraud Office (SFO) began a court case that came to trial in 1991 and ended with the conviction of four people in February 1992. Six months later, all four convictions were overturned on appeal. The case

[101] Max Thum, "Investigating, Prosecuting Corporate Fraud in England: Time for Reform?" *Defense Counsel Journal* 60, no. 2 (1993): 213–222.
[102] Lawrence Lever, *The Barlow Clowes Affair* (London: Macmillan, 1992), 2.

cost British taxpayers £35 million.[103] The Bank of England came under intense criticism for having turned a blind eye to County's dishonesty. *The Economist* wrote that "The Bank confused its regulatory role with its role as sponsor of the City's interests."[104] The DTI reopened the inquiry, and, although it found that "at no stage did the Bank of England obstruct or impede the DTI in relation to its investigations into the Blue Arrow transaction,"[105] this finding was not nearly enough to satisfy critics howling at the ineffectiveness of the regulatory regime.

Maxwell, 1991

Robert "Bouncing Bob" Maxwell, the extroverted head of the media empire Mirror Group, engaged for years in misusing the pension funds of approximately 4,000 of his staff. He both stole money from the funds or used them as collateral for other loans. Maxwell finally came under investigation in 1991, but he soon died in mysterious circumstances, apparently drowning after falling off his yacht. By then, some £350 million were missing from his company's pension funds. The SFO, unable to pursue the dead Maxwell, brought his two sons and several other Mirror Group officials to another long and fruitless trial. The case revealed an interesting new flaw with the Financial Services Act. The purpose of the act was investor protection, with an assumption that investors would always be the victims of crime and financial intermediaries the crooks. The drafters of the act never envisaged that an investor might himself be dishonest, and there were no rules guarding against this contingency. It was through this loophole that Maxwell had squeezed himself.[106] The trial cost £25 million, which included a highly controversial £10 million in legal fees for the defendants. Maxwell's sons, who were technically insolvent, had successfully claimed that they were entitled to state funds under the Legal Aid program, whereby the legal fees of the poor and unemployed are paid out of public funds. This cost, needless to say, raised a furor among taxpayers.

BCCI, 1991

The Bank of Credit and Commerce International (BCCI) was founded in 1972 by Agha Hasan Abedi. Based in Pakistan, it had branches throughout the Middle East, in the United States, and in London. Both U.S. and British authorities had suspected since the mid-1980s that it had links to drug cartels and terrorists, including Abu Nidal.[107] By the late 1980s, regulators in both countries were investigating fraud, and in July 1991 the U.S. Senate Banking Committee announced a full-scale investigation of the bank. Meanwhile, the accounting firm Price Waterhouse had completed an investigation in the United Kingdom that found extensive fraud.

---

[103] Michael Gillard, "Flawed Squad," *The Observer*, Sunday, 21 January 1996, 32.

[104] "The Blue Arrow Affair," *The Economist*, 7 March 1992, 26.

[105] "NatWest and the Bank of England: An Apology," *The Economist*, 23 January 1993, 76.

[106] Confidential interview with IMRO official, July 10, 1992.

[107] Nick Kochan and Bob Whittington, *Bankrupt: The BCCI Fraud* (London: Victor Gollancz, 1991), 11.

Later that month, the Bank of England closed BCCI, which promptly collapsed, owing millions of pounds to thousands of individual depositors, who were left stranded. The Bank of England was criticized for what appeared to many to be an abject failure of supervisory oversight in three separate inquiries—a British parliamentary report, a U.S. Senate subcommittee report, and a special inquiry conducted by Lord Justice Bingham. Bingham described the Bank of England's role in the affair as "a tragedy of errors, misunderstandings and failures of communication."[108] In 1999, the liquidators of BCCI sued the Bank of England, threatening to go even to the European Court of Justice if they were unsuccesful in the British courts.[109]

An unpleasant aspect of the case, aired by Labour MPs such as Hattersley and Keith Vaz, was that the British victims of the BCCI collapse were concentrated chiefly among the South Asian, mostly of Pakistani origin, immigrant populations in inner cities such as Birmingham. BCCI had specialized in lending to this population and had shown a far greater degree of concern for immigrants' businesses than had other British banks. Hattersley publicly questioned whether racism, or at least a studied unconcern for the well-being of the South Asian immigrant population, had lain behind the Bank of England's indifference to the warning signs about BCCI's affairs.[110]

Barings, 1995

Nicholas Leeson, a twenty-eight-year-old high school graduate who had failed math and statistics, was head of futures trading at the Singapore branch of Barings PLC, a highly prestigious investment bank whose clients included the queen. Between 1993 and 1995 Leeson accumulated trading losses of £750 million through a series of spectacularly wrong bets on Japanese stock-index futures and covered them up in a secret account. The fact that he was simultaneously the head of back-office operations and trading greatly facilitated the coverup and pointed to a failure of both internal and external regulations that should never have allowed such a situation to arise. Leeson's trading losses, discovered in February 1995, were enough to bankrupt Barings, which was eventually bought for £1 by a Dutch bank. Leeson was tried for fraud and found guilty in Singapore, where he served four years in prison. British bondholders of Barings collectively lost £100 million in the collapse and demanded that Leeson be tried in London, since the fraud had been in a British bank with British customers. The SFO declined, arguing that Leeson had been operating under Singapore law.

All these scandals were precisely the events the Financial Service Act had been designed to prevent, in which small retail savers and pension fund

---

[108] Quoted in Jason Nisse, "BCCI Liquidators in Plan to Sue Bank," *The Times* (London), 29 September 1999, 1.

[109] Ibid.

[110] Neil Buckley, "Tragedy for Asian Traders," *Financial Times*, 8 July 1991, 6.

holders were the main victims. With each new trial, calls for the reform of the act grew from both the public and the city. However, in contrast to the failure of the regulatory authorities to oversee the retail markets effectively, British regulators were proving to be extremely conscientious in their attempts to stamp out financial fraud in which big institutional investors and liquidity traders rather than small savers are the real victims, as the campaign to eradicate insider trading illustrates.

Rethinking the Financial Services Act

In 1989, stung by public criticism over the Barlow Clowes affair, the Conservatives established a specialized form of public prosecutor, the SFO, to pursue white-collar crime. Yet the seeming inability of the SFO to secure convictions for financial fraud attracted continuous criticism throughout the 1990s. The belief grew that rather than relying on criminal prosecutions, the powers of the SIB and the other regulators should be strengthened so that they could administer punishments with greater speed and ease, as is the case in the United States. The example of the SEC's ability to levy fines was frequently cited. Such a shift of responsibility to the regulators was thought to be conducive to tougher enforcement of the laws because the standards of proof required for the successful prosecution of a criminal case are much higher than those needed for a regulatory discipline. As one commentator put it, "By raising acts of cheating, however serious, into heinous criminal offenses, the priority becomes justice rather than cleaning up the financial community."[111] This point was illustrated by a regulator at IMRO, the SRO that came under severe criticism for allowing Maxwell to defraud his pension-fund holders. The regulator explained: "In fact, we had long suspected that he was up to no good. But we couldn't ring any alarm bells because we weren't allowed just to voice suspicions without having the evidence to prove them in a criminal case. If we had said to people, 'look, I'd be careful of him if I were you' he could have sued us and would probably have won."[112]

In a 1994 case, the SFO brought fraud charges against two stockbrokers at Thomas C. Coombs. Presiding Judge Clark dismissed the case and remarked, "I cannot help thinking that this sort of inquiry, where there has been no financial loss to any individual, would be far better left to the regulatory jurisdiction of the appropriate bodies rather than a full-blown criminal trial."[113]

The complaints grew louder as the list of scandals that had gone unpunished grew longer. A £19 million fraud at Brent Walker resulted in the chairman, George Walker, being cleared of all charges in October 1994. The company had been accused of artificially raising its share price

---

[111] Graham Seargeant, "The City Should Mind Its Own Business," *The Times* (London), 26 August 1993, 23.

[112] Confidential interview, IMRO official, July 10, 1992.

[113] Quoted in Seargeant, "The City Should Mind Its Own Business," 23.

throughout the mid-1980s by inflating its profit figures, which it had done by lending money to third parties to enable them to buy its products. It then took advantage of its high share price by issuing equity and using the capital to make acquisitions. "The news was greeted by financial commentators [with] . . . a ritual groan to the effect that the U.K.'s SFO had done it again: another failed prosecution at a cost of millions to the taxpayer."[114] In the soul-searching that followed, the U.S. approach of classifying many cases of financial fraud, such as insider trading, as both criminal and administrative offenses was again brought up. SIB Chairman Large favored this American approach: "The knowledge that the criminal route is available is a deterrent while the availability of civil settlement provides a quick—and public—disposal of cases where prosecution is not essential."[115]

The inability of the 1986 regulatory structure to protect small investors appeared to be so endemic that in 1993 the Treasury commissioned bureaucrat Sir Kenneth Clucas to investigate retail investor protection. His recommendation was that the SIB establish a new SRO specifically for retail investors, consisting of a merger of LAUTRO, FIMBRA, and those parts of IMRO and the new Securities and Futures Association (SFA)[116] that represented private clients. The result was a Personal Investment Authority (PIA), proposed in 1992, to intense criticism from the big banks and life insurers.[117]

Even this did little to assuage public complaints that small investors and savers were not adequately protected by the new regime. One source of criticism came from an SIB report on the mismanagement of personal pensions, a £4 billion industry, which concluded that in over one and a half million cases, investors had been wrongly advised by firms. The SIB came under criticism from consumer groups, trade unions, and Labour MPs for its failure both to protect individuals or to punish adequately corporate wrong-doers. Alistair Darling, Labour's city spokesman, was reported as saying that, "The regulators must . . . act for the public good."[118]

The continued failure of the new regulatory regime to represent small investors adequately was demonstrated by the founding of a new pressure group, The Guild of Shareholders, in 1995. Its founder was a former Conservative MP, Tom Benyon, and its goal was to ensure better representation for small investors on company boards. The last straw had been a fight during the 1995 British Gas annual meeting, when private shareholders had attempted to block what many believed to be the excessive new pay package for Chief Executive Cedric Brown. The attempt had been beaten by the

[114] John Plender, "Arbitrary Justice in the City," *Financial Times*, 2 November 1994, 13.

[115] Andrew Large, quoted in Plender, "Arbitrary Justice," 13.

[116] The SFA was created by the merger of the securities and futures regulators in 1992, themselves creations of mergers from the original SROs.

[117] "Self-Regulation's Last Stand," *The Economist*, 5 December 1992, 77.

[118] Robert Miller, "SIB Accused of Weak Stance in Pension Scandal," *The Times* (London), 17 January 1996, 23.

proxy votes of institutional investors. According to Benyon, "The Guild is banding private shareholders together to give a lobby big enough to stop them being pushed around."[119]

A 1996 editorial in *The Times* was headlined "In the Dock: Britain's Financial Regulation Has Been Tried and Found Wanting." The article went on to assert:

> The idea of creating a powerful financial regulator, modeled on the U.S. Securities and Exchange Commission, is finding growing support even within the City and the Bank of England, which have traditionally insisted on the lightest possible financial supervision, based on self-regulation . . . the Government and the City cannot afford simply to ignore the evidence that the present system of financial regulation has failed.[120]

As the scandals continued, the idea of consolidating the various regulatory authorities along U.S. lines became more and more attractive not only to private investors and taxpayers but also to large city institutions, who were becoming increasingly concerned with the havoc the scandals were wreaking on London's international reputation.[121] By the time of the Labour party victory in 1997, there were few defenders of the Financial Service Act's original structure. Even so, the speed and comprehensiveness of Labour's structural reforms took many by surprise.

In 1997, less than three weeks after taking office, Labour's new chancellor of the exchequer, Gordon Brown, wrote that "It has long been apparent that the regulatory structure introduced by the Financial Services Act of 1986 is not delivering the standard of supervision and investor protection that the industry and the public have a right to expect."[122] He went on the call the Financial Services Act inefficient and confusing, although he praised it for involving practitioner-based regulation and for recognizing different levels of regulation for wholesale and retail business.[123] Brown then stunned observers by scrapping the remaining three SROs and consolidating all supervisory powers into a new, greatly strengthened, and vastly expanded super SIB. For good measure, he stripped responsibility for banking supervision from the Bank of England and transferred it to the SIB, a telling comment on how badly the BCCI and Blue Arrow affairs had undermined the bank's reputation for competence. The staff at the SIB was expanded by a factor of eight, to 1,500 personnel. Its supervisory powers now stretched undiluted across the entire spectrum of financial services. Britain's new, consolidated

[119] Colin Narbrough, "Private Shareholders Promised More Clout," *The Times* (London), 28 August 1995, 6.

[120] "In the Dock," *The Times* (London), 20 January 1996, 1.

[121] "Stitched Up," *The Economist*, 15 February 1997, 70.

[122] Gordon Brown, letter to Sir Andrew Large, chairman of the SIB, quoted in *International Financial Law Review* (August 1997): 26.

[123] Ibid.

**Figure 4.1 Consolidation of the Regulatory Structure of Finance
in the United Kingdom, 1986–1997**

1986				
		SIB		
		+		
SA	AFBD	FIMBRA	LAUTRO	IMRO

1992		
	SIB	
	+	
SFA	PIA	IMRO
(SA + AFBD, 1991)	(FIMBRA + LAUTRO, 1992)	

1997
SIB

Abbreviations: AFBD, Association of Futures Brokers and Dealers; FIMBRA, Financial Inter-mediaries, Managers and Brokers Association; IMRO, Investment Management Regulatory Organisation; LAUTRO, Life Assurance and Unit Trust Regulatory Organisation; PIA, Personal Investment Authority; SA, Securities Association; SFA, Securities and Futures Association; SIB, Securities and Investments Board.

1997 regulatory regime, with its powerful and independent supervisor, looks much more like the centralized institutions of the SEC in America or the MOF in Japan than like the fragmented system of 1986. (See Figure 4.1.)

V. Insider Trading

Britain's traditional reliance on self-regulation in financial markets makes it hard to quantify exactly the extent to which insider trading occurred or was tolerated. On the other hand, there is considerable anecdotal evidence to suggest that the practice was common. It is not hard to understand why. The LSE was, until the Big Bang, a small, relatively closed, and socially cohesive community. In the clubs, pubs, and wine bars around Moorgate, or in the estates, gardens, and weekend retreats in the South of England to which most of the financial community repaired on weekends, it was and actually still is extremely easy to pass on tidbits of information to an old school chum working in a different bank or law firm. Compared with the United States, there was little legislation on acceptable market conduct, and guidance was normally conducted on a nod-and-wink basis from the Stock Exchange Council, the Bank of England, the Treasury, or the Takeover Panel. Moreover, there is the strong sense that until the 1980s there was no particular stigma attached to the practice. I was told on several occasions that giving or taking an insider's tip was a perk of the stockbroker's job, and that doing someone a favor by "tipping them the wink" was no more undesirable than giving a client a bottle of port at Christmas.[124] It is striking that even today we can find brokers harking back to the good old days and referring to insider trading as "a victimless crime."[125] Conventional wisdom, then, is that insider trading was both common and widely accepted socially.

However, there is also evidence that the authorities took the crime seriously. The Prevention of Fraud (Investments) Act of 1958 stipulated that "the dishonest concealment of a material fact" in a securities transaction was illegal, and carried a maximum seven-year penalty, although there was only one case when it was applied.[126] The city Takeover Panel had rules against it, although these lacked the force of law. Both the Conservative government in 1973 and the Labour government of 1978 attempted to introduce amendments that would have made insider dealing a criminal offense, but both governments fell before the bills were passed. In other words, although it is true that until 1980 insider trading was technically legal and probably commonly practiced, this is not to say that it was regarded as entirely acceptable, at least by the regulators. In this regard, Britain almost certainly fell somewhere between the laxity of the Japanese and the increasingly severe standards of the Americans.

Insider trading was eventually made illegal in Britain under the terms of the Companies Act of 1980. For the first time, it was explicitly defined and proscribed. An insider was defined as anyone who was connected with the corporate issuer, including people outside the company whose job "might reasonably be expected to give him access to [inside] information." Such information was defined as "specific, non-public and price-sensitive." The penalties for violations included two years in prison and unspecified fines.[127] In 1981, the LSE set up a surveillance team to monitor suspicious trades, expanded in 1983. Manual inspection of trades made its work impossibly slow until the automation of the LSE for the 1986 Big Bang, which brought down the time needed to inspect trades from six weeks to two hours.[128]

The next step in the campaign against fraud was the Company Securities (Insider Dealing) Act of 1985, which expanded the definition of insiders by making outsider advisors to the company more responsible for their actions

---

[124] Interviews, London, August 1992. Getting a "nap" was often the word used, from horse-racing slang, where a "nap" is information on a horse gleaned from its stable.

[125] To further illustrate the socially acceptable nature of insider trading in Britain, it is instructive to consider the case of the Lloyd's Insurance Market, where, until the early 1990s, it was legal for members' agents to place their own money or that of their friends into profitable underwriting syndicates, popularly known as "Baby syndicates," while putting their clients into syndicates known to be less profitable. This was regarded as morally acceptable because, as one Lloyd's employee put it, "If I trusted my money to an agent, I should bloody well hope that they were well-informed enough to know which were the good syndicates and bright enough to put their own money in them." Confidential interview, London, June 1993.

[126] Barry A. K. Rider, *Insider Trading* (London: Jordon and Sons, 1983), 48.

[127] Ibid., 13.

[128] "Hiccoughs Cured," *The Economist*, 7 February 1987, 76.

in dealing in a stock or recommending it to others. An amendment to the Financial Services Act of 1986 extended the 1985 act to futures and options as well as securities.

In June 1989 the European Community passed a directive making insider trading illegal in all community countries.[129] To bring U.K. legislation into line, new legislation was introduced into the Criminal Justice Act of 1993. This extended the scope of existing legislation to the all-securities markets, not just listed stocks, and widened the definition of inside information to include all price-sensitive information, not just information specifically referring to the company. An insider was defined as anyone "with direct access" to inside information, rather than someone connected to the company. Originally wider in scope, it was heavily redrafted as a result of pressure from financial institutions in the city.[130] The objections centered around the needs of stock analysts to conduct and profit from legitimate research.[131] According to critics, the new rules are still weaker than those in the United States, most notably in the absence of civil liability and in the division of regulatory responsibility between the SIB, the Treasury, the DTI, the LSE, and the Takeover Panel.

It is interesting to note which groups were most likely to be charged with insider trading offenses after the laws were put in place. Revealingly, it was not financial professionals or even company executives who were the biggest insider traders. It was, in fact, members of the general investing public. A profile of those people suspected of insider dealing and interviewed by the London Stock Exchanges Insider Dealing Group between April and June 1990 shows that 20 percent were from the financial sector, defined as anyone whose business was regulated by the Financial Services Act; 13 percent were company directors; 11 percent were company employees; and the remaining 56 percent were the general public.[132]

Although the authorities received constant criticism for their poor prosecution rate, the ratio of successful prosecutions to cases referred grew steadily during the 1980s. Between 1980 and 1984 eighty-four cases of insider trading were referred to the courts, but only 6 percent were successfully prosecuted. Between 1985 and 1989, 101 cases were referred, with 17 percent resulting in prosecutions.[133]

VI. Financial Regulation and Capital Mobility

Events in Britain in the 1980s lend support to the hypothesis that changes in the international capital markets prompted deregulatory reforms in domes-

[129] Com 87 111, based on Article 100 (a) (1) of the Treaty of Rome. It is discussed in J. H. Dalhuisen, *The New U.K. Securities Legislation and the E.C. 1992 Program* (Amsterdam: North-Holland, 1989), 128–139.

[130] *Financial Times*, 14 September 1992, 8; "Balancing Act," *The Economist*, 22 May 1993, 84.

[131] Patricia Tehan, "Tougher Insider Dealing Law in Force Next Month," *The Times* (London), 2 February 1994, 23.

[132] *Quality of Markets Quarterly Review* (summer 1990): 27.

[133] Ibid.

tic markets. Competition, in particular from New York, stimulated reform of the LSE. The critical factor in explaining the Big Bang was the threat of exit exercised by institutional investors. Until 1980, despite their attempts to set up a rival exchange, they had no real alternative but to deal on the official LSE and to accept the regulatory structure, even though it did not operate in their favor, and they ended up subsidizing small investors. Once the door was opened for them to escape to foreign markets, notably the NYSE, they did so with a vengeance. This is a case, then, when competitive pressures on an institution, brought about by internationalization and spearheaded by disgruntled large customers, were necessary and perhaps sufficient stimuli to reform. Of course, the story of the Big Bang is more complicated, and domestic considerations also played a role, as we have seen. The OFT's case has been viewed by some as the vital catalyst in the process, although others have described it as an unnecessary distraction at best and a damaging delay at worst. In any event, domestic considerations had an impact on both the timing and the details of the reforms. Given that the Big Bang was in its turn the stimulus for reform in rival European exchanges, with deregulation of the Paris Bourse, tellingly known as *Le Petit Bang*, these domestic factors must therefore be deemed to have had at least some systemic effects as well as vice-versa.[134]

The triumph of the high-flying financiers and the success of the city in attracting hot money from abroad was the subject of much adverse criticism in the late 1980s and 1990s, and the alleged division between city and manufacturing interests was debated anew. The cartoon strip "Alex" depicted investors in an unflattering light as shallow, greedy, upper-class yuppies engaging in dubious activities from insider trading to infidelity. A 1991 Fabian pamphlet argued that "if a Labour Government is to create world class manufacturing strength it will need to tackle short-termism head-on."[135] The pamphlet went on to advocate harsher taxes on speculative investments, defined as those held for less than five years. More seriously, in 1995, the Labour Party announced that it was taking a fresh look at the problems of City short-termism. Shadow Chancellor Brown proposed a tax break to encourage investors to hold onto their shares for a longer period.[136] The new Labour leader, Blair, promised a stakeholder rather than a shareholder economy, an explicit acceptance of the belief that the Anglo-American model of shareholder-driven capital markets was at least partly responsible for Britain's poor economic performance compared to, say, Germany and Japan. To that end, according to Darling, Labour's city spokesman, a Labour government would consider scrapping those laws introduced by the Conservatives that encouraged speculative rather than

---

[134] See Philip Cerny, "The 'Little Big Bang,'" *European Journal of Political Research* 17 (1989): 169–192.

[135] David Pitt-Watson, *Economic Short-Termism: A Cure for the British Disease*, Fabian Pamphlet no. 547 (London: Fabian Society Press, 1991). Quoted in Barry Riley, "Long-Termism and the Left," *Financial Times*, 10 August, 1991, 1.

[136] "Short-Term Solution," *The Economist*, 13 May 1995, 56.

long-term investment, and he explicitly included the prohibition on insider trading as such a law.[137]

The evidence that such short-termism existed was, as when the Wilson committee first investigated the issue in 1980, less than fully compelling. Indeed, the 1995 edition of the Pension Fund Indicators, put out by fund managers PDFM showed that on average pension funds held British shares for an average of five years in 1994, about the same length of time they had held them in 1986. The holding period had dropped after the Big Bang to a low of two years in 1989. Since pension funds owned around one-third of U.K. shares, while insurance companies owned around one-fifth, many commentators took this as evidence that in fact British shares were in relatively long-term hands.[138] Once in office, as we have seen, Labour quickly dropped its antagonism to the city and began loudly extolling the virtues of an open and internationally competitive financial system.

The 1986 Financial Services Act at first glance appears to be reform-driven, essentially by domestic political factors, the result simply of the desire by both politicians and regulators to avoid (or at least be seen to be trying to avoid) the sorts of financial scandal involving widows and orphans losing their life savings. The act as it was first passed bears out this view. Yet again, it was the largest customers of financial services who were able, in the ten years after the act was passed, to revise the regulatory framework more closely to their own liking. While many regulations deemed burdensome to institutional investment have been quietly dropped, the laws of concern to these investors, such as the prohibition on insider trading, have been continuously strengthened. This has had the effect both of favoring large British investors and of attracting investors in internationally mobile assets and financial intermediaries from abroad. The Labour Party's decision to scrap the two-tier structure and replace it with a single, all-powerful regulatory agency similar to the SEC was only the logical conclusion of a process of consolidation begun almost as soon as the act was passed.

Various points of interest emerge from the story of financial reform in the United Kingdom. First is the refusal of the Conservative Party to save the old LSE; this is especially noteworthy given the common misconception that Conservatives are invariably friendly to the city. Second is the concern demonstrated by the drafters of the Financial Srevices Act to avoid financial scandals at any cost, despite their expressed interest in London as a competitive financial center. But finally and most important, the story shows the ultimate success of the big investment institutions, epitomized by Prudential, in getting what they wanted over the objections of all other actors. This strongly supports the model of regulatory reform that stresses the crucial connection between openness, mobility, and political power. In the next two chapters we see the same dynamic shaping regulatory reform half a world away in Tokyo.

[137] Anthony Harris, "At Long Last, a Darling Idea from Labour," *The Times* (London), 1 May 1996.
[138] "Short-Term Solution," *The Economist*, 13 May 1995, 56.

Chapter 5

Japanese Financial Deregulation in the 1980s

Chapters 5 and 6 chart the passage of Japanese securities regulation from the producer-friendly, bureaucratically controlled system of the 1970s toward the more investor-friendly, market-oriented system of the late 1990s. The first section of this chapter puts the events in historical context. Later sections examine the process of internationalization of finance that undermined the ability of the Japanese securities industry to maintain its cartel and so caused a series of deregulatory reforms beginning in the early 1980s. Chapter 6 examines the 1990s. For the first half of this decade, the story is predominantly one of combating fraud and restructuring the system of financial oversight. The government's goal was to curb practices that Japan's banks and brokers had been using to exploit their customers. The means to this end were a series of reforms that included the establishment of the SESC, a legislative campaign against financial fraud, and the overhaul of the MOF itself. Together, these reforms represented a major shift away from Japan's traditionally producer-friendly regulatory structure and toward one in which investor interests were given greater priority. In the latter half of the 1990s, the focus shifted to the complete liberalization of the Tokyo Stock Exchange (TSE)—the *Biggu Bangu*. I argue that while these reforms were usually undertaken either at the request of the financial services industry or proactively by the Ministry of Finance (MOF), the primary beneficiaries were the internationally mobile customers of the industry, notably the corporate borrowers and institutional investors. Some foreign firms also benefited, almost invariably the investors in the most highly mobile assets or financial service intermediaries.

I. The Prewar Origins of Japanese Financial Regulation

Three features of the postwar financial system had their origins as far back as the seventeenth century: the use of financial instruments for speculation, the dominance of bank credit for fund-raising, and the government's use of the financial system to control the economy.[1] But it was not until after the

---

[1] Japan was host to the first recorded futures markets. The Dojima Rice Market in Osaka, founded in 1688, at one time had more than 1,300 registered rice dealers. Ulrike Schaede, "The Development of Organized Futures Trading: The Osaka Rice Bill Market of 1730," in *Japanese Financial Research: Contributions to Economic Analysis*, ed. Walter T. Ziemba, Warren Bailey, and Yasushi Hamao (Amsterdam: North Holland, 1991).

Meiji Restoration in 1868 that a formal capital market for corporate and government securities developed. The restoration was followed by intensive industrialization, which created a very strong demand for more efficient capital markets.[2] Finance Minister Matsukata Masayoshi drew up the Banking Act of 1882, creating a series of specialized lending institutions including the Bank of Japan, a foreign-exchange bank (Yokohama Specie Bank, later renamed the Bank of Tokyo), a long-term industrial lending bank (Industrial Bank of Japan), and a series of commercial banks and credit associations.[3] The TSE was opened in 1878, and until the 1930s the securities markets were a key source of investment capital.[4] By the 1930s, however, the MOF and the banks had firmly replaced bonds with bank loans as the primary source of corporate funds, with credit allocation often directly guided by the government.[5] In the 1930s the growing concentration of economic power in the hands of the giant *Zaibatsu* ("financial cliques") industrial groups made external financing even less important for corporate funding and so reinforced the speculative use of stock investments.[6]

The Allied occupation forces that ruled Japan following World War II set out to break the power of the prewar economic establishment, and the financial system was a central target for the reformers.[7] The Allied authorities, strongly influenced by New Deal progressivism, were at pains to ensure that the new system of finance would prevent the concentration of economic power.[8] The existing structure of Japanese finance, in fact, appeared to facilitate this since it was marked by a high degree of fragmentation among the various sectors of the market. The Americans were concerned, however, that too many of Japan's prewar rules had taken the form of ministerial ordinances rather than formal laws, and so the U.S. reforms tended to codify and formalize the existing arrangements wherever possible.

II. The Postwar Japanese Financial System

The Securities and Exchange Law, 1947

The blueprints for Japan's present securities law were drawn up hurriedly by SCAP in 1946.[9] As with most Occupation reforms, the new laws were

---

[2] See Hugh Patrick, "Japan, 1868–1914," in *Banking in the Early Stages of Industrialization*, ed. Rondo Cameron (Oxford: Oxford University Press, 1967), 318–340.

[3] Andreas Prindl, *Japanese Finance* (Chichester: John Wiley, 1981), 7.

[4] Japan Securities Research Institute, *Securities Markets in Japan 1994* (Tokyo: Japan Securities Reserve Institute), 14.

[5] Kent Calder, *Strategic Capitalism: Private Business and Public Purpose in Japanese Industrial Finance* (Princeton: Princeton University Press, 1993), 29.

[6] Japan Securities Research Institute, *Securities Markets in Japan 1994*, 14.

[7] Eleanor Hadley, *Antitrust in Japan* (Princeton: Princeton University Press, 1970).

[8] Kazuo Kawai, *Japan's American Interlude* (Chicago: University of Chicago Press, 1960), 142–159.

[9] SCAP (Supreme Commander for the Allied Powers) was the nickname given both to General Douglas MacArthur, who commanded the Allied occupation, and his staff more generally.

modeled very closely on—and in some cases translated almost verbatim from—existing U.S. financial law. SCAP had the explicit goals of encouraging democratic capitalism and destroying the power of the *Zaibatsu*, which had, so conventional thinking went, contributed strongly to Japan's prewar policy of colonial aggression.[10] The task of dissolving the *Zaibatsu* went to the Holding Company Liquidation Commission, which was immediately confronted with the problem of disposing of some ¥7,500 million shares previously held by *Zaibatsu* holding companies. The commission stated that "Since it is a conspicuous fact that present-day enterprises are operated under capital in the form of securities, the democratization of the ownership of enterprises requires the democratization of the ownership of securities.... [T]he democratization of securities may be called the finishing touch to the dissolution of the *Zaibatsu*."[11]

It was to encourage this end—the wide ownership of stock—that the Securities Exchange (or Transactions) Law (*shoken torihiki-ho*; referred to as SEL) was drawn up by the securities division of the MOF, under SCAP supervision, and passed by the Diet in March 1947. The key pieces of American legislation informing the SEL were the Securities Act of 1933, the Securities and Exchange Act of 1934, and the Banking Act of 1933 (Glass-Steagall Act), which separated commercial from investment banks. In Japan, Article 65 of the SEL performed the same function as Glass-Steagall. The 1934 Securities and Exchange Act had been passed in response to the Stock Market Crash of 1929 and the subsequent revelation of widespread corruption. This act established the Securities and Exchange Commission (SEC) to oversee the new reforms and enforce fairness. SCAP founded an equivalent agency, the Securities Commission for the Supervision of Securities Business, in 1948. As was its U.S. counterpart, it was intended to be independent of political control and was entrusted with the administration of the 1947 law.

Securities trading on the Tokyo, Osaka, and six other Japanese exchanges recommenced in 1949. As intended, the sale of *Zaibatsu* shares led to a surge of individual share ownership, and the early years of stock trading were dominated by individual investors. Margin transactions and an investment trust system were introduced in 1951, and bond trading, which had been suspended during the war, was resumed on the Tokyo and Osaka exchanges in 1956.

However, although both the United States and Japan began postwar life with almost identical financial regulations on paper, securities markets in the two countries developed along very different lines. The break came immediately after the Americans departed, when the bureaucrats began to reestablish the control over economic life that they had held before the war.

[10] J. A. A. Stockwin, *Japan: Divided Politics in a Growth Society*, 2d ed. (London: Norton, 1982), 49.

[11] The Holding Company Liquidation Commission Laws, *Rules and Regulations Concerning the Reconstruction and Democratization of the Japanese Economy* (Tokyo: Kaiguchi Publishing Company, 1949), 6.

The Securities Commission was abolished in 1952 and replaced by an advi-sory council to the Securities Bureau of the MOF.[12] Various other articles designed to establish American standards of investor protection were also scrapped.[13] So, by the early 1950s, the Japanese financial system was begin-ning to assume the major structural features that marked it for most of the postwar period.

The Japanese Financial System, 1950–1970

Japan's postwar financial system was characterized by a high degree of frag-mentation or functional segmentation.[14] Financial institutions were divided along functional lines, with each sector offering a different type of financial service such as long-term banking or securities underwriting. The entry of new participants to any sector was almost impossible, but within each sec-tor, competition was strictly controlled and no major institution was al-lowed to go bankrupt. Domestic markets were largely insulated from for-eign competition. In this respect, the financial services industry operated as a series of cartels, primarily benefiting the cartel members rather than their customers. Bank lending was the dominant form of corporate financing. Regulatory and supervisory authority was centralized in the MOF, but fair trading, investor protection, and market surveillance were not priorities for the regulators. Again, the interests of financial service consumers—specifi-cally stock market investors—were poorly served.

The main lines of banking business were divided up as follows. City banks (*toshi ginko*) were the large national commercial banks, numbering ap-proximately twelve. Their main business was providing loans, usually to large corporations, and often in their capacity as main bank for large *keiretsu* (industrial groupings).[15] Funds came at first from retail deposits, but in the high-growth period of the 1950s to 1970s, deposits were usually inadequate

[12] Thomas Adams and Iwao Hoshii, *A Financial History of Japan* (Tokyo: Kodansha, 1972), 51–52; Hiroshi Oda and R. Geoffrey Grice, *Japanese Banking, Securities and Anti-Monopoly Law* (London: Butterworths, 1988), 86.

[13] Oda and Grice, *Japanese Banking*, 86.

[14] There are a plethora of journalistic, economic, or descriptive practitioner-oriented works on all aspects of Japanese finance. English language sources include James Horne, *Japan's Financial Markets* (Sydney: Allen and Unwin, 1985); Prindl, *Japanese Finance*; Takagi Shinji, *Japanese Capital Markets* (Oxford: Blackwell, 1993); Steven Bronte, *Japan's Financial Markets* (London: Euromoney Publications, 1982); and Aron Viner, *Inside Japan's Financial Markets* (London: Economist Publications, 1987). On recent reforms, see Walter Ingo and Hiraki Takako, *Restructuring Japan's Financial Markets* (New York: New York University Press, 1993). In Japanese, see Royama, *Nihon No Kinyu Shisutemu* [Japan's financial system]; and *Zenginkyo* [Federation of Japanese Bankers], *Nihon no Ginko Seido* [The banking system in Japan] (Tokyo: Zenginkyo, 1989).

[15] For discussions of the relationship between banks, *keiretsu*, and other companies, see Richard Caves and Mass Auks, *Industrial Groupings in Japan* (Tokyo: Dowel, 1976); Michael Girlish, *Alliance Capitalism: The Social Organization of Japanese Business* (Berkeley: University of California Press, 1992); Takatoshi Ito, *The Japanese Economy* (Cambridge: MIT Press, 1992); and Masahiko Aoki, ed., *The Economic Analysis of the Japanese Firm* (Amsterdam: North-Holland Press, 1984).

to meet the demand for loans, and thus banks relied on short-term financing from the interbank call market, the bill market, and the BOJ. This, it is argued, is what gave the BOJ leverage over their lending decisions. The biggest of these banks took turns chairing the National Federation of Bankers' Associations (*Zenkoku Ginko Kyokai* or *Zenginkyo*), the powerful industry association and lobby group. In the early postwar years, these banks were restricted to domestic business, the Bank of Tokyo functioning as the sole bank for foreign exchange. Three long-term credit banks provided much of the government-guided long-term capital for industry, and seven specialized institutions provided trust banking services. Below these came a plethora of smaller institutions: regional banks, foreign banks, approximately seventy mutual (loan and savings) banks, nearly one thousand small credit cooperatives (*shinkyo kumiai*) and credit associations (*shinkin kinko*), labor credit cooperatives, and approximately ten thousand agricultural cooperatives grouped in the *Norinchukin Ginko* (Central Cooperative Bank for Agriculture and Forestry). Finally, the National Post Office, with twenty-two thousand branches, dwarfed all of its rivals in its capacity to collect private deposits: in 1980 the system controlled more deposits than all thirteen city banks combined. The MOF decided how the funds were lent, but there were, and still are, fierce fights on regulatory policy between MOF and the Ministry of Posts and Telecommunications over control of these funds.

The Securities Industry

Japan had several regional stock exchanges (*shoken torihiki shijo*), but Tokyo and Osaka were by far the largest and most important. The TSE has steadily outpaced all its rivals since World War II. In 1949, the TSE accounted for 60 percent and Osaka for 28 percent of all stock trading. By the mid-1990s, the TSE accounted for 80 percent and Osaka for 14 percent of trading volume.[16] The economic rivalry between these two exchanges is real and has acted as a catalyst for several product innovations, such as index futures.

The securities companies (*Shoken gaisha*) engaged in all aspects of the stock (equity) and bond markets, including underwriting new issues and secondary market trading.[17] In 1949 there were over one thousand securities companies in Japan, but these had been consolidated to approximately 290 in the late 1990s, of which approximately half were members of the TSE.[18] The Big Four brokers, Nomura, Daiwa, Yamaichi, and Nikko, dominated the market, accounting for over 70 percent of TSE trading volume for most of the 1960s. This combined share dropped to around 60 percent in the

[16] Tokyo Stock Exchange, *Fact Book* (Tokyo: Tokyo Stock Exchange, 1995), 100.
[17] See Megumi Suttee, *Nihon no Shoken-Gyo: Soshiki to Kyoso* [The securities industry in Japan: organization and competition] (Tokyo: Toyo Keizai Shinpo-Sha, 1987); and Okumura Keiichi and Kawakita Hidetaka, *Nihon no Kabushiki Shijo* [The Japanese stock market] (Tokyo: Toyo Keizai Shinpo-sha, 1992).
[18] Tokyo Stock Exchange, *Fact Book* (1999), 116.

1980s and is now around 40 percent.[19] The Big Four dominate industry pol-icymaking and the industry association, the Council of Securities Organiza-tions (*Shoken Dantai Kyogikai*).

The smaller brokerages were, however, able to develop some balancing power on the TSE by virtue of their numbers, and by the ties they devel-oped to politicians they were able to help with fund-raising both legally and illegally. In addition, each large city bank or long-term credit bank (LTCB) had very close ties with at least one medium-sized securities firm. This gave these companies some leverage against the Big Four when their interests diverged.

The ability of securities companies large and small to feed Japan's money politics machine was an important part of their political power. Stock trades, in the opaque markets of the early 1980s and before, were a good way for politicians to launder money that had been raised in violation of Japan's notionally strict campaign financing laws.[20] With lax controls over the paper trail of exactly when and at what price a trade was made, it was rel-atively easy for a securities company to conjure up seemingly highly prof-itable trades which they could book to favored clients. The absence of tight laws on insider trading also allowed companies to favor politicians by giving them stock recommendations that were extremely valuable, but, since no money changed hands, were not in violation of any laws. The ability of the big companies to corner the market in a particular stock, thanks to their powerful market share, also allowed them to manipulate prices. One type of fraud worked like this. A securities company would privately recommend to a favored few politicians that they buy a particular stock at a low price. A few hours or days later, the securities company would coordinate a massive up-surge in the buying of that stock by aggressively recommending its purchase to all of its clients. The buying would drive the price up, at which point the securities company would quietly inform the favored few to sell. Once the favored clients had sold out, the company would stop ramping up the stock, and its price might or might not fall again. For the scam to work, the bro-kerage must have sufficient market power to move the price of a chosen stock, and the regulators must have little power or motivation to detect or deter the price manipulation.[21] The practice of stock manipulation was so common in the 1980s that market participants would refer to particular

[19] In 1985, a fairly typical year for the 1980s, the market shares of stock transaction volume on all exchanges were as follows: Nomura, 15.1 percent; Daiwa, 10.9 percent; Nikko, 10.2 percent; Yamaichi, 10.5 percent. Daiwa securities quoted in Hayes and Hubbard, *Investment Banking*, 173. See also Suto Megumi, "The Securities Industry in Japan: An Overview" in Japan Securities Research Institute, *Capital Markets and Financial Services in Japan* (Tokyo: Japan Securities Research Institute), 85–86.

[20] Robert Zielinski and Nigel Holloway, *Unequal Equities: Power and Risk in Japan's Stock Market* (New York: McGraw Hill, 1992), 95–99.

[21] The mechanics of this type of price ramp were repeated to me often in the course of inter-views in both Tokyo and London from 1992 to 1994. For obvious reasons, however, it is diffi-cult to find specific concrete evidence, since securities companies and politicians generally deny that the practice went on. My reasons for believing that the stories have some truth are

shares as being "political stocks" (meaning that they were owned by politicians and were therefore subject to sudden upward and downward movements), or "ambulance stocks" (meaning that they had been selected as the vehicle by which a securities company would compensate a favored client for losses on another stock).[22]

Investors

During the early postwar period, individual investors dominated both ownership and trading of stock, assisted by the armies of door-to-door saleswomen sent out by the securities companies. The high number of individual investors was in part a result of the forced sell-off of *Zaibatsu* shares in 1947, most of which went to former employees. It was also a testimony to the skill and persistence with which the securities companies sold shares. Nomura Securities pioneered the use of door-to-door saleswomen who sold stock to housewives, who traditionally maintained control over family finances.[23] One highly successful tactic employed by Nomura was to leave locked savings boxes (known as "million-*ryo* chests") in every house or shop in which they could get a foot in the door. When the box was half-full of change, the savings were unlocked and the equivalent sum, less commission, was paid into a Nomura investment trust.[24] In the period immediately following the *Zaibatsu* sell-off, individuals owned around 70 percent of all equities.[25]

However, as in Britain, the relative importance of individuals on the exchanges dropped dramatically during the postwar period. The share of total stock owned by investors fell from 46 percent in 1960 to approximately 40 percent in 1970, 29 percent in 1980, and 23 percent percent in 1990.[26] There were two significant reasons for this. First was the deliberate attempt by Japanese corporations to buy up shares in order to use cross-shareholdings "for the purpose of stable stockholder operation."[27] Second was the growing importance of corporate customers to the securities companies and their reluctance to make the market more appealing to individuals. According to the Japan Securities Research Institute, the decline in the relative value of individual shareholdings was in part due to "the stance taken by

---

partly personal: as a fund manager in London in the late 1980s I was approached by more than one (British) salesman from a Japanese securities company who privately claimed to be able to move the price of certain stocks by up to 5 percent for up to two or three days.

[22] Interviews, securities company and fund management officers, Tokyo, July 1994. See also Zielinski and Holloway, *Unequal Equities*, 98. The loss compensation scandal is discussed in greater detail in chapter 6.

[23] Nomura believed, apparently correctly, that women customers would be much more likely to trust another woman's financial advice. In 1962, the company employed over 2,000 low-paid women for door-to-door sales. Albert Alletzhauser, *The House of Nomura* (New York: Arcade Publications, 1990), 145.

[24] Ibid.

[25] Japan Securities Research Institute, *Securities Markets in Japan 1994*, 72.

[26] Ibid.

[27] Yosho Suzuki, ed., *The Japanese Financial System* (Oxford: Oxford University Press, 1987), 141.

securities companies and issuing corporations [which] was short of making the securities market attractive to individual investors."[28] The period was therefore one in which securities declined somewhat as a medium for household savings. In 1965, approximately 24 percent of net personal financial assets were in securities including stocks, bonds, and investment trusts. By 1995, the figure had declined to approximately 12 percent, with 6 percent in stocks.[29] In contrast, in the United States, approximately 33 percent of net financial assets were in securities, with 17 percent in stocks. Moreover, the decline in the relative significance of individual investors in Japanese securities markets was just as dramatic when measured by their contribution to trading volumes. Individual investors' share of total stock trading fell from around 60 percent to approximately 20 percent between 1975 and 1995. (See Figure 5.1.)

On the other hand, while institutional investors grew in importance over the period, they had not yet acquired the overwhelming importance in Japan that they had in Britain. This is partly due to the fact that the two biggest groups of shareholders, banks and insurers, were until the 1990s relatively inactive as stock traders, a situation that did not begin to change until the 1980s. In the Japanese case, these investors included insurance companies, investment trusts, mutual aid associations, and pension funds. The Japan Securities Research Institute and other Japanese sources also include as institutional investors Japan's 153 banks and corporations and other entities that are engaged in securities investments on a continuing basis.[30] The banks became major holders of stocks to cement long-term *keiretsu* relationships and from the mid-1970s became the biggest single group of shareholders.[31] However, for the same reason, they did not become active traders on the market until the mid-1980s. The second biggest class of institutional investors were the forty-eight life and casualty insurers, and in particular the seven biggest life insurers: Nippon, Dai-Ichi, Asahi, Meiji, Yasuda, Mitsui, and Sumitomo. Unlike their British counterparts, these insurers were forbidden by the MOF to count capital gains as investment income, with the result that they engaged in almost no stock trading until 1989. Accordingly, until then they were not as interested as their British counterparts in pressing for liberalization of trading rules and commission rates. But institutional investors' share of stock holdings grew rapidly as that of individuals fell. Banks and other financial institutions held approximatey 23 percent of all stocks in 1960 but approximately 42 percent in 1990. Nonfinancial corporations also saw their share of holdings rise from approximately 18 percent to approximately 25 percent in the same period.

The implications of this shift in investor composition were to be the

---

[28] Japan Securities Research Institute, *Securities Markets in Japan 1994*, 72.

[29] Ibid., 9. The picture is a little more complicated over the whole period, with the proportion of stockholdings rising somewhat during the Bubble Economy period in the late 1980s, but the trend is unmistakable.

[30] Japan Securities Research Institute, *Securities Markets in Japan 1994*, 9.

[31] Zielinski and Holloway, *Unequal Equities*, 35.

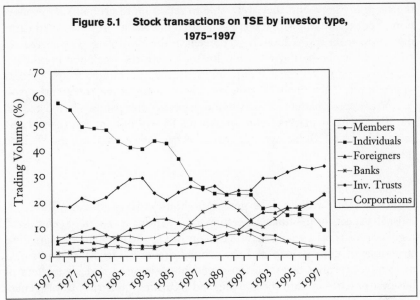

Figure 5.1   Stock transactions on TSE by investor type, 1975–1997

Source: Tokyo Stock Exchange

same in Japan as they were in Britain. Larger consumers of financial services have a greater ability to exploit the opportunities of exit to international markets than do small investors. To the extent that the sellers of financial services—in this case the securities companies—became more reliant on the business of large customers, they were more vulnerable to the changes in bargaining power that internationalization brought in the 1980s. If my argument about the exit option is correct, we would expect to find that the securities companies became less resistant to the idea of regulatory reform when they thought it would stimulate market changes of benefit to their largest customers. As I discuss later, developments in the market bear out this interpretation of events.

Borrowers

Japanese corporations did not rely much on the stock market for their funding needs during the postwar period, when bank lending dominated the market for private capital. In 1965, approximately 11 percent of new corporate funds came from stock and bond issues, while 89 percent came from borrowing.[32] These proportions remained about the same until the early 1980s.[33] One major trend was that corporations in Japan were able to rely less on any form of external funds (either securities or bank loans) as

[32] Bank of Japan, *Shinkin Junkan Kanjo* [Flow of funds accounts] (Tokyo: Bank of Japan, 1994).

[33] In 1980, for example, the figures for external corporate funds were 11.9 percent debt and equity and 87 percent for bank borrowing.

the economy grew and they were able to retain more profits. The proportion of corporate funds that were generated internally, from retained earnings, grew from approximately 30 percent in the late 1960s to an average of 50 percent in the period 1980–84. By 1995, with the stock and bond markets in seemingly terminal slump, internal capital accounted for 84 percent of new funds.[34] Yet the TSE grew steadily throughout the 1960s and 1970s. In 1965, approximately one thousand Japanese companies were listed on the TSE, with a market value of around ¥6,000 billion. By 1980, 1,400 companies had TSE listings, with a market capitalization of around ¥80,000 billion.[35]

Ministry of Finance

The MOF (*Okurasho*, The great storehouse) exercised control over almost all aspects of the financial system, representing a system of centralized regulatory authority that was in sharp contrast to the fragmented regulatory structures of both Britain and the United States.[36] The MOF controlled matters concerning taxes, customs, and interest rates; and all matters of business practice in both the banking and securities industries. It was generally considered to be one of the top (and perhaps *the* top) bureaucratic agency in Japan, more prestigious and arguable more powerful than even the Ministry of International Trade and Industry (MITI).[37] As such, its upper echelons were staffed almost exclusively by elite graduates of the Faculty of Law, Tokyo University (*Todai*). The ministry is divided into seven bureaus, each responsible for a different aspect of the financial system.[38]

There is considerable debate over the extent of the MOF's influence over domestic economic and political affairs. According to John Creighton Campbell, MOF staff refer to it as "the Ministry of Ministries" because it has a dominant position in the policymaking arena due to its power over the budget. As Campbell puts it, "the spending ministries propose, the MOF disposes."[39] He notes the ministry's ability to protect itself, when it wants to, from political interference so that "even high-level promotions are screened from interference from the LDP."[40] Steven Vogel shares this view of the MOF's dominance, at least over the issue of financial market regula-

---

[34] Economic Planning Agency, *Economic Survey of Japan* (Tokyo: Economic Planning Agency, 1997–1998), 194.

[35] Tokyo Stock Exchange, *Fact Book 1995*, 101.

[36] See John Creighton Campbell, *Contemporary Japanese Budget Politics* (Berkeley: University of California Press, 1977), 143–115, for a description of the MOF and its decision-making procedures. See also Eamon Fingleton, "Japan's Invisible Leviathan," *Foreign Affairs* 74, no. 2 (1995): 69–75. For Japanese sources, see Suzuki Yukio, *Keizei Kanryo* [Economic bureaucrats] (Tokyo: Tokyo Keizai Shimbunsha, 1969); and Kawakita Takako, *Okurasho: Kanryo Kiko no Choten* [MOF: Pinnacle of the system] (Tokyo: Kodansha, 1989).

[37] Campbell, *Contemporary Japanese Budget Politics*, 44.

[38] These are Budget, Banking, Securities, Tax, Finance, Customs, and International Finance.

[39] Campbell, *Contemporary Japanese Budget Politics*, 43.

[40] Ibid., 49.

tion. He argues that bureaucrats in the MOF "have still managed to run their financial revolution their way" and that "the evidence from the financial system reform case strongly supports my contention that MOF officials have followed their own priorities—and not those of financial institutions or party politicians."[41] Eamon Fingleton refers to the MOF as "the invisible Leviathan," claiming it is the single most powerful bureaucratic agency in the world.[42] Many Japanese concur, and use the term "MOF-ocracy" to describe the power that the ministry has over policymaking.[43]

Other scholars agree that the MOF is important, but do not accept its overwhelming centrality. Rosenbluth recognizes the MOF as one central actor in the field of regulatory politics, but argues that its function is often that of "an enforcer of private bargains" rather than the main protagonist of change.[44] She argues that "the bureaucracy plays a key role in policy making, even if its function is more one of mediating and equilibrating the interests of politically powerful interest groups than of formulating policy objectives or controlling policy outcomes."[45]

Rosenbluth also notes the importance of the Liberal Democratic Party (LDP) in making financial policy since the beginning of the LDP's long period of one-party rule in 1955.[46] While she notes that the LDP has "a strong preference for delegating to the MOF" tasks of balancing the interests of different groups, she gives evidence of "the party's substantial influence and indeed satisfaction with how matters were proceeding."[47] The latter point is a significant one. For much of the postwar period the LDP and the MOF shared the same broad goals, including the encouragement of high, export-led economic growth, conservative monetary policy, and the protection of the domestic industry from foreign competition. Hence, conflicts were less likely than in a country such as Britain, where the goals of at least one group in the politician-bureaucracy relationship—the ruling party—changed dramatically and frequently as the two main political parties alternated in government.

On other hand, the LDP's influence over financial policy is surprising for two reasons. First, many aspects of financial policy are technically demanding, and elected politicians in Japan usually lack the research and support staff to master the complexities of the policy issues. As such, the better-informed and better-supported bureaucrats were able to sway policy. Second, since the MOF controls the disposition and geographic allocation of

[41] Steven Vogel, "The Bureaucratic Approach to the Financial Revolution," 237.

[42] Fingleton, "Japan's Invisible Leviathan," 6.

[43] Interviews, Tokyo, June 1994.

[44] Rosenbluth, *Financial Politics in Contemporary Japan*, 5.

[45] Ibid., 13.

[46] The importance of the LDP is the subject of much debate, with bureaucratic-dominance models of politics, such as Johnson's being questioned by more pluralist accounts such as Muramatsu and Krauss, "The Conservative Policy Line"; and T. J. Pempel, "The Unbundling of 'Japan Inc.': The Changing Dynamics of Japanese Policy Formation," in *The Trade Crisis: How Will Japan Respond*, ed. Kenneth Pyle (Seattle: Society for Japanese Studies, 1987), 117–152.

[47] Rosenbluth, *Financial Politics in Contemporary Japan*, 28.

most of the budget, politicians wishing to divert resources to their own constituencies, which in effect means all Japanese politicians, have strong incentives to cultivate friends in the ministry. The MOF has the power, through its control of the tax agency, to threaten recalcitrant politicians with a tax audit, something no politician involved in money politics wants to be subjected to.

The power of the MOF over private industry was great. Its main source of power lay in its ability to use Japan's strict regulatory structure to punish companies that did not follow its suggestions. Given the MOF's tight and discretionary control over such company-specific issues as granting licenses for new offices or subsidiaries, the ministry could single out specific companies for regulatory retaliation, which gave it the ability to divide and rule. Each specific company often had stronger incentives to toe the MOF line than to organize collectively to oppose it. The ministry did not usually need to resort to actual threats. Its use of administrative guidance (*gyosei shido*) was sufficient in most cases to persuade financial intermediaries to do what it wanted. The practice of retiring bureaucrats taking up positions in the industry they regulated, a process known as *amakudari* (descent from Heaven), strengthened business-government ties.[48] The effects of *amakudari* on power relationships cut both ways. Private companies could offer retiring bureaucrats a nice office and high salaries to compensate for their meager public pension, but the bureaucrats in turn could offer contacts and privileged access to current ministerial decision makers. Such a *paipu* (pipeline) could, of course, be extremely valuable, especially to a smaller firm. So important is the relationship between firms and the ministry that all the major private financial institutions use *MOF-tan*, employees whose full-time job is to cultivate relationships in the ministry and anticipate regulatory decisions.[49]

MOF authority also derived from the enormously high regard in which it was held. The intellectual abilities of its staff were unquestionably the highest in the country, and it enjoyed a high reputation for the successful administration and application of regulatory policy, at least until the scandals and policy mistakes of the 1990s that so dramatically tarnished its reputation. The social and intellectual cohesion provided by the old school ties of *Todai* also contributed to the persuasive power of the ministry.[50]

Observers differ about the degree of internal unity in the MOF. Campbell states that intraministry infighting occurs less in the MOF than in other ministries. He states: "Rivalries and tensions there may be, but among Japanese ministries, Finance is famous for unity—the "finance family"

---

[48] Neither the salaries nor the pensions of Japanese bureaucrats are especially high, especially considering the long hours and sacrifices the jobs entail, so these lucrative *amakudari* positions are especially attractive to retiring mandarins.

[49] The American equivalent would be the "Fed-watchers," although this term does not capture the extent of the personal interactions *MOF-tan* are expected to make.

[50] In Japanese the term *gakubatsu* (school faction) denotes the importance of educational ties in policymaking.

(*Ookua ikka*) is a term often heard. . . . [F]or the most part intrabureaucratic factionalism is not as intense [as in other ministries]."[51] On the other hand, he concedes that there is less cohesion in the ministry because it is, as he describes it "all bureaus and no ministry," in part because of the greater degree of departmental specialization of its officials. This lack of cohesion may be indicative of a more serious lack of unity than Campbell allows. Other observers point to considerable rivalries between bureaus, and there have been many sharp disagreements. The battles between the Banking and Securities Bureaus are particularly fierce, with each bureau tending to take the side of its sector in turf wars between the industries. The Securities Bureau was frequently and somewhat contemptuously referred to as "the Toranomon Branch of Nomura Securities," a reference to the district in Tokyo where the ministry is located. The loss-compensation scandals in 1991 began to sour relations between the ministry and the securities industry, and the rift remains.

Other observers have argued that inter-bureau infighting is actually worse in the MOF than in other government agencies. In part this may be due to the interests of key constituents, notably the city banks and large securities companies, who are extremely sensitive to regulatory policies and often at odds with one another. Bureaucrats who wish to take up lucrative *amakudari* jobs in the private sector have a strong motivation to keep their potential employers happy with favorable policies. This can lead them into conflict with their colleagues.

Another possible explanation for the greater degree of interagency infighting in the MOF is that the tendency toward infighting in other ministries is dampened by the fact that managerial staff are typically rotated between divisions every two years. This prevents senior staffers from becoming too closely identified with the interests of a particular division. In the MOF, by contrast, rotation can be somewhat stickier since the best and most ambitious staff tend to try to work as long as possible with the most prestigious bureaus—Budget, which wields the purse strings and therefore the most power, and Banking, which controls the cream of the financial institutions.[52]

Development of the Securities Markets, 1953–1971

The procurement boom prompted by the outbreak of the Korean War in 1950 led to a stock market boom that lasted until the crash following Stalin's death in 1953. The market boomed again in 1955–61, pushed in part by the rapid development of investment trusts.[53] A period of credit stringency beginning in 1961 put severe downward pressure on stock prices, and the Nikkei-Dow Average fell 44 percent between 1961 and 1965.[54] The

[51] Campbell, *Contemporary Japanese Budget Politics*, 47.

[52] Interviews, MOF officials, summer 1995.

[53] Japan Securities Research Institute, *Securities Markets in Japan 1994*, 16–17; Hayes and Hubbard, *Investment Banking* (1990), 156–157.

[54] Japan Securities Research Institute, *Securities Markets in Japan 1992*, 277.

MOF responded by propping up stock prices artificially, a policy they pursued continuously from 1961 until 1968. The Japan Joint Securities Corporation, a cooperative effort between the banks and the securities companies, funded by the BOJ, was founded in 1964 in order to prevent any further reduction in stock prices.[55] It attempted to accomplish this by buying up some ¥189 billion of stocks, approximately 3 percent of the entire market.[56] Meanwhile, sixty or so of the largest securities companies organized the Japan Securities Holding Company, again with BOJ help, to buy up the excess stocks being sold off by the investment trusts.[57] This organization bought up another ¥230 billion of stock.[58] Yet these attempts to support prices were unsuccessful, at least in the short term, and the continuing sell-off of stock caused the near-collapse of the then-largest Japanese securities company, Yamaichi Securities.[59] Yamaichi had run into trouble by using the securities it was managing in investment trusts as collateral for bank loans, which it then used to buy shares for own-account trading.[60] In addition, the company had invested heavily in land, anticipating a property boom. It had also taken out large positions in several small companies for which it had acted as underwriter.[61] By 1965 it was so deeply in debt that there was a panic sell-off of shares and a bad stock market crash, known as the *Yamaichi Shokku* (Yamaichi shock). The BOJ was forced to undertake a series of measures to keep the market from collapsing further, including arranging a bail-out of Yamaichi by the Industrial Bank of Japan and extending a series of emergency loans to both Yamaichi and another, smaller broker, Ohi Securities, in July 1965.[62]

In the aftermath of the scare, the SEL was amended to introduce a more rigorous system of licensing for securities companies. This prompted a sharp consolidation of the industry and a dramatic drop in the number of smaller securities houses. The total number of securities companies in Japan was halved, from 598 in 1962 to 277 in 1968, the year the new licensing system came into effect.[63] An important side-effect of the new system was the consolidation of the market power of the Big Four, since only the biggest firms had sufficient risk capital to qualify as lead managers for stock issues. In part as a result of these measures, and also buoyed by the resurgent economy, the market picked up again in 1968 and rose steadily until 1970. The Japan Securities Holding Association was dissolved in 1969 and the Japan

[55] Ibid., 18.

[56] Zielinski and Holloway, *Unequal Equities*, 62.

[57] Japan Securities Research Institute, *Securities Markets in Japan, 1992* (Tokyo: Japan Securities Research Institute), 18.

[58] Zielinski and Holloway, *Unequal Equities*, 62.

[59] For more on the stock market panic and the Yamaichi shock, see Adams and Hoshii, *A Financial History of Japan*, 170–172.

[60] Japan Securities Research Institute, *Securities Markets in Japan 1992*, 18.

[61] Hayes and Hubbard, *Investment Banking*, 157.

[62] Japan Securities Research Institute, *Securities Markets in Japan 1992*, 18.

[63] Tokyo Stock Exchange, *Fact Book* (Tokyo: Tokyo Stock Exchange, 1998), 116.

Joint Securities Corporation in 1971.[64] But these events clearly illustrate the political power of the securities companies and the extraordinary lengths to which the MOF would go in order to protect them.

III. Pressures for Change, 1970s–1990s

The first major changes in the long-run reform of the Japanese financial market were domestic in origin. There is general agreement among scholars about the list of domestic economic changes that were responsible for the first cracks to appear in the tightly controlled financial system. Hamada Koichi and Horiuchi Akiyoshi, for example, argue that "the recent liberalization of financial markets was an inevitable response by the monetary authorities to the fact of structural change."[65] The most important of these structural changes was the escalating government debts of the 1970s, detailed next. A second important trend was the diversified demand for financial services following a rapid increase in the level of privately held financial assets, which was caused in turn by steady growth. Examples of this new type of demand include the *gensaki* (forward repurchase) market, occasioning the negotiable CD market introduced in 1979, and the demand for postal savings accounts. A third important trend was the changing pattern of corporate finance. From 1973 to 1977, big business relied on bank loans for an average 30.2 percent of investment funds, but by 1978–82, this figure had dropped to 17.5 percent. This was prompted by a greater reliance on internal funding from retained earnings, itself a by-product of decades of high growth and economic success. Also influential were technological developments, which facilitated the "joint production of financial services";[66] and (5) inflation, which became a problem in 1973–74 in the aftermath of the 1973 oil shocks. Inflation greatly increased the interest-rate sensitivity of all Japanese savers, prompting demands for a liberalization of the fixed interest-rate structure of Japanese banks.

Growth in Government Debt

For most of the period from 1949 until the early 1970s, the Japanese government ran a balanced budget. High economic growth, a relatively inexpensive welfare system, a young population, a small defense budget, and a strong national desire to encourage growth all combined to counter demands for greater government spending. Accordingly, the market for government bonds

---

[64] Japan Securities Research Institute, *Securities Markets in Japan 1992*, 19.

[65] Koichi Hamada and Akiyoshi Horiuchi, "The Political Economy of the Financial Market," in *The Political Economy of Japan*, vol. 1: *The Domestic Transformation*, ed. Kozo Yamamura and Yasukichi Yasuba (Stanford: Stanford University Press, 1987), 223–262. The view is shared by Suzuki, *Japanese Financial System*, 25–34, who writes that "The internationalization of finance thus helped to ignite financial liberalization in the domestic economy. But the more basic causes of financial liberalization in Japan were to be found in internal factors" (30).

[66] Hamada and Horiuchi, "Political Economy of the Financial Market," 257.

was tiny. However, the high-growth miracle came to an end with the first oil shock of 1973. Real GNP growth that year fell by 1 percent, compared to the real growth rates of 9 percent the preceding year.[67] One result was a sharp drop in the tax revenue base, especially from corporate taxes. At the same time, the ambitious plans of Prime Minister Tanaka Kakuei to "remodel the archipelago" put new upward pressures on government spending. In addition, structural increases in expenditures such as the continuous expansion of social security spending, kept pressure on the budget even in the later 1970s after tax revenues had recovered with the upswing in economic performance.[68] The result, inevitably, was the large-scale issuance of government bonds. The bond-dependency ratio jumped from 9.45 in 1974 to 34.7 percent in 1978.[69]

The market could not handle the vast increase in the volume of bonds.[70] Its segmentation into distinct sectors made it impossible for the sectors that were allowed to trade the bonds, principally the securities firms and the general public, to assimilate them. At first, the BOJ absorbed the majority of the newly issued Japanese government bonds (JGBs), but this soon put intolerable strain on the money supply, threatening severe inflation. The only financial institutions capable of taking on such a large quantity of bonds were the banks, and they were subjected to considerable bullying by the authorities to buy them. The problem for the banks was that according to Article 65, they were not permitted to sell the bonds, since this would have been securities business. Yet the prospect of taking these loss-making bonds onto their books and holding them "under water" indefinitely was particularly unappealing for the banks at a time when the demand for corporate loans was declining sharply. The banks therefore insisted that the financial structure be reformed to allow them both to absorb the quantities of bonds that the BOJ was forcing on them and to recoup in other areas the profitability that they were losing in other areas.

In 1978, the MOF agreed to let banks sell government bonds on the open market. This was to prove the first break in the segregation of the system. In addition, the money market was liberalized in various ways to allow the banks to fund their bond positions. In an effort to attract more investors to the bond market, additional measures were taken to increase the market's attractiveness, including the introduction of medium-term (five-year) bonds in 1977, three-year bonds in 1978, two-year bonds in 1979, and four-year bonds in 1980. In other words, by the late 1970s, Japan's financial system was beginning to liberalize. The process was about to be given added impetus by developments in international capital markets.

[67] Bank of Japan, *Economic Statistics Annual* (Tokyo: Bank of Japan, 1985).

[68] See Yukio Noguchi, "Public Finance," in Yamamura and Yasuba, *The Political Economy of Japan*, 1:186–222.

[69] Bank of Japan, *Economic Statistic Annual* (Tokyo: Bank of Japan, 1979). The bond dependency ratio refers to the percentage of annual government expenditure that is dependent on issuance in the bond market.

[70] M. Colyer Crum and David Meerschwam, "From Relationship to Price Banking: The Loss of Regulatory Control," in *America versus Japan* (Boston: Harvard Business School Press, 1988), 261–298.

Internationalization and Financial Reform in the 1980s

Internationally, two structural changes created pressures for financial market reform in Japan in the 1970s. One was the growth of large current-account balances, which stimulated the need to recycle surplus balances abroad. The ratio of foreign trade, exports and imports, to GNP rose from 23 percent in 1970 to 28 percent in 1975 and 29 percent in 1985. Although this pressure was international in the sense that it was caused by international trade, it was endogenous to Japan because it was created by domestic factors, notably the competitiveness of Japanese industry and the protectionist policies implemented by the Japanese government. In contrast, the other structural change was *kokusaika* (internationalization) and, in particular, integration of financial markets. By the mid- to late 1980s, internationalization was putting severe constraints on the ability of Japanese regulators to control the borrowing and lending practices of the private sector.[71] Corporate borrowers were able to tap international markets with increasing ease and at decreasing cost, undermining the value of the regulatory cartel that the securities companies and the banks had hitherto been able to impose.

The 1984 Yen-Dollar Talks

By the early 1980s, the liberalization of the Japanese markets was under way. The trend was given a big boost by the yen–dollar talks, when the United States put pressure on Japan to liberalize its financial system.[72] As with many cases of *gaiatsu* (outside pressure), this U.S. pressure was effective in achieving its immediate goals principally because it was pushing against a door that was already opening.

At the United States–Japan summit in Japan in November 1983, President Ronald Reagan and Prime Minister Nakasone Yasuhiro agreed to discuss the opening of Japan's capital markets. The purpose was to strengthen the yen against the dollar, which was regarded as massively overvalued. The belief was that if the yen were to take a greater role as an international currency, the supply of yen would increase and hence strengthen the relative value of the dollar. This, the participants believed, would in turn help reduce the trade imbalance between the two countries. Increasing the yen's international role would be facilitated by increasing the demand for yen-denominated instruments and that would, in turn, be facilitated by liberalizing Japan's relatively closed markets, allowing a greater inflow of capital and

[71] Hamada and Horiuchi write that the internationalization of finance "has exerted increasing pressure to open and deregulate the Japanese financial system and made it impossible to sustain cartel-like behavior in the banking sector supported by the monetary authorities." Hamada and Horiuchi, "Political Economy of the Financial Market," 257.

[72] See Kinyu Zaisai Jijoo Kenkyukai, *Kinyuu Jiyuka to En no Kokusaika* (Financial liberalization and the internationalization of the yen) [Tokyo: Financial System Research Council, 1985]; and Frankel, *Yen/Dollar Agreement*.

diversifying yen instruments. Many were skeptical of the reasoning, since an increase in the supply of any commodity (in this case, the yen) is normally associated with a decrease rather than an increase in its price. One Japanese economist noted that although the United States's motive was to strengthen the yen in the yen–dollar talks, "economically . . . it is not clear to me why the yen should appreciate when it is more widely used."[73]

The result of the summit was the establishment of the Yen-Dollar Committee, jointly chaired by Japanese Finance Minister Noburu Takeshita and U.S. Treasury Secretary Donald Regan. The committee submitted its report in May 1984, and the MOF simultaneously issued its report, "The Current Status and Future Prospects for the Liberalization of Financial Markets and the Internationalization of the Yen," which made essentially the same points.[74]

In April 1984, the rules governing the issuance of resident euroyen bonds were liberalized following the U.S.–Japan negotiations of 1983–1984. In June 1984, the regulations on conversion of foreign funds into yen were liberalized. "These liberalizations are expected to accelerate the internationalization of Japanese Financial Markets and to promote structural change in the financial system."[75]

Exercising the Exit Option: Raising Funds Abroad

But while the Japanese and American governments argued about the need for Japan to liberalize, another dynamic was emerging. This was the tendency of Japanese borrowers and investors to use international capital markets for services that were prohibited—or prohibitively expensive—at home.

For several years after World War II, Japanese companies did not borrow abroad, but in 1959 they began to issue foreign-currency bonds in the American market, starting with dollar-denominated convertible bonds.[76] In 1960, Kobe Steel issued the first nonconvertible corporate bond, and the first convertible bond was issued by Hitachi, Ltd., in September 1962.[77] Both were made in the form of private placements. The first equity issue was a Sony Corporation ADR offered in June 1961. However, the imposition of the Interest Equalization Tax in 1963 caused the Japanese, along

[73] Yoichi Shinkai, "The Internationalization of Finance in Japan" in *The Political Economy of Japan*, vol. 2, *The Changing International Context*, ed. Inoguchi Takashi and Daniel Okimoto (Stanford: Stanford University Press, 1988), 249–275.

[74] Japanese Ministry of Finance and U.S. Department of the Treasury Working Group on Yen/Dollar Exchange Rate Issues, *Report by the Working Group on Yen/Dollar Exchange Rate, Financial and Capital Market Issues to Japanese Minister of Finance Noburu Takeshita and U.S. Secretary of the Treasury Donald T. Regan* (Tokyo, 1984).

[75] Hamada and Horiuchi, "Political Economy of the Financial Market," 254.

[76] The first overseas bonds issued by Japanese corporations came shortly after the Meiji Restoration of 1868, but overseas issues were suspended during World War II.

[77] From 1962 to 1982, 539 convertible bonds and 357 non-convertible bonds were issued abroad by Japanese companies.

with other nationalities, to shift to the eurocurrency markets. Issuance of eurobonds by Japanese corporations was active, with issues of convertible bonds reaching $235 million in 1969, of which $185 million was by corporate issuers. The first samurai bonds were issued in 1971.[78] The Law on Foreign Securities Firms was also enacted in 1971, and in July 1971 the government lifted the ban on investment in foreign securities by Japanese investors. Restrictions on the overseas flotation of debt securities were lifted in 1973. "Out-out" issues, which were funds raised overseas for use overseas, were allowed in principle, subject to approval. "Out-in" issues, which were funds raised overseas for use in Japan, were still tightly controlled due to the policy of tight money. But in May 1974, out-in issues of electric power bonds were allowed "because of the public character of their service."[79] In November 1974, all restrictions on out-in issues were lifted for business corporations.

The first listings of six foreign stocks on the TSE took place in December 1973. However, offerings of yen-dominated foreign bonds were suspended from November 1973 to July 1975, following an issue by the Brazilian government, in the wake of the oil shocks. In 1974, the MOF lifted the ban on the issuance of Japanese corporate bonds on overseas markets. In 1975, the MOF authorized the issue of a Finnish government bond as the first yen-dominated sovereign foreign bond.

The total amount of overseas financing by Japanese corporations jumped dramatically from ¥15 billion in 1973 to ¥73 billion in 1974, and to ¥421 billion in 1975.[80] Then came a big jump from ¥567 billion in 1978 to ¥904 billion in 1979. By 1982 the year's total was ¥1,426 billion, raised in 105 overseas stock issues. This represented approximately one-third of the total securities finance raised by Japanese companies.[81] By the mid 1980s, more and more Japanese companies were escaping the restrictions of the domestic market to raise money abroad, and the relative importance of overseas financing grew even greater.[82] From 1984 to 1987, about half of all new securities financing by Japanese companies was taking place outside Japan. A variety of new products were developed to service the demand. For example, the first issuance of bonds with stock subscription warrants, or warrant bonds, was made by Mitsubishi Chemical Industries in Europe in January

---

[78] A samurai bond is a yen-denominated bond issued in Japan by a foreign borrower.

[79] Japan Securities Research Institute, *Securities Market in Japan, 1994*, 262.

[80] See MOF, *Kokusai Kinyu Kyoku Nenpo* [Annual report of the international finance bureau of the MOF] (Tokyo: Ministry of Finance, 1994).

[81] Foreign bond issues accounted for approximately 21 percent of total bond funding by Japanese corporations in 1977 but approximately 48 percent in 1982. Bond Underwriters of Japan, *Bond Review* (Tokyo: Bond Underwriters of Japan, 1983).

[82] On the asset side, in contrast, the use of foreign securities as portfolio instruments by Japanese companies was not particularly significant in the 1980s. Such use was growing, but from a tiny base. The shares of foreign securities holdings in the total securities holdings of financial institutions was 5.4 percent for banks, 4.1 percent for trust banks, 19.8 percent for life insurance companies, and 10.9 percent for property insurance companies in 1985. Bank of Japan, *Economic Statistics Annual* (Tokyo: Bank of Japan, 1986).

1982.[83] Yet much of the money raised abroad was brought back for use in Japan.[84] By 1991, the amount of debt securities issued abroad by Japanese firms rose to about $68.4 billion, representing nearly 60 percent of all new securities financing.[85] Table 5.1 illustrates the exit option in action.

This use of exit by Japanese borrowers played a key role in persuading the MOF that Japan's domestic markets had to be liberalized.[86] As Hamada and Horiuchi write, "The increased borrowing in foreign capital markets by Japanese corporations is a result of their rapid expansion overseas. This implies that corporations have effective alternatives to borrowing in domestic markets, and domestic financial markets are inevitably receiving impacts from abroad. This is especially true of corporate bond markets."[87]

It was curious, to say the least, that Japanese corporations should need to tap foreign markets at all given the massive trade surpluses the country had generated. The reason why Japanese corporations were such enthusiastic borrowers on the euromarket was that the costs of raising money in the domestic markets was significantly higher. High domestic costs were, in turn, due to the many restrictive regulations passed partly for the benefit of the politically powerful banks and securities companies and partly to facilitate control over the markets by the MOF. In particular, the registration requirements set forth in Article 4 of the SEL and the requirement to pay trustee fees to the banks were onerous to borrowers.[88]

[83] Tokyo Stock Exchange, *Fact Book* (Tokyo: Tokyo Stock Exchange, 1983), 62.

[84] Hamada writes that "It has been common knowledge in financial circles that a considerable portion of the securities floated by Japanese companies in the Euro-market without any registration under the SEL tends to find its way back to the Japanese market rather immediately after the closing date [of the flotation]. In recent years this trend has been quite conspicuous in particular for Japanese equity warrants initially attached to Euro-dollar BEWs [Bonds with Equity Warrants]." Kurio Hamada, "External Issues of Securities by Japanese Companies," in Japan Securities Research Institute, *Capital Markets and Financial Services in Japan* (Tokyo: Japan Securities Research Institute), 253.

[85] Dollar values were derived by translating the foreign currency amount into dollars at rate prevailing at time of issuance. Japan Securities Research Institute, *Securities Market in Japan* (1994), 227.

[86] Hamada and Horiuchi write that the use of the euromarkets "created competitive pressure in domestic markets, thereby contributing to the deregulation of these [domestic bond] markets." They go on to argue that the increase in the issuance of convertible bonds in Switzerland in 1981—1982 was so rapid that "it induced some liberalization in the conditions applying to bond issues in the domestic market." Hamada and Horiuchi, "Political Economy of the Financial Market," 250. This assessment is shared by Rosenbluth, who stresses that the politically powerful banks conceded to deregulation of domestic bond markets as a "second best option" once corporations began using the flexibility of foreign markets. She writes that "Deregulation of the domestic bond market was a reaction to, rather than a cause of, changes in Japanese corporate finance. . . . the pressure on banks to accommodate the corporations increased as a growing number of firms began scaling down their bank debt and obtained access to the Euromarket." Rosenbluth, *Financial Politics in Contemporary Japan*, 165.

[87] Hamada and Horiuchi, "Political Economy of the Financial Market," 254.

[88] In 1988, the costs of issuing a straight bond in the domestic market were 5.5 percent for a six-year bond and 5.32 percent for a twelve-year bond. In contrast, costs for a straight euroyen bond were 5.43 percent and 5.28 percent respectively. While these differences may

Table 5.1. Foreign and domestic securities financing by Japanese corporations, 1975–1991

	1975–79 (average)	1980	1981	1982	1983	1984	1985	1986	1987	1988	1989	1990	1991
Total funds raised (billions of ¥)	2,926	3,106	5,010	3,954	4,449	5,943	6,437	6,499	9,301	13,432	19,215	28,308	9,472
Foreign issues	560	856	1,401	1,426	2,038	2,793	3,202	3,264	4,118	5,378	6,907	11,465	5,436
Foreign issues (% of total)	19.1	27.6	28.0	36.1	45.8	47.0	49.7	50.2	44.3	40.0	35.9	40.5	57.4

Source: Bond Underwriters Association of Japan, *Bond Review* (Tokyo: BUAJ, 1992).

The dissatisfaction of corporations with regulations in domestic markets was repeatedly made clear in surveys conducted by the Bond Underwriters Association of Japan. The first, commissioned in 1986, surveyed 533 listed companies to determine their reasons for issuing different types of bonds. The companies were asked to list the top five factors underlying the decision to issue the bond in question. The results were as follows (the figures in parentheses indicate the percentage of respondents who listed the factor among their top five).[89]

Foreign currency–denominated convertible bonds
1.   Issuing coupon rate can be lower than in Japan. (84%)
2.   Issuing procedures (excluding disclosure) are simpler than in Japan. (50.9%)
3.   Unsecured bonds can be issued. (34.8%)
4.   Useful to consolidate stockholder's equity since the bonds are quickly converted into stock. (24.1%)
5.   Disclosure procedures are simple. (21.4%)

Foreign currency–denominated straight bonds
1.   Real yen cost declines due to use of swap agreements. (70.0%)
2.   Issuing coupon rate can be lower than in Japan. (50.7%)
3.   Issuing procedures (excluding disclosure) are simple. (29.3%)
4.   Issuing possible with bank guarantee without secured mortgage. (28.0%)
5.   Issuing terms are set voluntarily and flexibly through negotiation. (28.0%)

Foreign currency–denominated warrant bonds
1.   Real yen cost declines due to use of swap agreements. (60.0%)
2.   Issuing coupon rate can be lower than in Japan. (57.1%)
3.   Compared to foreign currency–denominated convertible bonds, warrants are exercised more slowly, giving the issuer an advantage regarding dividend payment burden. (47.1%)
4.   Issuing procedures (excluding disclosure) are simple. (20%)
5.   Issuing terms are set voluntarily and flexibly through negotiations. (20.0%)

The survey found that the ability to issue bonds at an unregulated (and therefore lower) coupon rate was a vitally important factor in the decision to

---

appear small, the difference of even seven basis points on a ¥50 billion issue created huge savings. Hiroko Okumura, "Japanese Capital Exports" in *Japanese Financial Growth*, ed. C. A. B. Goodhart and George Sutija (New York: New York University Press, 1990), 95–120.

[89] Bond Underwriters of Japan, quoted in Tatsuro Tamura, "Changes in Corporate Fundraising," Foundation for Advanced Information and Research (FAIR), *Japan's Financial Markets*, vol. 29 (Tokyo: Look Japan, 1987), 3.

use offshore markets rather than domestic ones. The simpler issuing procedures found abroad were another attraction for corporate borrowers. A similar survey conducted in 1991 revealed similar attitudes. Foreign bond issues were cheaper and simpler, the required financial covenants were less severe, less time was needed to prepare issues, and there was a greater variety of debt instruments available.[90] For these reasons, Japanese manufacturers made clear their desire for change. *Keidanren* (the Japanese Federation of Employers' Association), the leading corporate association, insisted that "the merit of liberalization is high."[91]

The MOF Responds to Internationalization

The MOF had been long opposed to internationalization, fearing an inevitable loss of control. On this issue, at least during the 1970s, all three major bureaus were in agreement. The Banking, Securities, and International Finance bureaus allied to impose regulations and strict limits on the foreign underwriting activities of Japanese banks under the Three Bureaus Agreement (*Sankyoku Goi*) in 1975.[92] This agreement remained in effect until the 1990s.[93] The MOF also prohibited Japanese banks, with the exception of the long-term credit banks, from using in Japan funds raised from the issuance abroad of long-term liabilities. But although these and other regulations tended to delay adaptation of the Japanese financial institutions to the internationalization of the markets, the regulations were increasingly relaxed after the amendment of the Foreign Exchange Law in 1980.

Article 21 of the Foreign Exchange and Foreign Trade and Control Law covered capital transactions requiring a license from the MOF. Any foreign-exchange transaction had to be placed through an authorized foreign-exchange bank or be subject to approval by the minister of finance. According to the Ministerial Ordinance Concerning Foreign Exchange Control, Article 17–1, the foreign-exchange banks' forward foreign-exchange transactions with resident customers had to be based on real demand. That is, they had to be based on the demands of nonfinancial transactions such as import or export transactions. The foreign-exchange bank's forward transactions with nonresident customers did not have to be for purposes of "real demand," but were subject to the restriction that "the capital transactions with a non-resident . . . must not be those whose purposes are clearly for speculation" (Article 17–2 of FEFTCL). In 1980, the government revised the law limiting foreign exchange according to the principle "With freedom as a principle, we will seek to control the exceptional trade imbalance and rapid changes in the foreign

---

[90] Bond Underwriters of Japan, *Survey of Corporate Borrowers* (Tokyo: Bond Underwriters of Japan, 1991), quoted in Hamada, "External Issues of Securities," 249.

[91] Atsushi Nama, *The Yen-Dollar Relationship, Macroeconomic Policy, Financial and Capital Markets and Related Issues,* Keidanren Papers no. 10 (Tokyo: Keidanren, 1992), 48.

[92] Viner, *Inside Japan's Financial Markets,* 26.

[93] Rosenbluth discusses the Three Bureaus Agreement in some detail. Rosenbluth, *Financial Politics in Contemporary Japan,* 150–157.

exchange market by treating them as 'special cases.'"[94] The borrowing of foreign capital (impact loans) held by residents was completely deregulated, as were restrictions on foreign currency deposits held by Japanese residents. The effect was the abolition of the real-demand rule on spot foreign-exchange transactions, although the rule still applied to forward transactions.[95] In April 1984, the real demand principle in foreign exchange was abolished.[96]

Meanwhile, the government was moving ahead with the liberalization of the bond market. In 1981, the Diet amended the Commercial Code to allow issuance of warrant bonds.[97] The big banks initially opposed reform. The Bond Issuance Committee, dominated by the big city banks, was in charge of corporate bond issues and was hostile to the liberalization of the corporate bond market. They believed that liberalization would threaten the dominance of bank loans in corporate financing patterns. They were, however, fighting a losing battle even before the yen–dollar talks. A 1982 report on industrial finance by MITI's Industrial Structure Council "vividly presents the dissatisfaction of nonfinancial firms with the existing domestic financial system. The report recommends reexamination of the traditional requirements for commercial loans and corporate bonds."[98] By the mid-1980s, the banks had realized that the game was up: they risked losing too much business if they did not agree to liberalization.[99]

The MOF publicly recognized the importance of the international markets in 1989 with the release of the interim report of the Second Financial Subcommittee of the Financial System Research Council. This report was clear about the need to liberalize markets. The reasons for reform were both domestic and international, but the changes at the international level were obviously important. Also of interest was the concern the report showed for efficiency and the expression of the idea that the efficient allocation of funds was facilitated by freer competition: "It is now recognized that competition in free, open markets serves to promote the efficient use of funds and resources.... As the current financial system restricts financial institutions from entering fields other than their own, it is believed that the time has come to review this system and thereby promote competition among such institutions to the maximum degree possible."[100]

[94] Foundation for Advanced Information and Research (FAIR), *Japan's Financial Markets*, vol. 22 (Tokyo: FAIR, 1988), 10.

[95] As of September 1983, at least partial restrictions on forward foreign-exchange transactions were in effect in France, Italy, Sweden, the Netherlands, Denmark, Norway, Australia, Argentina, and Mexico: most of these had some version of the real demand rule. There were no such restrictions in the United States, West Germany, the United Kingdom, Canada, Switzerland, New Zealand, Hong Kong, and Singapore. FAIR, *Japan's Financial Markets*, 10.

[96] Japan Securities Research Institute, *Securities Markets in Japan 1994*, 28.

[97] Ibid., 27.

[98] Hamada and Horiuchi, "The Political Economy of the Financial Market," 250.

[99] Interviews with Japanese bankers, Tokyo, June 1995.

[100] Second Financial System Subcommittee of the Financial System Research Council, *On a New Japanese Financial System*, Interim Report (Tokyo: Financial System Research System, May 1989).

The report noted four factors that had created needs that the present system did not meet.

1. The accumulation of assets held in the private sector, due to high savings rates and a general rise in income levels. It was noted that in 1987 the total balance of financial assets held by individuals was ¥700 trillion, or 2.0 times GNP, whereas in 1975 total assets held by individuals accounted for 1.2 times GNP. (In 1987, corporations held ¥350 trillion.)

2. The slowdown in growth, which had ended the previous shortage of funds. Accompanying this had been a trend toward securitization: "Large and medium-sized corporations have shifted the bulk of their fund-raising from bank loans to securities."[101]

3. Financial innovations, in particular the development of new products.

4. Integration of world financial markets.

According to the report "the distinction between domestic and overseas financial transactions is losing much of its significance, and 'trading without borders' has become a reality throughout the world." Since financial assets are very liquid, it continued, "the consolidation of their market had progressed the furthest."[102]

> Financial liberalization and internationalization have become world-wide trends. . . . with the consolidation of world money and capital markets, the choice of whether to raise and manage funds domestically or abroad had come to depend entirely on the attractiveness of financial products offered in each country's markets, and on the convenience and efficiency of those markets. Money, in other words, now moves freely in search of more attractive markets.[103]

The report noted that in fiscal year 1988 Japanese companies had raised ¥7 trillion in international markets compared with ¥12 trillion domestically—that is, 40 percent of funds were raised internationally compared with less than 10 percent in the 1970s. Finally, the report noted other factors prompting change, which included the trend toward securitization of assets and the greater financial risk caused by interest rate deregulation, and including interest rate risk, and (significantly) foreign-exchange and liquidity risk caused by the sudden outflow of funds. A final factor concerning the council was Japan's place in the world. The report noted that in 1988 Japanese banks accounted for 10 percent of the loans to industry in the United States and 25 percent of the bank assets in the United Kingdom. It noted also that foreign banks accounted for 4 percent of bank assets in Japan. The report then argued that policy reforms "must be based on an adequate consideration of the international position of the nation's money and capital

---

[101] Ibid., 4.
[102] Ibid., 6.
[103] Ibid.

markets. It must aim to ensure that Tokyo can fulfill its responsibility as one of the big three financial centers alongside New York and London, and *that it allows for easy operation by foreign institutions and users* as well as Japanese."[104]

These quotations make it clear that the drafters of the report were very well aware that the insulated and uncompetitive nature of the Japanese financial structure was becoming increasingly unsustainable in a world of international money. Moreover, it is clear from the quotation about financial liberalization that what worried the council most was not the threat of retaliation from foreign governments, but rather the possibility that those who had "the choice of whether to raise and manage funds domestically or abroad"—in other words, the mobile-asset holders at the center of my argument—would choose not to raise and manage funds in Japan because of the relative unattractiveness of its financial products. This is the clearest possible evidence of the twin threat of exit and promise of entry working to shape policy. The council made reform proposals that appealed to those who had the choice of where they raised and managed funds, without those actors having had to say a word or engage in a single piece of lobbying.

To summarize, the process of deregulation of the Japanese securities markets, initiated to accommodate the large government deficits of the mid-1970s, was given added impetus by the internationalization of finance. This impetus worked in two ways. First, internationalization led to an increase in direct pressure on Japan to reform by foreign governments, especially the United States. Moreover, the Japanese government was facing pressure from foreign firms with internationally mobile assets—both financial services intermediaries and investors—and their government representatives, who wanted to conduct business in Japan. But a more profound transformation was taking place in the markets. Japanese corporate borrowers, who long had chafed at the high costs and restrictive regulations governing the issuance of securities in Japan, had begun to turn to the increasingly cheap and liquid international markets for funds. At the same time, Japanese investors were beginning to see the possibilities of investing in overseas markets, benefiting from the lower transaction costs and greater product choice. Japanese financial firms were confronted with a loss of business, and the Japanese government was confronted with worsening relations with important allies such as the United States and the United Kingdom. Moreover, the government was aware of the positive revenue and image boost it would earn by hosting an internationally first-class financial center. For all of these reasons, Japanese securities markets were overhauled dramatically over the course of the 1980s.

---

[104] Ibid, 11. Emphasis added.

IV. Reform at the Tokyo Stock Exchange

The Tokyo Stock Exchange was at the heart of the liberalization process. Reforms increased its accessibility to foreigners, deregulated dealing costs, and increased the number and nature of financial instruments that could be traded.

Opening the Toyko Stock Exchange to Foreign Membership

Article 8 of the original TSE charter prevented foreign firms from becoming members of the exchange. The TSE authorities amended the article in 1982 to allow foreign membership in principle. The measure was meaningless at the time because no spare membership seats were available. When one became available in 1984, the TSE auctioned it off. The auction was officially open to foreign as well as domestic brokers, but the process quickly became embroiled in controversy and accusations of rigging. A high bid by U.S. broker Merrill Lynch was rejected, and the seat was awarded to an obscure local securities house, Utsumiya, which had reportedly bid significantly lower. Utsumiya happened to be an affiliate of Yamaichi Securities, who in turn happened to have acted as broker for the auction.[105] Merrill Lynch was outraged, but the MOF responded that since the TSE was a private company, the whole affair was a private matter over which the MOF could not claim jurisdiction. However, the MOF bore the brunt of foreign criticism of this affair, chiefly from the U.S. Treasury Department, and in turn leaned on the TSE to do more to open up. The TSE presented a number of excuses about why it could not admit more members, including that it had run out of floor space, but none were particularly convincing. In late 1984, the MOF ordered the TSE to review its membership regulations in order to quell criticism from abroad.[106]

Part of the pressure to open the TSE to foreigners came from foreign investors, whose interest in Japanese stocks was rapidly rising as the Japanese economic miracle continued into the 1980s. In 1975, foreigners had accounted for 4.7 percent of share trading volume on the TSE, but by 1984 they accounted for 14 percent.[107] This pressure was compounded by foreign brokerages interested in cornering a part of that business. The *gaijin* (foreign) brokers were helped by lobbying from their governments. In 1985, during a visit to Japan, British Prime Minister Thatcher demanded reciprocal access to British brokers in advance of the Big Bang opening of the London market. At the time, Nomura and Daiwa were hoping to win approval to become primary dealers in gilts under the new government-bond auction system being prepared. Thatcher made the unsubtle threat

[105] Joseph Tompkins, "Foreign Financial Firms in Japan: The Perspective of a Global Securities Firm," in *Capital Markets and Financial Services in Japan,* ed. Japan Securities Research Institute, 281.

[106] Viner, *Inside Japan's Financial Markets,* 52.

[107] Okumura and Kawakita, *Nihon no Kabushiki Shijo* [The Japanese stock market], 62.

that Japanese brokers would be denied this privilege if concessions to U.K. brokers were not forthcoming from Japan. In 1985, in the face of this threat, the TSE agreed to create new seats and admit foreign firms. In 1986, it accepted bids from six foreign firms, both British and American, to become full members.[108]

The number of foreign brokers increased in May 1988 after the TSE increased the physical size of its trading operations, allowing sixteen foreign and six domestic members to join the ranks. In November 1990, ten new seats were created, of which three went to foreign firms.[109] By 1994, 24 of the TSE's 124 member firms were foreign.[110] Their impact on the market deepened slowly. During the market boom of the late 1980s, foreigners did not make much of an impact, but by 1990 they accounted for approximately 6–7 percent of all TSE dealing—a significant marginal change.[111] Their presence after the 1990–91 crash increased as trading volumes shrank and speculative futures transactions took on greater importance. Foreign firms, notably U.S. firms, had far greater experience and expertise in futures trading and soon came to dominate that section of the market. By the late 1990s, foreign brokers and investors were a very powerful force in the market, both in terms of the amount of trading they conducted, and in terms of setting sentiment. In 1997, for example, foreigners accounted for almost one quarter of share trading. (See table 6.1.) That same year, the *Nikkei Weekly* newspaper began their annual survey of stock market trends with the headline "Foreign Investors Guide Market."[112]

Once foreign brokers held seats on the TSE, they didn't have to pay commissions on stock trades and could bid at auction for JGBs. One of the strongest hidden benefits of buying the seat was the trust it instilled in potential Japanese clients that the broker was committed to the Japanese market.[113] The cost, however, was high: ¥1 billion on the direct cost of buying the seat, plus numerous hidden costs, such as responsibility for settlements problems and so on.[114] Nevertheless, in the boom years of the late 1980s, such seats were greatly sought after by investment houses anxious to boast of their truly international credentials. Big international investment houses clamored to buy exchange seats with much the same enthusiasm that they had snapped up British brokerages prior to the Big Bang and often with the

[108] These firms were Goldman Sachs, Merrill Lynch, and Morgan Stanley (all American); Jardine Fleming and Warburgs (both British); and Citicorp Scrimgeour Vickers. The last seat had been given to the British broker Scrimgeours, which was promptly and not coincidentally bought out by the U.S. giant Citicorp as it geared up for London's Big Bang.

[109] Interview with Tokyo Stock Exchange officials, June 1995.

[110] Of these, eight were American, eight British, four French, two Swiss, and two German.

[111] Rex Brown, "Medium-Sized Firms Prosper through Their Banking Links," *Financial Times*, 15 May 1990, vi.

[112] *Japan Economic Almanac* (1997), 58.

[113] Interviews, British and American brokerage officials, summer 1995.

[114] Joseph Tompkins, managing director of Morgan Stanley Japan, calculated that just the start-up costs of becoming a member of the TSE were in the order of $15–20 million in the late 1980s. Tompkins, "Foreign Financial Firms in Japan," 279–297.

same disastrous consequences for their bottom line. As a corollary, the number of foreign companies who chose to list on the TSE also rose dramatically during the 1980s, indicating the greater flexibility of rules on the exchange.

Abolishing Fixed Commissions

In the 1980s and earlier, commission rates on stock transactions on all Japanese stock exchanges had been fixed and non-negotiable, according to Article 131 of the SEL.[115] The actual amount and the method of collection were to be set by each exchange and stipulated in that exchange's Brokerage Agreement Standards. The establishment and validation of such standards were all subject to approval by the MOF, and the finance minister also had the right to alter them. In the early 1980s, nonmember securities firms paid 27 percent of the normal brokerage fee to exchange members for putting through a transaction.[116]

As might be expected, the securities houses were hostile to the idea of liberalizing brokerage commissions, which were a very important component of their revenues. In 1985, commissions accounted for 70.4 percent of total income for all brokers on the TSE.[117] However, the Big Four were less dependent on commissions than the smaller brokers. Estimates for the early 1980s suggest that the Big Four earned around 50 percent of their revenues from commissions, while smaller brokers earned about 75–80 percent from commission.[118] By the mid-1980s the share of Nomura's income from brokerage commissions had fallen slightly to 43 percent, and it fell further to 32 percent in 1990, but these commissions were always the biggest single source of revenue.[119] Ironically, the foreign securities companies who had argued loudly in favor of liberalization when they were trying to obtain membership on the TSE fell very silent on the subject of fixed commissions. Having paid so much to join the cartel, they were reluctant to get rid of one of its primary benefits, despite their ideological convictions about the benefits of free markets.[120]

Equally predictably, large investors were anxious to see rates come down, despite a discount of up to 20 percent on large trades. This was a particularly pressing concern for the big investors, since the practice of continuation was not allowed on the TSE, unlike the LSE. As in Britain, there were a number of ways in which fixed commissions could be circumvented for fa-

---

[115] General background is given in Okumura and Kawakita, *Nihon no Kabushiki Shijo* [Japanese Stock Market], 46–49.

[116] Interview, Tokyo Stock Exchange official, June 1994.

[117] MOF, *Shoken kyoku Nenpo* [Securities Bureau Yearbook], cited in Okumura and Kawakita, *Nihon no Kabushiki Shijo* [Japanese Stock Market], 46.

[118] Viner, *Inside Japan's Financial Markets*, 60.

[119] Stefan Wagstyl, "Diversification is on Trial," *Financial Times*, 15 March 1990, vi.

[120] Interviews, foreign brokerages, Tokyo, August 1991. See also Stephen Church (director of UBS Phillips and Drew International), "Foreign Financial Firms in Japan: The Market, Issues, and Concerns," in *Capital Markets and Financial Services in Japan*, ed. Japan Securities Research Institute, 298. Christopher Wood reports that heads of the foreign securities companies formed a delegation to argue the case for fixed commissions to the MOF. Christopher Wood, *The Bubble Economy: The Japanese Economic Collapse* (Tokyo: Charles Tuttle, 1992), 117.

vored clients.[121] For example, small securities firms were reported to buy worthless research from institutional clients as a way to offset the cost of the fixed fees, and billings errors in favor of large customers were not unknown.[122] Still, these measures were not enough for the institutional investors who used both exit and voice to affect change. First, they turned increasingly to intermediary transactions, in which the buyers and sellers find each other and pay a small nominal commission to a securities firm that acts as a nominal intermediary. This represented money for doing nothing for the securities firm, albeit less than a full brokerage fee. But in 1985, galled by the massive profits earned by the securities firms, institutional investors demanded that the TSE investigate commission rates, which it agreed to do.[123] In the 1980s, under pressure from ballooning trade volumes, the commission rates were revised downward several times. From 1980 to 1990, commission rates on large stock transactions were cut by 58 percent.[124] However, despite repeated proposals by institutional investors, the MOF refused to consider a complete liberalization of rates until the early 1990s.[125]

The arrival of foreign brokers as full members of the TSE in 1986 finally tilted the scales in favor of the full deregulation of commission rates rather than a downward revision of rates within a fixed structure. The first six foreign members, ironically, did not continue to favor liberalization once they were admitted to the cartel. On the contrary, they were happy to receive artificially high prices for their services. But their global reach was used by Japanese institutional investors to bypass the entire exchange. The share of Tokyo trading commanded by the foreign brokers was pitiful, but their presence allowed Japanese institutional investors with foreign offices to bypass both the TSE and the high commissions of the Japanese brokers by off-market block trading. Block trading worked by the institutional investor's arranging for its foreign office to place an order to buy or sell a large block of Japanese securities through the foreign broker's office; the foreign broker filled the order by finding a buyer or seller, charging a lower negotiated commission on both sides of the transaction.[126]

Faced with pressure from this potentially serious loss of business, the TSE gave ground. It cut rates on all transactions, with the biggest cuts for the largest transactions, which meant those greater than ¥10 million. In 1990, rates stood at 1.15 percent for trades up to ¥1 million, with a ¥2,500 minimum, ranging down to 0.1 percent for trades over ¥500 million and 0.075 percent for trades over ¥1 billion.[127] Commissions for futures trades were also cut.(See table 5.2.) The slashing of rates on large transactions resulted in an interesting distribution of benefits. Obviously those who bene-

[121] Interviews, fund managers, Tokyo, July 1994.
[122] Both examples from Viner, *Inside Japan's Financial Markets*, 60.
[123] Ibid.
[124] Brown, "Medium-Sized Firms Prosper," vi.
[125] Naoki Tanaka, "Face the Problem Squarely," *Japan Times*, 10 July 1991, 8.
[126] Viner, *Inside Japan's Financial Markets*, 61.
[127] Tokyo Stock Exchange, *Fact Book* (1991), 92.

Table 5.2. Changes in commission rates for Japanese government bond futures contracts, 1986–1995

Face value up to (millions of ¥)	1986	1995	
¥500	0.06%	0.015%	
¥1,000	0.06%	0.01%	+ ¥25,000
¥2,000	0.05%	0.005%	+ ¥75,000
¥3,000	0.0467%	0.005%	+ ¥75,000
¥5,000	0.044%	0.005%	+ ¥75,000
¥10,000	0.032%	0.0025%	+ ¥20,000

fited most from the cut in rates for large transactions were the large investors. Those who had most to lose were the Big Four securities companies, who depended to a greater extent on institutional business than did the myriad small and medium-sized brokers, for whom a higher proportion of revenues came from individual retail business.[128] For these actors, in contrast, the shift in commissions was believed to be good news; securities industry analyst Paul Heaton observed in 1990 that "securities firms whose business depends on individuals will continue to prosper."[129]

Further pressure to liberalize fixed commissions happened as an aftershock of the crash and the resulting scandals. A report by the LDP in August 1991 suggested that deregulation of commissions on large-lot trading could help to prevent a repetition of the loss-compensation scandal by forcing brokers to compete on price and not on other factors such as compensation for losses. Finance Minister Hashimoto Ryutaro announced in the Diet that he might support a further cut in rates. The LDP report also recommended further tightening of the regulation of markets, including improvements in self-regulation.[130]

The MOF, the securities industry, and the TSE were opposed to the deregulation of rates in 1990–91.[131] For the securities firms, the matter was a simple one of economic self-interest. Fixed commissions were an enviable source of profit. The interests of the brokers in turn prompted opposition to

[128] In 1990, the fifth largest securities company in Japan was New Japan Securities, which earned over 80 percent of its revenues from retail business. Brown, "Medium-Sized Firms Prosper," vi. Nomura earned 41 percent of revenue from commissions, compared with 16 percent for the U.S. broker Shearson Lehman and 2 percent for Salomon Brothers. James Sterngold, "Financial Giant's Slippery Slope," *New York Times*, 10 March 1991, 36.

[129] Brown, "Medium-Sized Firms Prosper," vi.

[130] Stefan Wagstyl, "Japan's Scandal-Hit Traders May Lose Fixed Commissions," *Financial Times,* 10 October 1991, 3.

[131] Ibid.

deregulation by the regulators. Another concern for the authorities after the 1990 crash, however, was to attract small investors back into the market, which they had deserted in droves. (See figure 5.1.) Sato Mitsuo, deputy president of the TSE in 1992, offered the following defense of fixed commissions:

> Japan's securities industry is characterized by high concentration of market share in a limited number of large broker/dealer firms. Given the economy of scale inherent in securities business, drastic deregulation will lead to serious financial turbulence which not only severely hit smaller firms but also render the whole system quite unstable to the ultimate detriment of benefits of investors in general.[132]

The TSE's defense of fixed commissions may have been motivated as much by self-interest as by economic theory. The argument that market stability can be ensured by maintaining a cartel does not follow. In theory, system stability is better ensured by encouraging more competition among brokers rather than less. It is also hard to imagine what "serious financial turbulence" would follow deregulation other than a steep loss of income for the big securities companies. Wharton Finance Professor Morris Mendolson, discussing Sato's comments, described his defense of fixed commissions as "weak," noting the similarity to the self-serving and economically questionable arguments put forward by NYSE member firms in 1975 that deregulation would lead to serious turbulence: "The experience of the NYSE does not bear that out and I know of no evidence that it does."[133]

More plausible was the defense that deregulation would damage the interests of small investors. Mendolson recognized the validity of the claim, criticizing it on the grounds that "I see no real economic grounds for subsidizing them [small investors]."[134] Of course the reasons for subsidizing them were not primarily economic, but a reflection of the intense desire by both the MOF and the TSE to get small investors back into the market.[135] In addition, both sets of regulators were anxious to protect the interests of the smaller brokerages who, as previously discussed, wielded some political clout. For this reason, it was alleged that the MOF had brokered an informal deal with the Big Four. In return for the continued protection of fixed commissions, which were of primary benefit to the big securities houses, these firms were asked to lend financial support to the smaller and uncompetitive brokers.[136] According to one source, in the early 1990s every single

[132] Sato Mitsuo, "The Tokyo Equity Market," in *Capital Markets and Financial Services in Japan*, ed. Japan Securities Research Institute, 49.

[133] Morris Mendolson, "Comment," in *Capital Markets and Financial Services in Japan*, ed. Japan Securities Research Institute, 54.

[134] Ibid.

[135] Interviews, Tokyo Stock Exchange, August 1991.

[136] See Tanaka, "Face the Problem Squarely."

small broker on the exchange was being kept in business by assistance from one or more large brokers.[137]

Regulators, brokers, and investors reached a compromise in 1992. The Securities and Exchange Council's report *On the Promotion of Fair Competition in the Securities Market* noted that "It is necessary to liberalize the stock brokerage commission rates applicable to wholesale trading . . . and then weigh the advisability of further deregulating the stock brokerage commission rates in light of the impact that liberalized commissions on wholesale trading will have on the securities market."[138] As a result of this report, and following further investigation of the issue by a specially appointed working group, commission rates on trades over ¥1 billion were completely deregulated.[139] As in Britain, the institutional investors and the big traders had won the regulatory battle. Underpinning their success was the fact that internationalization had given them new opportunities to escape from the old regulatory structure. Unlike in Britain, however, the process had been long, and the MOF and the TSE had attempted to protect for as long as possible the economic interests of all the financial intermediaries under their charge.

Introducing Futures and Derivatives

Futures trading was banned in Japan until the 1980s. Pressures to introduce futures came at both the domestic and international levels, but the driving force for reform was the institutional investors. According to the Japan Securities Research Institute, the two main factors in the opening of a bond futures market were the rise in the volume of government debt, which caused "the need for institutional investors holding large chunks of government bonds to hedge their positions against price fluctuation";[140] and the increasing use of futures trading in overseas markets, which made it "of vital importance for Japan's money and capital markets to offer investors hedging opportunities in order to compete with overseas markets."[141] The fact that overseas exchanges, most notably Singapore, Hong Kong, Chicago, and London, were beginning to offer trading in futures derived from Japanese instruments, such as the Nikkei index, added to the problem. Singapore launched a bond futures market in 1984 and began futures trading on JGBs. Yen bond futures were started on LIFFE, the London futures exchange, in 1987, and Chicago followed suit in 1988.[142] Japanese investors flocked to these markets. By 1989, over half of the euroyen trading in Hong Kong and

---

[137] Interviews, securities company executives, Tokyo, February 1994.

[138] Securities and Exchange Council, *On the Promotion of Fair Competition in the Securities Market* (Tokyo: Securities and Exchange Council, 1992).

[139] Commission rates from 1990 to 1994 were 1.15 percent for stock trades less than ¥1 million and 0.075 percent for trades over ¥1 billion. As of 1996, fixed commission rates for trades under ¥1 billion have remained the same. Tokyo Stock Exchange, *Fact Book* (1998), 92.

[140] Japan Securities Research Institute, *Securities Market in Japan* (1994), 119.

[141] Ibid.

[142] Viner, *Inside Japan's Financial Markets*, 124.

eurodollar trading in Singapore was being conducted by Japanese traders.[143]

Japanese regulators tried at first to persuade other exchanges not to allow the trading of financial instruments based on Japanese securities, but were soon faced with the reality that their influence did not extend very far abroad. TSE Deputy Chairman Sato, in one unsuccessful attempt to restrict foreign trading of Japanese futures, reportedly yelled, "You don't understand—no new products!" at the vice-president of the American Stock Exchange. He is reported to have threatened to throw an ashtray at the head of the uncooperative president of the Singapore Exchange.[144]

In December 1984, the Securities and Exchange Council recommended the establishment of a market in futures for long-term (10-year) JGBs. The Diet passed an amendment to the SEL to this effect in 1985. Among its conditions were the authorization of direct participation by banking institutions in futures trading. The rules on margin requirements were taken from the London model: on this occasion the Japanese eschewed the U.S. role model.[145] Trading in these futures was begun in Tokyo in October 1985. The first stock index futures contract, the Stock Futures 50, was introduced on the Osaka exchange in 1987, following another recommendation by the Securities and Exchange Council.

The introduction of financial futures was a ticklish subject for the MOF. Liberalization created potentially vast profit opportunities, and the city banks were reluctant to let the securities companies capture them all. The Federation of Bankers' Associations (*Zenginkyo*) issued its report, "View of the Banking Community on Financial Futures Trading," in March 1987. The bankers wanted a new, unified exchange to deal specifically with financial futures, and they wanted a unified new law to govern it. The unwritten subtext was that a unified exchange should treat banks and securities companies equally. The most obvious alternative would have been to place financial futures under the existing SEL. This could have resulted in greater business opportunities for the securities companies relative to the banks.

In light of this report, the Financial System Research Council and the Foreign Exchange Council issued a joint report in December 1987. This report agreed with the concept of a unified exchange. The stated advantages included that Tokyo, as a major financial center, would be required to provide an up-to-date futures exchange, especially in light of the wide range of futures contracts that could be traded elsewhere; a unified exchange would be cheaper for participants than membership on several different exchanges; and a unified exchange, under a single regulator and a new law, would facilitate the introduction of new instruments and contracts without the necessity to consider the possible breach of fire walls (divisions between banking and securities).

---

[143] *Japan Economic Journal, Survey of Tokyo Financial Markets* (summer 1989), 6.

[144] Gregory Millman, *The Vandals Crown: How Rebel Currency Traders Overthrew the World's Central Banks* (New York: Free Press, 1995).

[145] Interview, MOF official, May 1994.

The basic framework for the futures market was laid down in the Financial Futures Trading Law, passed in May 1988, and in further revisions to the SEL. The laws stipulate that those financial futures instruments derived from securities covered by the SEL may be launched and traded by any stock exchange. However, futures instruments not derived from securities explicitly covered by the SEL can only be launched and traded on a recognized financial futures exchange. As a consequence of these laws, the Tokyo Financial Futures Exchange (TIFFE) was established in April 1989. It launched futures contracts for euroyen and eurodollar interest rates and for yen-dollar currency rates. Trading in U.S. Treasury bond futures was promptly authorized on the TSE in December 1989, followed closely by the introduction of more index futures contracts such as the Nikkei 225 index future. Options on individual stocks and indices were also rapidly launched by both Tokyo and Osaka. Futures based on the Tokyo Stock Price Index (TOPIX) were launched in September 1988 and TOPIX options in October 1989. Options on JGB futures were introduced in 1990, to provide an additional hedging tool for institutional investors.[146]

The popularity of these instruments for institutional investors wishing to hedge trading risks and for traders using them for speculative purposes is demonstrated by the very rapid growth in trading volumes. Between its introduction in 1989 and 1990, trading volume for euroyen interest futures contracts almost doubled from 35,000 contracts per day to 58,000 contracts per day.[147] Trading volumes on stock index futures had grown to ten times the volume of the underlying cash markets by 1990.[148]

The Erosion of Article 65

The first major breach in Article 65 followed the pressure of domestic market forces in the mid-1970s, particularly the expansion of the JGB market. Since then, Article 65 has been eroded steadily and surely, albeit gradually, under the pressures of financial market growth and changing international circumstance. The matter has been one of intense debate in the MOF since at least 1985. The MOF decided in 1989 against an outright abolition of the bank–securities house division, and specifically rejected proposals to introduce German-style universal banking, but recent reforms have had the effect de facto if not de jure, of making the divisions decreasingly relevant.[149]

In April 1983 financial institutions were permitted to sell government bonds, government-guaranteed bonds, and local government bonds to the

---

[146] Tokyo Stock Exchange, *Fact Book* (1995), 52.

[147] Tokyo Stock Exchange.

[148] Japan Securities Research Institute, *Securities Market in Japan* (1994), 126–127.

[149] In which respect, of course, the Japanese policy decision most closely resembles the United States, where Glass-Steagall is still on the books (despite recent attempts to scrap it by the new Republican Congress) but is increasingly irrelevant, in practical terms, to market participants—most especially to market customers.

general public as long as they had held them for longer than one year. In effect, this let banks into the securities business. One year later, banks were allowed to sell these bonds to corporations. In June 1985, the one-year residual maturity requirement was dropped.

Banks supported the move to deregulation of the barriers: the deputy president of IBJ, Kurosawa Yoh, explained: "With the process of securitization going on, the separation between banks and securities companies is losing its meaning. We would like to get back the underwriting powers we had before the War. Our clients ask us to get in the securities business. Now, they have only four choices for corporate underwriting. If deregulation takes place they will have fifteen."[150]

His view was disputed by Kanzaki Yasuo, executive vice president of Nikko Securities, who argued: "I don't think that Article 65 can or should be amended regardless of what happens in the United States. I don't think that participation by banks in the securities markets will bring further development of Japan's securities market and benefits to customers unless there is a way to eliminate negative aspects such as conflicts of interest with an institution or group."[151]

Both sides had long anticipated the eventual abolition of the barrier and were preparing for it by gleaning whatever experience and knowledge they could in those areas of business that were officially closed to them. All of the big banks and the Big Four securities houses took advantage of the different regulatory structures of foreign markets to open subsidiaries through which they engaged in new business and actively rotated staff through them. For example, Daiichi Kangyo Bank (DKB), a large city bank, opened a London subsidiary, DKB International, which engaged in securities activities in the euromarkets. DKB bankers were seconded to this London office for periods of a few days to a few years to learn the mechanics of the businesses of securities trading, fund management, and so on. In another London subsidiary, Bank of Tokyo International, the average time for secondment from Tokyo was approximately two years. This training system was generally believed to be extremely expensive, since inexperienced staff were more prone to make mistakes and bringing them up to speed consumed the time and energy of highly paid local staff. It seemed to many frustrated locals that as soon as the new people got a firm grasp on the work, they were whisked back to Tokyo to be replaced by other clueless novices. The whole process of training from scratch then began again. Another form of training was via secondment to affiliates. For example, in 1987 Sumitomo Bank had over one hundred employees training at the second-tier securities house Meiko, while at least fifty of Ryoko Securities' 500–strong staff were on loan from Mitsubishi.[152] On the other side of the

---

[150] Seth Sulkin, "Views on Financial Reform," *Japan Economic Journal, Survey of Japan's Financial Markets* (summer 1989), 4.

[151] Sulkin, "Views on Financial Reform," 5.

[152] *Japan Economic Journal,* 5 December 1987, 6.

bank/broker divide, securities companies including Nomura and Daiwa quickly established foreign banking subsidiaries and undertook the same kind of training regimes.

Faced with pressure from banks and from corporate borrowers dissatisfied with existing arrangements, the MOF's banking bureau commissioned the Financial System Reform Council to investigate reform. The council delivered an interim report in May 1989, and a final one in June 1991, entitled "How the Basic System Regarding Capital Market Ought to be Reformed." The gist of the report was that competition in all aspects of the financial system was being hampered by the existence of intramarket barriers, and that greater competition should be encouraged by reducing the degree of specialization of different financial institutions. It did not go so far as to recommend the abolition of Article 65, instead proposing that banks and securities companies should be allowed to enter one another's business by the use of subsidiaries. German-style universal banking was specifically rejected. Moreover, the MOF retained the right to approve the establishment of such subsidiaries. Firewalls between parent companies and subsidiaries along American and British lines were mandated in order to deal with conflicts of interest. The report was put into action in 1983, when the first banks set up securities subsidiaries and vice versa. The results have been greater competition in the market and a clear step in the same direction as both the United Kingdom and the United States.

Banning Insider Trading

The scandals of the late 1980s and early 1990s, and the public outrage that ensued, have been cited as key reasons why the Japanese authorities moved so publicly to clean up the stock market. In fact, however, moves to stamp out unfair business practices had been going on for several years before these scandals surfaced. The moves against insider trading, for instance, began in 1988. In September of that year, the Securities and Exchange Council reactivated the Committee on Unfair Securities Trading, charged with submitting to the MOF recommendations to improve the fairness of initial public offering procedures and to reduce stock-price manipulation and the cornering of market shares.

SCAP had introduced U.S.-style insider-trading regulations with the Securities and Exchange Law of 1948. The act was closely modeled on the U.S. Securities Act of 1933 and Securities and Exchange Act of 1934.[153] Article 58 was the Japanese equivalent of the U.S. Rule 10b–5: a general, vaguely worded antifraud provision. Article 189, the equivalent of the U.S.

---

[153] This discussion draws on Misao Tatsuta, "Japan," and Shen-Shin Lu, "Securities Law in Japan: An Update," both in *International Capital Markets and Securities Regulations*, ed. Harold Bloomenthal and Samuel Wolff, vol. 10c, releases no. 13 and 14, Clark Boardman Callaghan Securities Law Series (Deerfield, 1993); and Oda and Grice, *Japanese Banking, Securities, and Anti-Monopoly Law*.

Rule 16(b), prevented short-swing trading by company officers in their company's stock: the maximum penalty was the requirement, when challenged, to disgorge profits. This was reinforced by Article 189, which required corporate insiders to notify the MOF of any changes in their stock holdings. Article 50 barred the officers of securities companies from trading on inside information gained in the course of their duties.

In Japan, as in the United States, there was no law or regulation explicitly banning insider dealing, but there were various provisions from which a ban could be inferred. However, whereas in the United States these provisions were used and interpreted to build a body of precedent against insider trading, in Japan the same provisions were either repealed or scarcely invoked until the late 1980s.

The first developments took place during the Reverse Course of 1952–53. With the onset of the Korean War and the Cold War, SCAP's overall policy changed drastically, from one favoring a New Deal style of democratic, anti-trust populism to one in which Japan's economic recovery and opposition to communism became paramount. The United States then encouraged Japan to revert to a more traditional, centralized form of policy-making. The Japanese Securities Commission was an early victim of a resurgent MOF, which subsumed it in 1952 and replaced it with a toothless Advisory Committee on Securities and Exchange. Thereafter, the chance of aggressive enforcement of existing regulations diminished rapidly. The extraordinarily close relationship between the MOF and the securities industry made it highly unlikely that the regulators would disturb the status quo by harassing and prosecuting the firms under their jurisdiction.

As if to reinforce this centralizing trend, Article 188 was revoked as not effective by the MOF in 1953, rendering any enforcement of the anti-short-swing trading provisions of Article 189 almost impossible. Article 58 remained on the books but was so vague that it was never invoked. The official regulators were scarcely given the resources to do their job. In 1992, the Securities Enforcement Division of the MOF had a staff of 17, compared to 299 in the SEC's Washington office. The TSE market surveillance team numbered 27, compared with 230 for the NYSE.[154] The difficulties of bringing successful trials under Japanese law also made the prosecutor's office reluctant to bring cases.

In other words, securities fraud in general and insider trading in particular do not appear to have been taken seriously by regulators or politicians in Japan, at least until the 1980s. On the other hand, there is no doubt that securities fraud and insider trading were common. There are various reasons for this. In one sense, insider trading was a natural consequence of the Japanese corporate culture of "long-term relationships and the exchange of information."[155] Allied to this, perhaps, was the more marginal nature of the stock market to Japan's economic life. With corporations relying on bank loans or

[154] James Sterngold, "Japan's Rigged Casino," *New York Times*, 26 April 1992, sec. 6, 30.
[155] Zielinski and Holloway, *Unequal Equities*, 97.

retained earnings more than on equity funding, the health and fairness of the stock market was of less concern to policymakers in Japan than in the United States. As the deputy president of the TSE forlornly remarked: "Unlike in the U.S. not many people in Japan regard the Stock Market as an important national asset."[156] A rigged stock market was also an ideal place to contravene the country's strict political-funding laws, as the Recruit Cosmos scandal was to reveal. Tip-offs to favored politicians about manipulated shares could be enormously valuable but virtually undetectable. In other words, there were strong incentives for both unscrupulous politicians and the financial community to keep the market as an *insaida tengoku* (insider's paradise).[157]

In 1987, however, the sleazy underside of Japanese securities trading was brought squarely to the public attention with the collapse of Tateho Chemical Company. The affair grew out of the stock market bubble of the mid- to late 1980s.[158] Tateho, in common with many other Japanese corporations, had been engaging in an aggressive form of financial engineering known as *zaiteku*.[159] Specifically, the company had run into trouble speculating in bond futures and had run up losses of ¥23 billion. Tateho's main bank, Hanshin Sogo, learned of the losses and promptly sold its holding of Tateho stock one day before the bad news was made public. Hanshin sold some 337,000 shares at ¥1,700, but news of the trading losses sent the price plummeting to ¥439. Needless to say, the investors who had bought Hanshin's stake were enraged.[160] The Osaka Stock Exchange investigated but did not find enough evidence to prosecute Hanshin. Nonetheless the Osaka Exchange concluded, with classic understatement, that "While there is no evidence of insider trading, we found trading which might cause misunderstanding. . . . We strongly point out that insider trading is unfair and damages investors' confidence in securities markets."[161] The outraged investors and the media were not satisfied with this finding and put intense pressure on the government to clean the market up.[162]

The result was an amendment to the SEL in May 1988, which came

---

[156] Mitsuo Sato, quoted in James Sterngold, "Japan's Rigged Casino," 28.

[157] The widespread practice of insider trading in Japan is documented in Nihon Keizai Shimbunsha, *Insaida Tengoku: Kenshoo Nihon Kabushiki Shijo* [Insider's paradise: The Japanese stock markets] (Tokyo: Nihon Keizai Shimbunsha, 1988).

[158] For background, see Gurupu NE, *Insaida Torihiki no Naimuku* [Inside information on insider trading] (Tokyo: OS Publishers, 1988), 22–38.

[159] *Zaiteku*, a play on "high-tech," is derived from *zaimu* (financial management) and the "tech" of high technology. The term refers, loosely, to the use of innovative financing techniques. In its benign form, *zaiteku* involved the use by manufacturing companies of sophisticated financial instruments such as interest-rate swap agreements for the purposes of hedging risks. As the stock market boomed, however, firms discovered that employing such instruments speculatively was also an easy way to make money— as long as things went well. In 1988, for example, approximately half of Sony Corporation's net income came from *zaiteku* profits. See Zielinski and Holloway, *Unequal Equities*, 115.

[160] Tateho's share price fell from ¥1,700 to ¥439 almost immediately.

[161] Quoted in Lu, "Securities Law in Japan," 16.

[162] Interviews with MOF officials, Tokyo, May 1994.

into effect in April 1989.[163] The new Article 166 clarified the concept of insider trading and explicitly made it illegal. Article 177 extended the rule to tender offers. It defined insiders as those with a contractual connection to the company and banned them and their primary "tippees" from dealing. However, a person who got the news third hand could deal legally, leaving a potentially big loophole for insiders to create chains of tippees. Penalties for violation were introduced, including up to six months in prison or a fine of ¥500,000. The law was extended to derivatives, including futures and options. Stricter controls on short-swing trading, relying on greater disclosure, were brought in.[164] Fire walls between departments in securities houses were made mandatory. On the related issue of takeovers, it became mandatory for investors to disclose a 5 percent or greater stake in a company.

In September of 1988, the Securities and Exchange Council, advisory body to the MOF, reactivated their Committee on Unfair Trading. There were public calls for an "SEC–type" independent regulator, but this was to wait until the aftermath of a series of extensive and heavily publicized financial scandals in 1991.[165] The laws against insider trading were further strengthened in 1992 when the existing regulations were extended to the over-the-counter markets. These changes made the legal climate much more hostile to insider trading, although anecdotal evidence suggests that many practitioners and even some regulators did not at first take the new rules seriously. A fund manager in Tokyo commented: "The MOF doesn't really care. The only real change that these laws have made is that companies have another excuse not to tell analysts things they don't want them to know."[166] An officer at Nomura Securities remarked, "There is no change following the law."[167]

Why did the Japanese authorities change their long-standing policy of toleration toward insider trading? Public outrage over the Tateho Chemical scandal appears to have prompted the MOF to implement tougher laws.[168] As important, however, was the need felt by the ministry to reassure international investors of the safety and soundness of the market. Japanese authorities appear to have been acutely aware of foreign, especially American, criticism of market practices. By 1988, of course, insider

[163] Showa 63, Law no. 75.

[164] Okumura Kazumi and Takeshita Chieko, *Laws and Regulations Relating to Insider Trading in Japan* (Tokyo: Commercial Law Center, 1989).

[165] See, for example, Quentin Hardy, "Japan Proposes Securities Agency but Finance Ministry Holds the Reins," *Wall Street Journal*, 16 September 1991, A12.

[166] Interview, fund manager, Tokyo, February 1994.

[167] Hisashi Taniguchi, quoted in "Insider Trading: Disclosure Law Heightens Corporate Awareness, But Little Changes," in *Tokyo Financial Markets, Japan Economic Journal* (summer 1989): 8.

[168] See Gurupu NE, *Insaida Torihiki no Naimuku* [Inside information on insider trading], who argue that the bubble economy in general and the Tateho incident in particular were "the triggers" for the campaign (part 1, 22–26).

dealing had become a major issue in the two other markets. Many within the MOF believed that Japanese regulations should reflect international norms, at least superficially.[169] One study argued that "the Tateho shock is not just domestic: it carried into London, New York, Frankfurt and the world's stock markets." Accordingly, they argued that it was necessary for Japan to control insider trading to maintaining the confidence of international financial markets, in which Japan has aspirations to be a major player.[170] The Japanese legal community was strongly in favor of the new laws.[171]

Moreover, there is evidence that the Japanese financial community recognized that stricter laws would ultimately be for its economic benefit. The privately funded Japan Securities Research Institute wrote that "In Britain and France, vigorous enforcement of regulation of insider trading has become an international tendency of the times."[172] Arai Isamu, president of the Japan Securities Research Institute, in explaining the 1988 bill, described the practice as: "grossly unfair . . . [it will] seriously undermine the public trust in the integrity of the securities market."[173] The Insider Trading Research Group, a semi-official group of academics, commented on Japan's need to build integrity in its markets: "The Tokyo market is now, along with New York and London, one of the three major global markets. . . . *As the internationalization of securities trading progresses, it is necessary from an international point of view for our country's regulations to keep step.*"[174]

This view was repeated to me many times during interviews with market practitioners. Significantly, many financial firms boast of having internal policies against insider trading that are stricter than those legally required. The Bank of Tokyo, for example, proudly claims credit for being the first Japanese financial institution to introduce internal guidelines against insider trading, that it introduced prior to the passage of the relevant regulations. The bank introduced internal policy guidelines in 1986 prior to their first use of futures to hedge their own portfolio. The rules prevented account officers from trading in the shares of any company owned by the Bank of Tokyo. The Bank of Tokyo Trust in New York greatly assisted in drafting the rules, drawing on their familiarity with U.S. practices. Shortly afterward, *Zenginkyo*, the Federation of Bankers' Associations, released its own

---

[169] See Naibusha Torihiki Kenkyukai [Insider Trading Research Council], *Insaida Torihiki Kisoku Ichimon Ittoo* [Insider trading regulations: Question by question] (Tokyo: MOF, 1988). This view is also reflected in interviews with market participants, Tokyo, February 1994.

[170] Gurupu NE, *Insaida Torihiki no Naimuku*, 28.

[171] For a legal perspective, see "Insaida Torihiki Kisei to Bengoshi Gyomu" [Insider trading regulations and lawyers' business], *Jurisuto*, no. 920 (1988): 58–59.

[172] Japan Securities Research Institute, *Securities Market in Japan 1992*.

[173] Ibid., 58.

[174] *Naibusha Torihiki Kisoku Kenkyukai*, 16. Author's translation; emphasis added.

guidelines, which all banks are now required to follow.[175] In other words, Japanese financial firms began to recognize the necessity of raising their business standards to the levels of their international competitors.

Progress toward Reform

By the end of the 1980s, the Japanese financial system had embarked on a fundamental shift of character. Previously protected markets had been pried opened to an unprecedented degree of competition from both foreign and domestic firms. Foreigners could become members of the TSE; banks could trade securities; investors could speculate in futures markets; and restrictions on international capital transactions had been greatly eased. Concurrently, the authorities were, for the first time in postwar Japanese history, seriously tackling the issue of financial fraud. The pace of change had seemed infuriatingly slow to many observers, and considerable differences still existed between the Japanese and the British or U.S. financial systems. But the trend toward a more liberal market was unmistakable. Robin Webster, assistant advisor on Japanese affairs at the Bank of England, wrote in 1990 that:

> The progress made in Tokyo in recent years has been remarkable in many aspects of deregulation and liberalization. There has been considerable progress in other areas, such as, for example, the setting up of the commercial paper markets, the development of certificates of deposit and other market instruments, the new offshore market and futures markets, quite apart from all the measures in the Euro-yen markets.[176]

But at the very end of 1990, just as the reform process seemed to be gathering real momentum, the stock market crashed and the asset price bubble, which had been the dominant feature of the economy in the late 1980s, collapsed. For financial policymakers, the issue of system liberalization was replaced by more immediate problems of damage control. The reform process was, in a sense, put on ice for the next few years while the MOF battled the crash and attempted to restore growth.

[175] Interviews, Bank of Tokyo, Tokyo, February 1994. The Bank of Tokyo introduced policy guidelines at least in part as a way of establishing that the *ringikan* (ethics) of the banks were superior to those of the securities companies and so to gain competitive advantage. According to one banker, Japanese securities companies "have no *ringikan* at all" and their current protestations to the contrary are *sononba shinogi* (temporizing). It is typical, he argued, that the brokers would only translate U.S. rules on insider trading in order to make the surface appear clean.

[176] Robin Webster, "Comment on Okumura" in *Japanese Financial Growth*, ed. C. A. B. Goodhart and George Sutija (New York: New York University Press, 1990), 128.

Chapter 6

Financial Reform in the 1990s: Creating a "Free, Fair, and Global" Market

In this chapter I examine the continued efforts of the Japanese government to improve both competitiveness and standards of investor protection in securities markets. The first section places the reforms in historical context: the Bubble Economy of the late 1980s, the rise and collapse of stock prices, and the series of financial scandals in the early 1990s that followed the crash. The next two sections consider the reforms themselves. The decline of MOF influence over the markets is illustrated by the founding of the *Shoken Torihiki Kanshi ii Inkai* (Securities and Exchange Surveillance Commission, or SESC) in 1992 and the Financial Supervisory Agency (FSA) in 1998. I also look at the raft of deregulatory policies implemented as the Japanese Big Bang in 1996.

The evidence presented in this chapter shows that regulatory reform benefited consumers, especially holders of internationally mobile assets, at the expense of producers. The abolition of fixed commissions and the introduction of greater competition on the Tokyo Stock Exchange were clearly designed to benefit institutional investors. The FSA and the SESC represent a significant strengthening of investor protection in Japan. As in Britain, the impetus for reform came from domestic financial scandals as much as from international pressure. Even so, the new regulations, most especially those governing insider trading, primarily benefited investors who were frequent, large-scale traders in the securities market.[1] In other words, while all consumers of financial services benefited from the new rules, large customers benefited relatively more than individual investors. Moreover, as was the case in Britain, the Japanese government chose to adopt the American regulatory model of investor protection.

I. The Bubble Economy and Financial Market Scandals

In the mid-1980s, the Japanese economy entered a period of massive asset price inflation known as the Bubble Economy. The Bubble was provoked by the rapid appreciation of the yen following the "Plaza Agreement" in September 1985, whereby the leaders of the the Group of Five Industrialized Nations (G-5) attempted to address persistent trade imbalances between

---

[1] See chapter 1.

Japan and the rest of the world by manipulating exchange rates.[2] The effect of the *endaka* (yen appreciation) was to slow real domestic demand for goods. Simultaneously, low interest rates and excess liquidity caused by lax monetary policy allowed corporations to compensate for the low demand for their products by borrowing at low rates and investing in real estate and financial markets. Trading volume and share prices on the TSE rose sharply. (See figure 6.1.)

The upward spiral in asset prices was driven by the fact that banks could use both shares and property as collateral for making loans. They could then use this collateral to make investments in stocks and loans to real estate companies. Stock market investments pushed up equity prices, which increased the value of the banks' asset base, allowing them to make more loans. Bank lending to real estate companies pushed up land prices, as buyers competed for the limited amount of usable land around Tokyo. The increase in land prices boosted the value of the banks' property holdings, which also increased their asset base, also allowing them to make more loans. The cycle was, for a time, self-reinforcing. This prompted many observers, both inside and outside Japan, to believe that the spiral would go on forever.[3] Investors, loan officers, and analysts alike were lulled by a series of ever more specious arguments that overlooked the now-obvious overvaluation of share and land prices. In 1989, price-earnings ratios on the TSE averaged 62.2, compared with 13.8 in the United States and 10.6 in the United Kingdom.[4]

Confidence that the market could rise forever was reinforced by the belief that the MOF would never allow the stock market to crash. This belief was fully justified by the actions of the MOF. The 1987 Black Monday stock market crash on Wall Street caused only a minor setback in Tokyo because the MOF instructed the Big Four securities companies to buy Japanese shares aggressively in order to keep prices and confidence high. Simultaneously, the BOJ flooded the economy with even more liquidity, pushing stock

---

[2] The yen appreciated by 60 percent against the dollar during 1986, rising from an average of ¥244 in 1985 to ¥153 in 1986.

[3] Karel van Wolferen, for example, termed this "The bubble that does not burst." He wrote of *zaiteku* that "In a Western setting the speculative activities in which Japanese firms have been engaged would have brought out the doomsayers out in crowds. A few did appear in Japan, predicting a 'bursting of the bubble'. . . in the near future. But the short- and medium-term pessimists overlook a critical factor: that the absence of a clear division of the public and private sectors in Japan, the cooperation . . . among the administrators and the ease with which the economic processes can be politically controlled all add up to a situation radically different from that in the other capitalist countries, whence such theories of bursting soap bubbles originally came" (Karel van Wolferen, *The Enigma of Japanese Power* [New York: Vintage Books, 1990], 401). The bubble burst within a year of the book's publication. (See Christopher Wood, *The Bubble Economy: The Japanese Economic Collapse* [Tokyo: Charles Tuttle, 1992].)

[4] Okumura and Kawakita, *Nihon no Kabushiki Shijo* [Japanese Stock Market], 104. See also Kenneth French and James Poterba, "Were Japanese Stock Prices Too High?" *Journal of Financial Economics* 29, no. 2 (1991): 337–363.

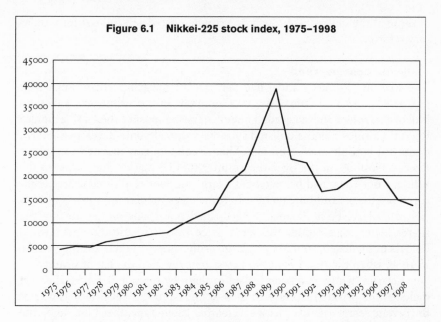

Figure 6.1   Nikkei-225 stock index, 1975–1998

and land prices still higher. The result was that equity and land prices almost tripled in value between 1985 and 1989, with the Nikkei 225 index rising from ¥13,113 at the end of 1985 to a high of ¥38,915 at the end of 1989.

Despite the predictions of some observers that this asset price inflation would never end because Japan did not obey Western laws of economics, reality set in in 1990. The Tokyo bubble and crash are reminiscent of the occasions when Wile E. Coyote, the cartoon character, keeps running on thin air long after he has gone over the edge of the cliff. Not until he looks down and realizes his predicament does he plummet to the ground, but he does so with a bump. The Nikkei 225 index fell by 40 percent during 1990. The market recovered somewhat over the next few years, but prices and trading volumes still did not return to the 1989 levels.[5] The crash in share prices brought about a concurrent collapse in the Japanese real estate market. By 1997, land prices in Tokyo had fallen more than 70 percent from their peak in 1991.

One effect of the crash was the increased interest in, and outrage about, financial fraud. During the Bubble years, financial firms had engaged in a variety of morally questionable practices such as insider trading and stock manipulation. A number of incidents were revealed just before or after the crash in a series of high-profile scandals. Together, these scandals drew the attention of Japanese and foreign observers to the overall laxity of investor protection legislation and the inadequacy of the supervisory regime in which regulators routinely placed the interests of the financial firms ahead

[5] The Nikkei 225 was ¥38,916 at the end of 1989, ¥23,849 at the end of 1990, and stood at approximately ¥19,823 on July 9, 1997.

of those of the investors. As such, the scandals acted as a catalyst for regulatory reform.

Recruit Cosmos, 1988

The Recruit Cosmos scandal had perhaps the most immediate impact on Japanese politics. Ultimately, it prompted Prime Minister Takeshita Noboru to resign and succeeded in embarrassing most of the LDP cabinet.[6] Recruit Cosmos was the unlisted subsidiary of real estate developer and recruitment consultant Recruit Co. The parent company planned to register Recruit Cosmos on the over-the-counter (OTC) market and, prior to the listing, from 1984, had parceled out a large number of allotted shares to favored politicians and bureaucrats. In some cases the Recruit Group's financial subsidiary, First Finance, even loaned politicians money to buy the shares. After registration, the share price rose dramatically, and favored holders immediately sold out at a large profit. News of these dealings broke in 1988, when the *Asahi Shimbun* newspaper revealed the list of seventy-six beneficiaries, which had been leaked to them by the police force.[7] The list included the private secretary to then-Prime Minister Takeshita, as well as the private secretaries of at least seven other cabinet members, including the minister of finance, Miyazawa Kiichi.[8] Miyazawa initially told the Diet that his private secretary had bought shares on his behalf, but without his knowledge and without using Miyazawa's money. When the press revealed this to be a lie, Miyazawa resigned in the face of intense hostility in the Diet in December 1988. Prime Minister Takeshita's problems were not over, however. The opposition parties were already in uproar over Takeshita's decision to ram through a 3 percent consumption tax measure and were using the Recruit Affair to attack the LDP. They boycotted or held up Diet proceedings, demanding that former Prime Minister Nakasone Yasuhiro appear before the committee investigating Recruit. Nakasone refused, thereby putting Takeshita in a very awkward position. Nakasone was one of Takeshita's most important political patrons, so for the prime minister to force him to

[6] See Asahi Shimbun Political, *Section Takeshita Seiken no Hokai—Rikuruto Jiken to Seiji Kaikaku* [The fall of the Takeshita administration—Political reform and the Recruit incident] (Tokyo: Asahi Shimbunsha, 1989). This scandal is also discussed in Brian Reading, *Japan: The Coming Collapse* (London: Weidenfield and Nicolson, 1992), 263–267.

[7] Asahi Shimbun, Yokohama Local Bureau, *Tsuiseki Rikuruuro Giwaku—Sukuupu Shuzai ni Moeta* [Covering the Recruit scandal—121 days of scoop newsgathering] (Tokyo: Asahi Shimbunsha, 1988). The practice by bureaucrats of using local as opposed to mainstream news sources as a pipeline for tactical leaks is common in Japanese politics. See Takesuke Nishiyama, *Za Reeku: Shimbun Hodo no Uraomote* [The leak: Press coverage inside and out] (Tokyo: Kodansha, 1992); and Maggie Farley, "Japan's Press and the Politics of Scandal," in *Media and Politics in Japan*, ed. Susan Pharr and Ellis Krauss (Honolulu: University of Hawaii Press, 1996), 133–163.

[8] Recruit employed the same practice again for two more share issues between 1984 and 1986. Eventually the names of approximately 159 favored power brokers were uncovered, including former Prime Ministers Suzuki Zenko, Tanaka, and Nakasone; the president of *Komeito* (the Clean Government Party); and the president of the Nihon Keizai Shimbun.

testify on the scandal would be political death for both of them. To appease the opposition without indicting his party boss, Takeshita admitted his own involvement in the scandal. It was then only a matter of time before continuing pressure from the opposition parties forced Takeshita to resign. In May 1989, Nakasone formally resigned from the LDP, but he retained enormous influence over his faction behind the scenes. The affair resulted in the prosecution of twelve people, including two politicians, and caused the resignation of a further forty-three people.

The impact of the scandal on securities market regulation was surprisingly slight in the short term. The TSE and the Japan Securities Dealers Association (JDSA) drew up new and somewhat tighter rules on the allocation of preregistration shares, limiting the number of shares allocated in advance to any one individual or corporation.[9] However, no legislative changes were made at this time. The impact of the affair on the political landscape was somewhat greater in the short run, since it so badly damaged the credibility of the LDP. It was the first major battle of a round of campaigning against money politics in Japan. However, it is hard to separate the unpopularity of the consumption tax from the fallout of Recruit. Arguably its long-term effect on politics was slight: Nakasone and Takeshita retained influence, and Miyazawa became prime minister a few years later. The influence of the Recruit Cosmos affair was to be felt later on, as a significant early element in the growing dissatisfaction felt by many Japanese with the inadequacies of their system of financial regulation.

Loss-Compensation Scandals, 1991

The Tokyo stock market boomed for most of the 1980s. The Bubble burst dramatically on the last trading day of 1989, and the market was in free-fall for most of 1990. The Nikkei 225 index fell from ¥38,916 at the close of 1989 to ¥23,849 at the end of 1990: a fall of approximately 39 percent. It continued to fall, more slowly, throughout 1992. The fall in share prices revealed a number of unsavory market practices associated with a special type of investment funds known as *tokkin* accounts.[10]

Tokkin accounts were trust funds held for corporations by trust banks with which an appointed investment advisor could engage in short-term trading.[11] The investment manager could be the trust bank in question, but

[9] Interviews, JSDA, July 1994. See also U.S. Treasury Department, *Report to Congress on Japanese Capital Markets and Global Finance* (Washington, D.C., 1995), 91.

[10] This scandal is covered by Okumura Hiroshi, *Shoken Sukandaru* [Stock scandal], Iwanami Booklet 223 (Tokyo: 1993). See also Wood, *Bubble Economy*, 118–126.

[11] *Tokkin* funds included both specified money trusts *(tokutei kinsen shintaku)* and fund trusts *(kingaishin)*. They had been around since 1948, but their popularity did not take off until the 1980s. Capital gains on *tokkin* funds could be converted into dividends, giving them attractive tax advantages in the mid-1980s as Japanese firms engaged in *zaiteku* activities on the back of the rising stock market. In 1984, insurance companies were permitted to hold up to 3 percent of total assets in *tokkin* funds, further boosting their popularity. See Viner, *Inside Japan's Financial Markets*, 211–213.

was often a securities company or an arm of a bank. One of the chief attractions of the *tokkin* funds was that they were anonymous and could therefore be used for ramping and other forms of market manipulation. They were widely used for speculative trading throughout the 1980s.

A special but illegal form of *tokkin* were the *eigyo tokkin* accounts. These funds were run by the institutional sales departments of securities companies themselves rather than by an officially authorized investment advisor. They bypassed the trust banks entirely, and were used either for the benefit of the securities company itself or on behalf of clients such as the cash-rich life insurance companies. Their popularity was due in part to the fact that the securities companies offered a guaranteed rate of return, which was usually 7–8 percent. Making such a guarantee was illegal, although, somewhat confusingly, compensating investors in order to meet the guarantee was not illegal. This guarantee and absolute anonymity made the *eigyo tokkin* very attractive vehicles for speculation. One source estimates that approximately ¥4 trillion was invested in *eigyo tokkin* funds, as much as was invested in regular *tokkin*.[12]

The MOF was aware of the existence of the *eigyo tokkin*, but did not initially attempt to curb their use.[13] Complaints by the trust banks that *eigyo tokkin* were drawing money away from their own, legal *tokkin* accounts were dismissed by the MOF in 1986.[14] In late 1989, the MOF, apparently worried about the effects *eigyo tokkin* were having in fueling the stock market rise, issued two directives. The first ordered securities companies to end the use of *eigyo tokkin* funds immediately. The second directive forbade compensation for losses suffered by investors. The Big Four securities companies denied managing such accounts, while beginning gradually to close them down.[15] Problems began when the stock market crashed almost immediately after the directives had been issued. The securities firms found it almost impossible to wind down the accounts quietly without paying compensation for the losses that accumulated rapidly as the market dived. The Securities Bureau of the MOF is alleged to have turned a blind eye to compensation payments in order to allow the funds to be paid off as soon as possible.[16]

Unbelievably, the securities companies then attempted to claim tax deductions for the compensation payments on the grounds that they were business payments. The Tokyo Regional Tax Bureau refused to allow such deductions. Attempts by the Big Four to use political influence on the National Tax Agency to force them to allow the deductions proved counterproductive. The National Tax Agency was so incensed by the strong-arm tactics of the brokers that in June 1991 it leaked to the press a report that

---

[12] Wood, *Bubble Economy*, 119.

[13] Brian Reading reports that Nomura managed an *eigyo tokkin* for the MOF pension fund (Reading, *Japan: The Coming Collapse*, 177).

[14] Ibid.

[15] There were 22,486 such nonexistent accounts in 1990. Ibid., 279.

[16] Wood, *Bubble Economy*, 119.

Nomura Securities had been making illegal compensation payments.[17] Once broken, the scandal spread quickly. On July 1, 1991, the Big Four securities companies admitted that they had made payments totaling ¥5 billion in 1990.[18] A few weeks later, it was revealed that the Big Four had made compensation payments totaling ¥128 billion to over 231 clients, including many of the most prestigious corporations in Japan.[19] Eighteen smaller brokers were also involved.[20]

There was a clash over whether the names of the companies that had received compensation should be disclosed. Initially the MOF was in favor of keeping the list secret. Yasuda Hiroshi, vice minister for finance, was quoted as saying that the ministry would not disclose the names.[21] The MOF argued that the information was privileged, having been supplied to them voluntarily by the brokerage houses. But Prime Minister Kaifu Toshiki promised that the Diet would order the MOF to disclose the list and would launch an investigation to probe the scandal if the brokerage houses did not volunteer the information. Faced with this threat, Finance Minister Hashimoto publicly urged the brokerage houses to volunteer the information. "The Prime Minister has the final say in the matter," he said, adding that "The securities firms should disclose the names by themselves in order to recover the public's trust in them."[22]

[17] "Nomura Allegedly Laundered Black Monday Compensation," *Japan Times*, 9 July 1991, 1. Nomura was first discovered to have used a global money-laundering scheme to compensate clients including Showa Shell Sekiyu KK for losses incurred during the 1987 Black Monday crash. Once again, note the use of the tactical press leak.

[18] "Big Four Paid Out ¥5 Billion," *Japan Times*, 2 July 1991, 1.

[19] The list included Hitachi, Nippon Steel, Toyota, and Nissan. Also included were a number of firms with un-Japanese-sounding names, written in *katakana*, which were generally believed to have been front organizations for politicians. Most beneficiaries fought a brief, unsuccessful battle to prevent the lists of compensated customers from being made public. (See *Quick News Service*, Tokyo, 29 July 1991.) Japanese insurance companies were believed to be the prominent beneficiaries of the compensation—reportedly receiving nearly $1 billion. Hence, Hata Kenjiro, chairman of the Life Insurance Association of Japan and president of the Meiji Mutual Life Insurance Company, insisted that the names of companies involved in the scandal not be disclosed. "Japanese Scandal Widens," *Financial Post* (Toronto), 22 July 1991, 5.

[20] According to the Japan Securities Dealers Association, the brokers had used securities transactions to transfer ¥160 billion in compensation out of a total of ¥172 billion. The most popular methods of compensation were the JGB market and the equity warrant market. Spreads of 4 percent in the JGB market meant that brokers could sell customers bonds at the bottom of the spread and buy them back at the top. The warrant market was an over-the-counter market not on an exchange, so price spreads were wide and trading was not very transparent. In addition, brokers sold unlisted bonds or newly issued convertibles at low prices and bought them back at high prices. The result was that the trades took place at prices that looked close to the genuine market price and so looked normal and reasonable. Large-volume transactions allowed large sums to be transferred. Wagstyl, "Japan's Scandal-Hit Traders," *Financial Times*, 26 June 1991, 8.

[21] "Japanese Scandal Widens."

[22] Quoted in Masaki Itagaki and Hisane Masaki, "Client Lists Could Be Disclosed," *Japan Times*, 29 July 1991, 8.

The Diet was in recess when the scandal broke, but the House of Representatives Finance Committee met in special session to investigate the affair. An extraordinary session of the full Diet met in August 1991, during which the opposition parties used the scandal relentlessly to attack the government. Tanabe Makoto, chairman of the Social Democratic Party of Japan, called the Finance Ministry "totally incompetent" and called for a new, independent regulatory agency similar to America's SEC. The criticism and the request for a Japanese SEC were echoed by Ishida Koshiro, chairman of the Clean Government Party (*Komeito*), who called it "quite unthinkable" that there would not be conflicts of interest when the agency responsible for supervising financial firms was also responsible for fostering their activities.[23] Their attacks were echoed by Prime Minister Kaifu, who was himself a proponent of clean government. He had recently been catapulted to power because he was one of the few LDP leaders untainted by the Recruit affair. He promised that "by taking necessary legislative and administrative measures, the government will do its best to restore investor trust in the stock and bond markets."[24] In addition, he ordered Finance Minister Hashimoto to begin to introduce tighter controls on the securities industry.[25] For their part, the presidents of two of the securities companies, Nomura and Nikko, had already announced their resignations.[26]

Hashimoto formally apologized to the Diet and admitted that the supervision of the MOF had been "insufficient."[27] He had already announced that he was giving himself a 10 percent pay cut to assume responsibility for the lack of supervision and that he had reprimanded four top ministry officials and cut their pay as well.[28] "This is a punitive measure I am imposing upon myself. It's very regrettable that the ministry did not properly control the market," he announced.[29] Meanwhile, the MOF had ordered the Big Four to suspend trading for four days.[30] For a while, Hashimoto avoided political damage.[31]

The MOF claimed that they were not to blame, since they had been duped by the securities companies. Hashimoto openly criticized the securities industry for a "lack of ethics" and announced that he had no plans to punish any MOF officials.[32] The ministry argued that compensation payments per se were not illegal, although they did contravene the administra-

---

[23] "Opposition Leaders Slam Ministry 'Incompetence,'" *Daily Yomiuri*, 8 August 1991, 1.
[24] Ibid.
[25] "Tokyo Scandal Spurs Tighter Controls," *International Herald Tribune*, 26 June 1991, 1.
[26] "Brokerage Heads to Quit," *Japan Times*, 25 June 1991, 1.
[27] "Hashimoto Gives Apology over Brokerage Scandal," *Japan Times*, 26 July 1991, 1.
[28] "Hashimoto Accepts 10% Cut in Pay to Take Responsibility for Scandals," *Japan Times*, 11 July 1991, 1.
[29] Hashimoto Ryutaro, quoted in David Sanger, "Tokyo Officials Take Pay Cut over Scandal," *New York Times*, 11 July 1991, 11.
[30] "Brokers Begin Four-Day Suspension," *Japan Times*, 11 July 1991, 1.
[31] Linda Sieg, "Hashimoto Appears Untarnished by Scandals in Financial Community," *Japan Times*, 17 July 1991, 8.
[32] "Brokerages Face Reprisal for Mob Dealings," *Japan Times*, 10 July 1991, 1.

tive directive of 1989, and that the MOF was unaware of any promises guaranteeing a rate of return, which would have been illegal. According to Matsuno Nobuhiko, director-general of the Securities Bureau of the MOF, "Compensation payments were not banned. On the other hand, they were not encouraged. Anybody who asked the ministry would have been told that they were improper, but nobody was required to ask."[33]

Utsumi Makoto, the vice minister of finance for international affairs, also sought to distance the MOF, insulating the ministry from charges of excessive coziness with the industry. "We should use this unfortunate event as leverage to get more distance [from the securities industry]. If we had clearly written laws on these issues, the situation might never have happened," he said.[34]

The attempt by the MOF to distance itself from the securities industry and the unpopularity in which it now found itself provoked fury and resentment in the industry and created a wide, perhaps permanent breach in the tradition of close cooperation between regulators and the regulated. The Big Four felt betrayed and let down by the ministry, which had previously protected them unquestioningly.

The split was public and nasty. At a meeting of Nomura shareholders on June 27, ex-President Tabuchi Yoshihisa publicly questioned the MOF's claim that it was blameless by suggesting that the ministry had known and approved of the compensation payments all along.[35] This, in turn, provoked a furious response by Finance Minister Hashimoto, who said of this suggestion, "The content was inappropriate and extremely regrettable. . . . If they [the Big Four] were to blame others for their own responsibility, it would be a moral issue. When I think about how they are handling such a serious social issue, I personally feel sorry.[36]

Indeed, Hashimoto was not content to let the brokers off with just verbal criticism, even with such unrestrained and abusive criticism as "deeply regrettable."[37] He hinted at economic retaliation in the form of withholding public money from the industry. "Whether investing in securities is appropriate for public funds may need to be reviewed," he threatened.[38] The MOF's denial of responsibility was never taken seriously within the industry, but may have been believed by the general public. The allegation by a senior ministry official that the Finance Ministry had known of compensation payments all along was therefore a severe blow to the MOF's reputation.[39] Hashimoto's initial denial of wrongdoing was exposed, and he resigned a few months later.[40]

[33] Quoted in Wagstyl, "Japan's Scandal-Hit Traders."

[34] Utsumi Makoto, quoted in Sanger, "Tokyo Officials Take Pay Cut over Scandal."

[35] "Scandal—Ministry Tie Alleged," *Japan Times*, 29 June 1991, 1.

[36] Sanger, "Tokyo Officials Take Pay Cut over Scandal."

[37] In Japanese public life this is just about as offensive as it gets.

[38] Sanger, "Tokyo Officials Take Pay Cut over Scandal."

[39] "Finance Ministry Turned Blind Eye to Payouts by Brokers, Official Says," *Japan Times*, 26 June 1991, 1.

[40] James Sterngold, "Japanese Finance Chief Announces Resignation," *New York Times*, 4 October 1991, 2. Many U.S. officials supported Hashimoto. Treasury Secretary Brady praised him warmly and publicly for his help in raising Japanese funds during the Gulf War.

Nomura and the *Inagawa-kai*, 1991

The compensation scandal was at its height in the summer of 1991 when a new scandal broke. In July 1991, Nomura Securities admitted to having made loans to Susumu Ishii, head of the *Inagawa-kai*, one of Japan's criminal *yakuza* gangs, for the purpose of ramping up the stock price of Tokyu Corporation.[41] In 1986, Nomura had opened an account for Ishii. The fact that Nomura knew he was a gang leader meant that this was illegal. Between 1986 and 1989, affiliates of Nomura and Nikko securities had helped Ishhii buy up to 23 million shares in the Tokyu Railways Corp., offering loans to the gangster of up to ¥35 billion. In 1989, Nomura helped manipulate the Tokyu share price by concentrated trading in the stock, in possible violation of the SEL.[42] The scandal prompted the resignation of two Nomura executives and a one-year 20 percent pay cut for all executives as penance for having violated Article 54 of the SEL, which prohibits excessive recommendation of a stock.[43] However, the MOF investigation in December 1991 found no evidence that Nomura had violated Article 125, which prohibits stock manipulation. Calls by the opposition to ban the *yakuza* from stock trading were considered briefly by the MOF but rejected. "Even gangsters have a right to engage in economic activities," claimed a senior MOF official.[44]

Tobashi, 1991

The morally dubious trading practice of *tobashi* claimed the head of another Big Four securities company president in 1991.[45] *Tobashi* is the practice whereby a securities company shuffles a client's stock from one account to another in order to manipulate the booked purchase price or market value of the stock. The usual purpose is for the broker to help a client "window dress" income and asset statements. *Tobashi* can achieve this aim by artificially (but only temporarily) inflating or deflating the book value of the stock. Typically, the securities company enters a verbal agreement to buy the stock from the client at an artificial price and sell it back at another, equally artificial price some time later—usually after the accounting period is over. Often the securities companies shift stock between client accounts, if the clients have different accounting periods or different accounting needs. Occasionally the securities companies do not tell both parties. Worse, some unscrupulous companies permanently shift the most poorly performing stock from the accounts of favored clients to the accounts of less-favored accounts.[46]

In March 1991, Daiwa admitted to having been involved in seven cases of

[41] "Nomura Is Linked to Mob Accounts," *Japan Times*, 4 July 1991, 1.

[42] The stock price of Tokyu surged from ¥1,700 to ¥3,600 in mid-1989.

[43] "Brokerages Face Reprisal for Mob Dealings."

[44] "Japan Halts Plan to Ban Stock Deals with Mob," *International Herald Tribune*, 18 July 1991.

[45] Quentin Hardy, "Daiwa Securities President Quits in Wake of Stock Trading Scandal," *Wall Street Journal*, 12 March 1991, A8.

[46] Interviews, Tokyo, February 1994.

tobashi, the largest involving the giant Tokyu Department Store. In August 1990, Daiwa had invested ¥90 billion in stock belonging to Tokyu that was only worth ¥30 billion. The public's hostile reaction was intense when the news broke, even though the practice of *tobashi* itself was not illegal. Daiwa's president, Masahiro Dozen, and two other senior executives resigned to take responsibility for the affair.

Foreign Reaction to the Scandals

Japan's reputation as a financial center plummeted as a result of the simultaneous revelation of at least three separate scandals in 1991. The loss-compensation scandal provoked the most angry reaction from abroad. In retaliation for the scandal, many foreign institutions shunned the guilty Japanese firms. The World Bank announced that it was excluding Nomura and Nikko from participation in its bond issues. Nomura had acted as a co-lead manager for every previous global bond issue of the bank. The World Bank had also suspended dealings with Salomon Brothers after the U.S. bond-auction scandal, although, unlike Salomon, the Japanese brokers were allowed to engage in secondary market dealings with the World Bank. The immediate effect was exclusion from $1.5 billion of underwriting, but the longer term effect would be a marked loss of prestige.[47]

In the United States, subsidiaries of the Big Four Japanese firms were put under intense hostile scrutiny.[48] Richard Breedon, chairman of the American SEC, rebuked the Japanese parent companies publicly. Breedon announced that, since only major clients had been compensated, it was likely that U.S. investors in Japan had been discriminated against. He promised that the SEC would pay closer attention to the business practices of all Japanese brokers' subsidiaries in the United States.[49] He also argued that the extravagantly large commissions were a cause of the compensation scandal, since clients had an interest in pressing brokers to pay back part of the excessive commissions they were charged. The SEC visited the U.S. subsidiaries of the Big Four Japanese brokers to question them about the degree of influence of their parent companies, and the possibility that the U.S. subsidiaries had been involved in the paybacks. Meanwhile the New York Stock Exchange launched its own investigation into the Big Four, all of whom were NYSE members.[50] The U.S. subsidiaries denied involvement in

[47] Simon London and Richard Waters, "World Bank Bans Nomura and Nikko," *Financial Times*, 13 September 1991, 19.

[48] All four had expanded the size of their American operations significantly in the late 1980s. Nomura's U.S. subsidiary expanded from 75 to 625 employees between 1985 and 1989. Daiwa U.S. grew from 80 to 450 people in 1990. Nikko U.S. had 250 employees in 1991. Stefan Fatsis, "Brokers Hampered in US," *Japan Times*, 27 June 1991, 7.

[49] Quoted in "Size of Fees Called Cause of Troubles," *Japan Times*, 2 August 1991, 1.

[50] "Wall Street to Investigate Big Four Subsidiaries," *Japan Times*, 29 June 1991, 1.

the affair and subsequent investigations found no evidence that they had contravened U.S. law.[51]

Several U.S. investors retaliated against Nomura all the same. They included the Illinois Municipal Retirement Fund and the giant California Public Employees Retirement System. Both employed Nomura Capital to manage part of their funds, and both instructed it not to put business through Nomura's brokerage arm.[52] Their reaction against Nomura was prompted as much by the gangster connection as by the loss-compensation issue. According to an executive at one foreign securities firm: "We've known for a long time that Japanese brokers offered compensation. But the added element of the *yakuza* makes it much more explosive. It's as if Goldman Sachs was caught lending to Al Capone."[53] Another British investment banker added, "The sheer mobility of money around the world is going to force Japanese firms to clean up their act. A lot of people will simply stop dealing with them if they feel the rules are rigged against them."[54]

Most foreigners did not appear to believe that the MOF was blameless either. Charles Stevens of Coudert Brothers (a Tokyo law firm) said that "the MOF's long-standing lack of will to enforce current Japanese securities laws" was the problem. He dismissed the argument of Japanese officials that compensation was banned only informally and argued that there were other Japanese laws that could have been used to prosecute cases, including Article 58.[55]

Reaction in Britain was more muted, but British officials questioned Japanese subsidiaries about possible wrongdoing. The British SIB and the relevant self-regulatory agency, the Securities and Futures Authority (the SFA), announced that they would "review the position" of Nomura and Nikko in London to ensure that the Tokyo scandal did not have repercussions in Europe.[56] Both the United States and Britain used a meeting of the International Organization of Securities Commissions (IOSCO), held in London in July 1991, to question the MOF delegation led by Securities Bureau Director-General Matsuno.

In the foreign finance community in Tokyo, the exposure of corrupt practices and the purge of powerful personnel was generally believed to remove obstacles to foreign participation. According to Paul Summerville, senior economist at Jardine Flemmings, "There's no moral high ground left for Japanese brokers. . . . [I]t makes foreign brokers look a lot more attractive."[57] There was a widespread view that the scandal had also boosted the

---

[51] "Broker's U.S. Units Deny Giving Payback," *Japan Times*, 4 July 1991, 14.

[52] London and Waters, "World Bank Bans Nomura and Nikko."

[53] Quoted in Tom Redburn, "Tokyo Brokers Face Global Backlash," *International Herald Tribune*, 27 June 1991, 18.

[54] Quoted in Redburn, "Tokyo Brokers Face Global Backlash."

[55] "Japanese Scandal Widens."

[56] "Tokyo Toughens Its Stance on Stock Dealings," *International Herald Tribune*, 27 June 1991, A1.

[57] Quoted in "Foreign Security Houses in Tokyo Hope to Benefit from Competitors' Scandals," *Japan Times*, 2 August 1991, 14.

standing of the pro-liberalization faction within the MOF at the expense of those favoring the interests of the securities industry.

II. Reform in the Aftermath of the Scandals

The scandals sparked a period of intense soul-searching in the securities industry, which collectively concluded that it needed to radically improve its image for reasons of sheer economic self-interest. One result was a strengthening of the powers of the Japan Securities Dealers Association (JSDA). All Japanese securities firms and foreign firms holding securities branch licenses in Japan are members of the JSDA, which listed 265 members in 1993, of which 49 were foreign.

In July 1992, the association changed its legal status from that of a nonprofit foundation under the Civil Code to an officially approved self-regulatory organization under the SEL. Its new responsibilities included registering sales representatives of securities companies and accepting financial institutions other than securities companies as members. Among its actions were the creation of a securities business guideline, to "promote clear understanding of the fundamental rules for salesmen"; the creation of a Sales Rules Inquiry System, which gave advice to members about the specific application of the new laws (or association regulations); and the encouragement of individual investors to join the market via stock investment funds.[58]

The political result of the scandals was a major revision of the Securities and Exchange Law. The Diet, in a special session in October 1991, passed a bill calling for an emergency revision of the law. There were two major areas of revision. The first focused on strengthening Article 125, which had prohibited stock-price manipulation but had clearly been ineffective in the *Inagawa-kai* case. One amendment mandated fire walls between a bank and its securities subsidiary and made limitations on activities by securities subsidiaries clearer. Another amendment increased penalties for brokers who had compensated clients for losses. The penalties now included prison terms for both brokers who gave compensation and for clients who asked for it.[59]

Dismantling the MOF, Round One: The SESC, 1992

The second major revision was the establishment of a new monitoring agency, the Securities Exchange Surveillance Commission (SESC). Recall that SCAP had established an independent financial supervisory agency in

[58] Interviews, Japan Securities Dealers Association, Tokyo, February 1994.

[59] "Japan's Ruling Party Drafts Tougher Laws for Broker," *New York Times,* 12 September 1991, D10; "Ministry Prepares for Revision of Law," *Japan Times,* 5 October 1991, 1.

1947 and that the agency had promptly been swallowed up by the MOF as that ministry reestablished its former powers over the financial system. From the 1950s on, the task of monitoring compliance with market regulations and protecting the financial industry's consumers fell to the same agency that was responsible for promoting the interests of the industry's producers. The inherent conflict of interest problems are clear. Yet it was not until the early 1990s that the situation came under real scrutiny and the task of enforcing the law was separated from the task of promoting the industry. This section discusses the events that led to this dramatic change in regulatory policy.

The SESC was inaugurated on July 20, 1992. It grew out of the backlash of the stock scandals of 1991. In particular, it was born of the widespread belief that the scandals were the result of the excessively close relationship between the securities industry and the MOF, especially the Securities Bureau. Many believed that the conflict of interest inherent in the MOF's role as both protector of the industry and its sole overseer was too strong to be overcome. Originally, therefore, Prime Minister Kaifu Toshiki proposed the establishment of a wholly independent watchdog. In the short term, the MOF was successful in blocking this proposal. The agency that emerged from the debates was considerably weaker than envisioned by Kaifu and others.

The first part of the story, then, appears to contradict my argument that international competitive pressures forced Japan to reform. The birth of the SESC is a story in which, for the most part, domestic political pressures prompted the reform and domestic political factors—in this case the political power of the bureaucracy—strongly influenced the outcome. At the same time, however, the influence of the American model of regulation was vitally important in shaping the final structure of the new agency. Moreover, the birth of the agency is only one part of the story. I argue that, once established, the SESC grew, and continues to grow, under the influence of international competitive pressures. By the late 1990s, it had developed as a stronger, more proactive agency, more concerned with policing markets fairly and evenhandedly than giving favors to domestic constituents. The founding of the FSA was, in a sense, the next logical step along the path begun with the SESC.

Fighting for an Independent Agency

The scandals of 1991 created an uproar in Japan so great that the ruling party could not ignore it. In July 1991, LDP Secretary-General Obuchi Keizo recommended to his party that an independent body be created to monitor the securities industry as part of an effort to prevent a recurrence of the compensation scandal.

Referring to the scandals, Nishioka Takeo, chairman of the LDP's Executive Council, said that "self-responsibility" must be respected and that

Japanese business should be conducted in accordance with "common rules" in the international community, given Japan's status as the world's second-largest economic power. He added, "Establishing conditions for fair competition in a free-market economy is the responsibility of politicians."[60]

In July 1991, Prime Minister Kaifu asked a government advisory panel to explore the possibility of establishing a watchdog agency similar to the SEC. This became known as the Ad Hoc Commission on Administrative Reform (Reform Commission). Its nine members were drawn from the ranks of business, labor, and academia.[61] Eiji Suzuki was appointed chairman. He was a former chairman of the Japan Federation of Employers' Associations *(Keidanren)*, and he was known to favor the establishment of a body that would resemble the SEC. Other members of the commission were Magara Eikichi and Ashida Jimosuke, both union leaders, who were also enthusiastic proponents of radical change in the policing of markets. Both were known to favor an independent, SEC-type regulatory agency.

Indeed, most of the debate over the new agency centered on how similar the new Japanese watchdog should be to America's SEC. Outside the securities industry and the MOF, most people were strongly in favor of an American-style agency.[62] This idea was supported by the heads of all the major business organizations. In addition to Suzuki of the *Keidanren*, these were Hayami Masaru, chairman of the Japan Association of Corporate Executives and Nagano Takeshi of *Nikkeiren*, the Japan Federation of Employers Associations.[63] Other supporters included *Rengo* (Japanese Trade Union Confederation) and the Democratic Socialist Party.[64] Bank of Japan advisor Suzuki Yukio wrote "Japan does not act promptly enough to prevent shady stock market transactions. . . . What Japan needs is a strict regulatory body like the U.S. Securities and Exchange Commission."[65]

The MOF's refusal to act when it had apparently known of abuses now fueled demands for an independent agency.[66] Many believed that the MOF had consistently erred on the side of supporting the securities firms at the expense of protecting the investing public. Indeed, it was not until the tax

[60] Quoted in Masaki Itagaki and Hisane Masaki, "Diet May Force Ministry to Act," *Japan Times,* 29 July 1991, 2.

[61] See Frank Schwartz, *Advice and Consent: The Politics of Consultation in Japan* (Cambridge: Cambridge University Press, 1997), for discussion of the dynamics of *shingikai* (consultative councils).

[62] The debate is discussed in Okumura and Kawakita, *Nihon no Kabushiki Shijo* [Japanese Stock Market]. See especially chap. 9, sec. 6, "Nihonban SEC ga Hitsuyo ka" [Is a Japanese SEC necessary?], 201–209.

[63] Clay Chandler, "Japan Finance Ministry's Harsher Tone Suggests New Suspicions of Wrongdoing," *Wall Street Journal,* 3 September 1991, A14. See also *Japan Times,* 26 July 1991, 1.

[64] "Calls Are Mounting for Broker Watchdog," *Japan Times,* 5 July 1991.

[65] Suzuki Yukio, "A Time For Soul-Searching," *Japan Times,* 9 July 1991. See also Okumura, *Shoken Sukandaru* [Stock scandal], who also calls for an American-style SEC, 51–53.

[66] Steven R. Wiesman, "Oversight Plan Loses in Japan," *New York Times,* 14 September 1991, D1.

agency had discovered widespread illegal practices that the ministry had acted at all. According to the *Nihon Keizai Shimbun:*

> The scandals were generated by a combination of factors—the absence of competition (which leads to excessive profits), legal laxity against fraudulent trading, ambiguous rules and a poor surveillance system. Common to these factors is an administrative policy that gives top priority to protecting and fostering the industry in a close symbiotic relationship between bureaucrats and business. Given such a state of affairs, *the only recommendation should be for a complete separation of a watchdog body from bureaucratic control* . . . [which] should be given as wide-ranging authority as possible.[67]

At the bottom of this symbiotic relationship was, of course, the *amakudari* system. MOF officials, like most Japanese bureaucrats, were relatively poorly paid, and thus the prospect of retirement to a wealthy securities firm was an attractive one. The monitors thus had strong personal incentives not to rock the boat by investigating those same firms.

It was not just the public who wanted reform. Foreign investors, especially the Americans, were loud in their demands for reform. "There were lots of complaints [about the scandals] from American companies," claimed one observer.[68] The point was not lost on the MOF, which recognized that, in the words of one official, "Fairer markets would help to attract not just small investors, but also foreign investors."[69]

Even without taking too critical or cynical a view of the closeness of the relationship between the ministry and the securities companies, it was clear that the markets suffered from a dearth of committed surveillance. The entire securities industry was monitored for fairness by only thirty or so staff from the Securities Bureau.[70] The TSE had about thirty more staff in its surveillance division, while the other self-regulatory organization, the JSDA, was not responsible for any monitoring function.[71] This would have made it very difficult for the authorities adequately to police the markets even if they were genuinely committed to doing so—a commitment that in any case many people doubted.

Missing from the debate about the new agency were the voices of the powerful securities companies, especially the Big Four. Their reluctance to take too prominent a position was understandable given their extreme unpopularity. As new revelations about their nefarious activities emerged, seemingly daily, they could do little more than hunker down and wait for

---

[67] "Securities Watchdog Should Not Be Muzzled," *Nikkei Weekly*, 14 September 1991, 6. Emphasis added.

[68] Interview with U.K. fund manager, Tokyo, February 1994.

[69] Interview, MOF official, May 1995.

[70] Interview, MOF official, February 1994.

[71] Interview, TSE official, Inspection Division, Tokyo, February 1994.

the storm of protest to subside. A senior official at one Big Four company explained this attitude, "Of course the securities companies hate new regulations. We didn't like the SESC because it could send people to jail, whereas the TSE and JSDA can only levy fines. But at the time we had no influence because of the scandals."[72]

Reformers versus the MOF

Unfortunately for the reformers, the staff of the commission was drawn from within the MOF: the director of staff, Masujima Toshiyuki, was a senior official in the ministry's Management and Coordination Agency. What resulted was a battle between the reformers on the commission and the ministry staff, who were determined not to give away any more power than they had to. They were implacably opposed to the creation of a new, independent regulatory agency.[73] Secret meetings with the finance minister, impossible deadlines, and bureaucratic pressures were some of the tools used by the MOF to water down the more far-reaching proposals.[74] They were helped by the solid support of Finance Minister Hashimoto, who was extremely sympathetic to the ministry. He is quoted as saying, "The securities industry is not so troubled as to need a watchdog like the SEC."[75] On September 3, 1991, when it appeared that the commission would recommend either an independent body or, at minimum, one with considerable discretionary powers, he declared "the ministry [of Finance] is prepared to accept [the commission's] recommendations, even if doing so entails much pain to us."[76] Hashimoto was to resign shortly afterward, but he clearly used his remaining influence in support of the ministry.

The decisive event in the MOF's rearguard action came in September 1991. Commission Chairman Suzuki stated at a news conference that he intended to make the new watchdog agency independent of the MOF. Shortly afterwards, Finance Minister Hashimoto Ryutaro met first with Suzuki and then, in secret, with Staff Director Masujima. After that meeting, Masujima began aggressively to argue against the idea of an independent body and is quoted as saying that "any new organization has to be in harmony with the existing structure."[77] His arguments began to sway the members of the

[72] Interview with Japanese securities company director, Tokyo, February 1994. In fact, the SESC does not itself have the power to send anyone to prison, but the statement is a telling illustration of the change in relationship between regulatory and regulated in Tokyo.

[73] See, for example, "Nihonban SEC Mikomaru" [A Japanese-version SEC looks in trouble], *Yomiuri Shimbun*, 6 July 1991, 9.

[74] James Sterngold, "Japanese Learn Lesson in Bureaucratic Rule," *New York Times*, 4 November 1991, D3.

[75] "Calls Are Mounting," *Japan Times*, 5 July 1991, 12.

[76] Hashimoto, quoted in "Rearguard Action," *The Economist*, 7 September 1991, 102.

[77] Quoted in Sterngold, "Japanese Learn Lesson," D3.

commission, who in any case had only until September 13, 1991, to make a final report to Prime Minister Kaifu.

By early September, all commission members except the two union leaders had agreed to the compromise that the agency would operate within the MOF. To achieve compromise, Magara and Ashida agreed to allow the agency to operate within the ministry, but only if it had powers to order a stop to violations of securities laws and to punish offenders unilaterally. This compromise was accepted, and the two provisions appeared on the draft given to commission members for review on September 11. When the final draft appeared before the council for the vote, however, the two provisions were gone, removed by the MOF staff. There was no time to make further amendments, and the draft presented to the prime minister was therefore considerably weakened even from the watered-down compromise agreed to by the commission. Masujima admitted that his staff had removed the provisions, claiming that "there was such limited time that, in the end, the most persuasive line had to be included in the report."[78]

In summary, as an embittered Magara stated, "There is no question the Ministry used its power, officially and unofficially, to make sure this new body was under its influence."[79]

The point was not lost on the Japanese press and public. "It is sad to admit that Japan is a country run by bureaucrats, of bureaucrats, and for bureaucrats," stated the *Yomiuri Shimbun*.[80] The *Nihon Keizai Shimbun* argued that "All through this mess the Finance Ministry has done nothing more than seek to defend itself. There are no signs that ministry officials feel responsibility for the scandals which were invited in part by their close relations with securities firms."[81] According to Kyoto University Economics Professor Sawa Takemitsu, "The Ministry of Finance ended up with what they wanted. In fact, the whole interdependence of the Government Bureaucracy and the securities industry will end up even stronger than it was before."[82]

The commission thus reported back, in September 1991, with "A Report on Basic Measures to Rectify Unfair Securities and Financial Dealings."[83] It addressed four separate matters. First, it reviewed current administrative practices and explored measures to ensure greater transparency. Second, it looked to strengthen the functions of the industry's self-regulatory bodies. Third, it looked at the way surveillance and inspection should be carried out. It recommended the creation of an independent watchdog within the MOF, and the concomitant reorganization of the various inspection agen-

---

[78] Masujima, quoted in ibid.

[79] Ibid.

[80] Ibid.

[81] Ibid.

[82] Sawa, quoted in Wiesman, "Oversight Plan," D1.

[83] Ministry of Finance, "Basic Measures to Rectify Unfair Securities and Financial Dealings" (Tokyo: Ministry of Finance, 1991).

cies already existing in the ministry.[84] Finally, it established the principle of self-responsibility for investors.[85]

Based on these recommendations, the MOF set up a special panel to study the securities and financial monitoring system, "canvassing views from many sectors and considering the matter in the widest perspective."[86] This included visits by MOF officials to the SEC in Washington in order to better understand how the Americans dealt with financial irregularities.[87] The result was a bill to partially amend the SEL, drafted in February 1992. The Law Amending the Securities and Exchange Law to Ensure the Fairness of Securities Trading, which established the SESC, was approved by the Diet in May and implemented on July 20, 1992. The purpose of the new agency was "to insure the fairness of securities trading and to retain investor confidence in the market."[88] Its activities were also to include "enhancing the credibility of the Japanese securities market among foreign investors and participants."[89]

The Securities and Exchange Surveillance Commission

The SESC is composed of a chairman and two commissioners, who are appointed to three-year terms by the minister of finance, subject to approval by the Diet.[90] Except under specific exceptional circumstances, their status is guaranteed and they cannot be discharged. Under the chairman and commissioners is the Executive Bureau, comprising two divisions, Coordination and Inspection; and Investigation. The agency's responsibilities include the examination of all market transactions by securities companies and others, and the supervision of self-regulatory organizations such as the various stock exchanges and the JSDA. The coordination section is also responsible for more general affairs, including the formulation of policy recommendations. While the SESC was authorized to review the activities of the SROs in order to check that they were providing services according to their rules, it was recognized that the SESC relied on the assistance of the SROs to oversee the markets adequately. According to the official publication, "In effect, the SESC and SROs share responsibilities, like the two wheels of a cart: both must work in tandem to be effective."[91]

The formal powers of the SESC are less than those of the SEC. It can investigate suspicious trading, but can only make recommendations to the

---

[84] "Ministry Plans Its Own In-House 'SEC,'" *Daily Yomiuri*, 11 August 1991, 8.

[85] Note here especially the parallels to the Pecora hearings and the American Securities laws of the 1930s, which also stressed transparency and self-responsibility as the best mechanisms for investor protection.

[86] Nakai Sei, "The Current State of Affairs of the SESC," *Kinyu Journal* (November 1993): 43–48.

[87] "Officials to Visit SEC," *Daily Yomiuri*, 11 August 1991, 8.

[88] Japan Securities Research Institute, *Securities Markets in Japan, 1994*, 179.

[89] Ibid.

[90] Securities and Exchange Surveillance Commission (SESC), *Outline of Activities 1992* (Tokyo: Securities Exchange Surveillance Commission).

[91] Ibid., 4.

MOF or the Public Prosecutor's Office for punitive action. Unlike the SEC, the SESC has no power to penalize market participants for abuses of laws, nor does it have subpoena powers when it is conducting investigations or enforcement actions. The Inspection Division is authorized to probe into suspicious cases, but it does not have the right to bring prosecutions. Instead, it may make accusations of suspected crimes to the Public Prosecutor's Office, which retains the right to bring cases to court. It may obtain a court order to search target premises and seize evidence. The SESC may recommend that the minister for finance take disciplinary action against a company it suspects of wrongdoing, and the minister is obliged to respect this recommendation and report back to the SESC on any disciplinary actions taken. It can also make policy recommendations to the finance minister.

However, others, included the commission itself, argue against the depiction of the SESC as weak. According to Ishizaka Masami:

> Some critics contend, erroneously, that the SESC of Japan has little power, but it, in effect, has as much criminal investigative powers as the S.E.C. has. For example, Japan's Commission, if armed with a court warrant, can enter the premise of a suspect and conduct compulsory investigation. In this sense, I have the feeling that Japan's Commission, legally speaking, has stronger power than its U.S. counterpart. The S.E.C. has no power to conduct compulsory investigations, such as the power to seize evidence. It can only subpoena witnesses or order them to submit evidence.[92]

The first chairman, Mizuhara Toshihiro, came from a career in the Public Prosecutor's Office. He had been deputy director-general of the Criminal Affairs Bureau of the Ministry of Justice in 1979. It was a significant and deliberate decision to appoint someone outside the MOF as the first chairman.[93] Of the two commissioners, one, Narita Masamichi, came from a career at NHK (Nippon Hoso Kyokei), the Japanese public television company (where he had been chief commentator), while Mihara Hidetaka was another bureaucrat, and former secretary-general of the Board of Audit. As of 1992 there was a staff of 202: 84 in Tokyo and 118 in regional offices, although about half of the regional staff members were assigned to monitoring the TSE.

Critics of the SESC have noted that its staffing numbers compare poorly to the 2,600–odd staff of its American counterpart, the SEC. This criticism is, however, rebutted by the SESC. Secretary-General of the Executive Bureau Ishizaka wrote:

> Some complain that with a ratio of 200 to 2,600, Japan's commission cannot hold a candle to the S.E.C. However, the comparison these critics make is

---

[92] Ishikawa Masami, "The Course of Action Planned by the Securities and Exchange Surveillance Commission,"CaMRI Speech 2 (Tokyo: Capital Markets Research Institute, 30 October 1992), 20.

[93] "Nihonban SEC Mikomaru" [Japanese-version SEC looks in trouble].

based on a wrong number. As the number of staffs assigned to the Enforcement Division of the S.E.C. is 800, not 2,600, the number of staffs of Japan's commission should be compared with 800. . . . However the 800 enforcement officers of the S.E.C. have to keep watch over 12,000 registered securities companies. By contrast, Japan's commission has only 200-odd licensed securities companies to ride herd on. When the two are compared in this light, our Commission is not so underhanded as these critics would have us believe.[94]

Independence from the MOF

Although the first three SESC commissioners came from outside the MOF, nearly all the other staff members were MOF insiders, assigned on a rotation basis. At first, they were drawn from the staff of the various inspection bureaus within the ministry. There were also a few staff members from the police or the Public Prosecutor's office, but, in common with their counterparts in the SIB, these individuals usually lacked training in securities fraud. Perhaps the most valuable outsiders were a contingent of fifteen from the much-feared Tax Agency, who had considerable experience launching highly successful investigative raids.[95]

In response to the criticism that drawing staff primarily from the MOF completely undermined the purpose of having a separate supervisory agency, the ministry defended the decision with an array of explanations that, frankly, varied in plausibility. First, MOF argued that there had been no time to recruit and train inspectors from anywhere else. One staffer explained that "The system was in crisis, so it was important to get it [the SESC] going as quickly as possible."[96] Finding talented staff would be more of a problem in Japan than in other countries because of the system of lifetime employment and the social stigma attached to job-hopping: few people would want to leave a post in a bank, securities company, or most especially a government ministry in order to work for the new organization if it were independent.[97] This made a reasonably plausible argument for the staff coming from within initially, but not, perhaps, for why the practice continues today.

Second, some claimed that the real problem had never been the close relationship between the ministry as such and the industry, but rather the problems had come from the relationship between the bureaus and their constituent industry sectors. The ministry claimed that, since the SESC drew staff from all bureaus, these old loyalties would be diluted, and there would be little opportunity for unhealthy new ties to form between the watchdogs and the regulated. In the words of one MOF official:

[94] Ishikawa, "Course of Action."

[95] Juzo Itami's 1987 movie *A Taxing Woman* contains a most enjoyable illustration of the awesome powers of this agency, and of the tactical value of the investigative raid.

[96] Interview, MOF official, February 1994.

[97] See also "Ministry Plans Its Own In-House 'SEC.'"

[The SESC's] neutrality is ensured by the fact that it is an amalgamation of the three monitoring departments in the three relevant bureaus of the MOF. Previously, each bureau owed loyalty primarily to its constituents—bank bureau to the banks, and so on. By removing staff from their bureaus, they will become more neutral and able to make policy for the good of the whole of Japan.[98]

A third, and perhaps the most convincing, argument was that the MOF genuinely believed that fragmenting the regulatory structure did not necessarily make for stronger or better supervision. This was especially true at a time when Article 65 and the other traditional barriers in the industry were being dismantled in favor of a unified system of finance. A senior official at the SESC argued that "With the erosion of Article 65, the difference between banking and securities business is declining. So there is a need for a single, central authority [the MOF]. The U.S. system of fragmented regulatory authority is crazy. Therefore the MOF wanted to keep it [the watchdog agency] under one roof."[99]

At the time of inauguration, as we have seen, many critics were deeply unhappy that the MOF had apparently managed to retain control over the SESC. Interestingly, however, the staff of the SESC went to considerable pains to stress its independence. The fact that all three commissioners had been chosen for their lack of ties to either the ministry or the securities industry was cited. And the first chairman, Mizuhara, was blunt about where he intended to put his loyalties." We will act independently of the MOF," he stated at a news conference to mark the inauguration.[100] Secretary-General Ishikaza stated in 1992, "We are not at all controlled by the finance ministry. . . . [E]ach institution has its own responsibilities."[101] In interviews, staffers stressed their independence, often citing the tax agency staffers as evidence of their commitment to objective and politically neutral law enforcement.

The performance of the SESC has been the subject of some debate. It was initially criticized for being too weak to be regarded as an effective watchdog. These claims were hotly disputed by the agency itself, which pointed to a growing series of successes in identifying and rooting out undesirable market practices. The commission inspected 170 cases of irregular share-price movements in 1992–93 and 217 in 1993–94.[102] It meted out punishments ranging from outright revocation of an individual's sales-representative registration (in effect barring him or her from the industry) to enforced suspension of business for firms. In four cases in its first two years of operation, the

---

[98] Confidential interview with MOF official, Tokyo, June 1995.

[99] Interview with SESC official, Tokyo, June 1995.

[100] "Securities Watchdog Panel Inaugurated," *Journal of Japanese Trade and Industry* 1 (October 1991): 5.

[101] Quoted in Robert Thomson, "Japanese Watchdog Aims to Silence Wagging Tongues," *Financial Times*, 30 March 1993, 31.

[102] Interview with SESC official, Tokyo, 6 June 1995.

SESC brought cases to the Public Prosecutor's Office resulting in criminal charges. These were Nihon Unisys (for market manipulation), Ipec (false disclosure), Nippon Shoji (insider trading) and Shimizu Bank (insider trading). The Nihon Unisys case is discussed briefly here.

The SESC took its first real investigative action in December 1991, launching an investigation into the share manipulations of Nihon Unisys, an affiliate of the American Unisys Corporation.[103] A series of well-publicized raids, including on the offices of suspected accomplices in the speculation scheme, netted sufficient evidence for the SESC to bring accusations against two individuals to the Tokyo Public Prosecutor's Office in May 1993, and both were formally prosecuted in August 1993. The ringleader, Makoto Araya, was a stock speculator who had led a group of speculators in buying and selling Unisys stock simultaneously to manipulate its price. The other indictee was his financial backer, an official at an affiliate of Sumitomo Realty and Development Co., one of the largest and most prestigious of Japan's real estate companies in Japan. The success of the raids in gathering evidence has been cited as proof of the SESC's effectiveness. "In reality, we have . . . much the same power as the American SEC," remarked Director Nakai Sei in relation to the Unisys case.[104]

In addition to the four cases in which criminal prosecutions were brought, the SESC has had other successes in curbing manipulative practices. For example, Cosmo Securities, a second-tier securities company, was found guilty of *tobashi* (the practice of shuffling stocks around client accounts to avoid booking losses). Cosmo's punishment was to suspend business for a week and stop dealing in convertible bonds on its own account for four weeks.

Critics of the SESC point out that the number of successful criminal prosecutions remains low. Nonetheless, the agency appears to be making its mark, as evidenced by the comments of market participants, many of whom acknowledge that the mere presence of the SESC has had the effect of reducing dubious market practices. A managing director of a Japanese investment trust commented, "The Japanese stock market has been unclear to foreign investors because of speculative price movements. The Commission's activities will keep the market clean."[105] The sentiment was echoed, albeit more cautiously, by the president of Fidelity Investments Japan, who remarked of the successful raids during the Nihon Unisys investigation, "It's a big step forward . . . but the Commission's still got a long way to go."[106]

In summary the activities of the SESC point clearly to the fact that the

---

[103] James Sterngold, "Japanese Regulators Seize Files in Stock Inquiry," *New York Times*, 8 December 1991, D1.

[104] Jonathan Friedland, "Watchdog Cuts Its Teeth," *Far Eastern Economic Review* 156, no. 26 (1993): 60.

[105] Endoh Takao (Asahi Investment Trust Management), quoted in Makino Yo and Ikeyo Akira, "Watchdog Raid Targets Illicit Speculation," *Nikkei Weekly*, 14 December 1992, 1.

[106] Akamatsu Yasukazu, quoted in ibid.

Japanese have, like the British, moved decisively if incompletely toward a much more American philosophy about what constitutes appropriate regulation of securities markets.

Dismantling the MOF, Round Two: The Financial Supervisory Agency

The MOF did not willingly relinquish its right to micromanage the Japanese financial system. Many, although by no means all, ministry officials continued their efforts to use informal guidance to influence the markets. But three events in the mid-1990s made it clear that while the MOF's desire to override market forces was as strong as ever, their ability to do so was becoming ever more limited. These episodes were the attempt to bolster Tokyo share prices at artificially high levels, the use of public money to support seven bankrupt housing-loan companies (*jusen*), and the alleged attempt to prevent Moody's Corporation from issuing disparaging reports on important Japanese banks. The MOF's failures in all three cases were to fatally damage its prestige.

The Price-Keeping Operation

The spectacular rise of the Tokyo stock market in the 1980s was, as discussed earlier, self-reinforcing. The crash of 1990 put the money machine into reverse and started a vicious downward cycle in share and land prices. As share prices fell, they hurt banks that had been counting as assets shares at market value. Banks cut back on loans, so there was less money to buy shares and land, causing prices to fall further.

The MOF therefore had good reason to believe that the stock market crash threatened the stability of the entire financial system. Indeed, if the banks were forced by falling share prices into contracting their loan operations, then investment in the real economy would also be threatened. When the Nikkei 225 index hit a low of ¥14,309 in August 1992, the MOF apparently decided to step in with an unofficial support operation—the Price-Keeping Operation (PKO).[107] Early tools of the PKO included blocking new share issues, which would have increased the overall supply of shares and therefore depressed prices, and guidance to securities companies to buy the market or attempt to talk it up. In addition, the MOF was reported to have compelled the use of public funds, including those held by the Postal Savings Bank and by the public pension funds to buy shares. Later, as it became harder to continue to use these sources, the ministry relied on less direct means, such as encouraging private funds to buy, or at least hold on to, shares. Ministry officials have always denied publicly that such a support operation existed, but many admit to it privately. There has certainly never been any doubt in the market that the operation goes on.[108] There has, however, been considerable doubt as to its effectiveness. Although share prices

[107] A play on the official PKO, the Peace-Keeping Operation Bill that was being discussed in the Diet at that time, which would allow Japan to send troops abroad on United Nations–sponsored peace-keeping missions.

[108] Interviews, Tokyo, June 1994. There are doubts about the effectiveness of this strategy even among MOF staffers. For example, it was believed in some quarters that the very exis-

picked up somewhat from 1994, the Nikkei 225 remained depressed for the rest of the decade, never rising above ¥23,000 and contributing to the longest and deepest recession of Japanese postwar history.

Jusen Bailout

Jusen were established in the 1970s by financial institutions as affiliates that would make home loans to individuals. The first was started by Kei-ichiro Niwayama, an ex-MOF official, and other MOF old boys were well represented in the top management of subsequent *jusen*.[109] But by the late 1980s, the banks wanted to break into this market themselves, forcing the *jusen* into riskier businesses, such as real estate lending. At the same time, however, the MOF limited the degree to which banks could engage in such lending. The result was that the *jusen* turned to agricultural cooperatives for funds. The collapse of the real estate market in the early 1990s thus threatened to destroy the agricultural cooperatives if they were forced to write off all the bad loans to *jusen*. In this case, though, the MOF were more afraid of the consequences of allowing this to happen than of using public money to bail the *jusen* out. In July 1996, the MOF set up the housing-loan Adminis-tration Corporation to unwind seven failed *jusen* and directed ¥685 billion of public funds to liquidate the bad loans. Public outrage ensued.

The Moody's Incident

In June 1995, the problems of the Japanese banking system were becom-ing very clear. During the Bubble period of unrestrained lending and the sharp contraction experienced after the 1990 crash, banks had accumulated bad debts that were officially admitted to be ¥40 trillion (approximately $500 billion), but which some private estimates put at up to four times that amount. This clearly was a cause of tension in a country in which it was a proud ministerial boast that no Japanese bank had been allowed to go bank-rupt since 1945. The unofficial but clear MOF guarantee that it would not allow a bank to go under was being strained to the limit.

Accordingly, Moody's, a private American credit rating agency, used two components in rating Japanese financial institutions. The first was the fi-nancial component, derived from a purely economic assessment of the firm's balance sheet and business prospects.[110] The second was a political component. Moody's took seriously the MOF's implicit guarantee of sup-port for Japanese banks, even though it was entirely unofficial, and rated Japanese banks higher because of it. However, by June 1995 the agency re-portedly became pessimistic about the ability and willingness of the MOF to

---

tence of the PKO paradoxically deterred potential investors who might otherwise have been tempted to "bottom-fish" the market, because they could not be certain that the market would not fall again if and when the artificial prop was removed.

[109] Peter Hartcher, *The Ministry: How the World's Most Powerful Institution Endangers World Markets* (Cambridge: Harvard University Press, 1998), 125.

[110] The Japan Premium of extra interest paid by Japanese institutions as a result of the bank-ing crisis was at least 0.25 percent in October 1995. Many smaller Japanese institutions were seeing their credit lines cut entirely.

make good on this guarantee, and it downgraded the ratings on two somewhat minor banks.[111] They stated, as the reason for the downgrade, their doubts about the MOF's ability to deliver on its guarantee to stand behind all banks.

The MOF was reportedly furious that its commitment was being questioned. Allegedly it summoned Moody's representatives and threatened them with the removal of their license as a recognized Japanese credit rating agency. The incident is officially denied by the MOF, and Moody's refuses to comment. It is, however, a significant comment on the declining influence of the MOF that Moody's did not alter its credit assessments.

Deteriorating Relationships between the MOF and Foreign Regulators

Meanwhile, even as the MOF's reputation was becoming ever more tarnished at home, two incidents involving the ministry's inadequate supervision of Japanese financial firms' foreign subsidiaries were to bring the wrath of foreign governments onto the heads of the beleaguered bureaucrats.

Until the mid-1980s, the lack of cooperation or active coordination between U.S. and Japanese regulators was striking. They began to work together as a perhaps unintended consequence of the yen–dollar talks of 1983, which brought the financial staff of the Japanese in Washington, as well as the MOF, into a closer cooperative relationship with their U.S. counterparts. One of the topics of the talks, first suggested by the Japanese Export-Import Bank, was the proposal to liberalize the issue of Yankee bonds in order to stimulate demand for yen-based financial instruments. One problem with this suggestion was the very complicated registration requirements in Japan for Yankee bonds compared with the far simpler registration for eurocurrency issues. To deal with this issue the Japanese proposed a system of shelf registration, but the Americans, in particular John Shad, then-chairman of the SEC, were less than enthusiastic about this suggestion. Thus, the need for a greater degree of common regulatory ground between the countries became more apparent, at least to the Americans. As a result, regular meetings between stock exchange regulators from the United States and Japan were proposed by Shad. At his suggestion, the MOF's Securities Bureau chief came to visit the SEC in 1985. This was apparently the first such official visit to the United States by a Securities Bureau chief. A series of annual bilateral talks began, in which Britain was "sometimes included."[112]

The MOF did not discuss the scandals of 1991 with any foreign regulators.[113] This was perhaps surprising, given the United States's reputation for

---

[111] David Holley, "Moody's Warnings of Downgrades Highlights East-West Differences," *Japan Times*, 22 June 1995, 8.

[112] Confidential interview with MOF official, Tokyo, May 1994.

[113] Ibid.

effective responses to financial misdeeds, but highlights the degree to which Japanese regulators were determined to maintain sole control over their own markets. At least one of the reasons for the reluctance by regulators to share information was the difference in institutional structures between the two countries. The exchange of information between the Japan and the United States was impeded by differences in which departments had access to what information. On occasions when the United States wanted specific information about a particular company or individual, the MOF were sometimes unable to oblige because of Japanese legal restraints. On the other hand, there were occasions when the Japanese were reluctant to impart information informally to their counterparts in the SEC, because they knew that the U.S. Justice Department had absolute rights to access to any information in the SEC's possession, a right that the Japanese Ministry of Justice did not have. This could have resulted in situations where the U.S. Justice Department knew more about the MOF's suspicions of Japanese wrongdoers than the Japanese Justice Ministry did, a situation intolerable to Japan.

The reluctance of the MOF to enter fully into cooperative relationships with either British or American regulators is well demonstrated by their handling of two crises involving the overseas subsidiaries of Japanese financial institutions, Daiwa Securities and Sumitomo Corporation.

The Daiwa U.S. Case, 1995   In the autumn of 1995, the Daiwa Bank Ltd. (New York) admitted that one of its traders, Iguchi Toshihide, had lost over $1.1 billion in bond trading, chiefly in U.S. T-bonds, over an eleven-year period. As head trader, Iguchi had also been in charge of the back office. In other words, like Barings rogue trader Nick Leeson, he had been responsible for the settlement of the trades he had made. Clearly this gave him the opportunity to cover up his losses, which ordinarily would have been known to at least one other person—whoever was responsible for settlements. Although financial irregularities at Daiwa had been known to the Federal Reserve Bank (Fed) since 1993, no action was taken against the firm. According to Federal Reserve Chairman Alan Greenspan, the Federal Reserve Bank of New York accepted the statements of Daiwa management that "the internal control problems identified in our examination had been corrected. With a more robust follow-up, the problem might have been found sooner."[114] In fact the New York Fed had told Daiwa to rearrange the oversight of its trading operations, but did not follow through. Neil Levin, superintendent of the New York State Banking Department, admitted that his agency's oversight had been inadequate. Federal and state banking regulations require that a bank operating in New York should immediately report any improprieties, but Daiwa claimed that it did not know that this was a legal requirement.[115]

[114] Keith Bradsher, "Lax Response in Daiwa Case Is Conceded," *New York Times*, 28 November 1995, D1.

[115] Sheryl WuDunn, "Japanese Delayed Letting US Know of Big Bank Loss," *New York Times*, 10 October 1996, A1.

In October 1995, the Fed, the Federal Deposit Insurance Corporation (FDIC; chair, Ricki Helfer), and six state bank regulatory agencies ordered Daiwa to shut down its U.S. offices by early 1996. They also outlined plans to make sure this would not happen again, for example, enforcing a rule requiring all bank employees to take at least ten consecutive business days off per year. But according to Greenspan, if internal controls fail, "it is exceptionally unlikely that we will be able ourselves to pick it up," nor would it be desirable to try: "Any system that attempted to be fail-safe would impose intolerable costs on the public, and the banking industry and would almost certainly stifle legitimate financial innovation," he added.[116]

The MOF admitted on October 9, 1995, that it had known of Daiwa's problems for six weeks during the summer without informing the Fed, a fact that enraged both the Fed and the U.S. Treasury. The MOF had known of the losses since at least July, when a letter from the trader admitting them came into their hands. But MOF officials argued that they were under no obligation to tell U.S. officials, and that it was the responsibility of the bank to inform U.S. authorities of their problems. Of course, it was possible for the MOF to have instructed Daiwa to admit the problems to the U.S. authorities itself, and the fact that the MOF did not do so strongly suggests that the MOF had reasons of its own not to disclose the problems. Daiwa stated that it had informed U.S. and Japanese regulators simultaneously of the losses on September 18, but later admitted that they had informally told the MOF's top banking official, Nishimura Yoshimasa, on August 8. Daiwa admitted to having told the MOF everything on September 12, and having told the Bank of Japan on September 14. Neither Japanese authority contacted U.S. officials until six days later. Greenspan argued that the Japanese had violated the spirit of their obligations under the Basle Concordat, an agreement between central banks about the coordination of bank regulation. But he said that Japanese officials had promised not to engage in similar delays in the future. Vice Minister for Finance Shinozawa Kyosuke admitted that "I am rather astonished" at the extent of the losses.[117] This admission did nothing to appease the American authorities, who remained furious with the MOF. Charles Schumer of the House Banking Committee was extremely dissatisfied with the laxity of the punishment, arguing that "the great area of weakness in bank regulation is foreign banks with major operations in the U.S."[118]

Sumitomo Corporation, London, 1996 In spring 1996. Sumitomo Corporation announced that it had lost $1.8 billion in unauthorized trading in copper. The company's star trader, Yasuo "The Hammer" Hamanaka, had

---

[116] Ibid.
[117] Ibid.
[118] Quoted in Bradsher, "Lax Response in Daiwa Case Is Conceded."

been engaging in unauthorized trading of copper futures on the London Metal Exchange (LME) for ten years. The affair highlighted both the degree to which financial regulators are already cooperating and the need for greater cooperation. The trades were conducted in London, but also involved an LME warehouse in the United States, which came under the jurisdiction of the U.S. Commodities Futures Trading Commission (CFTC). The LME was strongly criticized for its failure to heed warnings from Sumitomo's trading counterparties that its copper trades were highly suspicious. LME regulators reportedly did not investigate these claims until they had been "repeatedly assailed" by U.S. commodity-market regulators. In turn, the Japanese MOF did not begin to investigate Sumitomo's copper dealings until British regulators issued a "blunt warning" to them.[119] In October 1996, officials from Britain's Serious Fraud Office (SFO) and the SIB, and from the U.S. CFTC, all visited Tokyo to urge the Japanese authorities to cooperate in their investigations.[120]

International criticism of the MOF was embarrassing enough for Japanese politicians. But by the mid-1990s, such criticism was beginning to spill over to the politicians themselves. In September 1995, for example, the internationally respected journal *Euromoney* referred to Takemura Masayoshi as "the worst finance minister in the world."[121] The incident did nothing to improve relations between bureaucrats and politicians, which were already fraying.

Deteriorating Relationships between MOF and LDP

Attempts by the MOF to use traditional nonmarket means to resolve Japan's economic problems came to be seen as clumsy and counterproductive. The MOF's prestige waned, and one casualty was the relationship between the ministry and the LDP, which deteriorated sharply during the 1990s. According to one senior LDP politician, relations between the governing party and the bureaucrats had until the 1980s been like a marriage: both were united in the common aim of economic growth to catch up with the West, and both sides therefore acted like marriage partners, "who do not criticize each other in public."[122] The electoral defeat of the LDP in 1993 was like a divorce, after which many in the LDP realized that the bureaucrats work not as the administrative arm of the LDP, but for the people—or, some would say, for themselves.

Public disputes between the two organizations became more common. As an example, one politician described a fight he had picked with the MOF over *gyosei kaikaku* (administrative reform). The LDP wanted to abolish the

---

[119] Suzanne McGee and Stephen Frank, "Sumitomo Debacle Is Tied to Lax Controls by Firm Regulators," *Wall Street Journal*, 17 June 1996, A1.

[120] *Nikkei Weekly, Japan Economic Almanac*, 26.

[121] *Euromoney Magazine* (December 1995), 12.

[122] Confidential interview with LDP politician, Cambridge, May 1996.

Import-Export Bank, a quasi-official bank with the task of encouraging exports. Since Japan was under severe international criticism for its trade surplus, the LDP thought that there was no need to spend public money to encourage more exports. The proposed solution was that the Import-Export Bank be merged with the Japan Development Bank. Officially, MOF opposition to this plan was based on the banks' historical differences: one is domestic in orientation, the other international. Reformers noted that the same rationale had not prevented the MOF from blessing (and according to some actually arranging) the merger of Mitsubishi Bank and the Bank of Tokyo in 1995.[123] In reality, it was claimed, the MOF wished to preserve both banks only to maintain *amakudari* positions for retiring MOF officials. The LDP lost this particular fight, but the point had been made that it was possible to take on the MOF.

By the late 1990s the MOF's reputation for wisdom and virtue was in tatters.[124] Criticism of the ministry led to a spate of resignations by senior officials. In the summer of 1995, a leading official in the Budget Bureau, Nakajima Yoshio, was forced to resign when it was revealed that he had accepted gifts of low-interest loans. Another official in the same bureau was demoted for accepting free golfing trips to Hong Kong from a banker whose thrift institution had failed.[125] When in December 1995 the MOF announced the $6.8 billion *jusen* bailout, the public uproar was so great that Vice Minister for Finance Shinozawa resigned.[126] He was said to be "leaving behind an organization in near-turmoil."[127] Finance Minister Takemura said, "I have accepted Shinozawa's resignation to improve the morale of the ministry, which is under an oppressive atmosphere following scandals involving ministry officials." He added that "Shinozawa is not quitting to take the blame for any individual incidents, such as the failure of two Tokyo credit unions or the ministry's decision to use taxpayers' money for the liquidation of ailing housing loan companies."[128] Ogawa Tadashi, director general of the National Tax Administration Agency, was named new vice minister for finance. These resignations, however, did not stop the criticism.

Meanwhile, the financial scandals continued. One of the most spectacular involved gangsters and two of the largest and most prestigious of Japan's financial firms, Nomura Securities and Dai-Ichi Kangyo Bank.[129] Dai-ichi Kangyo had lent the equivalent of ¥30 billion (approximately $250 million)

---

[123] Interviews, Tokyo, June 1995.

[124] See, for example, Sandra Suguwara, "Japanese Public Opens War on Finance Ministry," *International Herald Tribune*, 27 October 1995, 1; Michael Williams, "Wiping Egg Off the Ministry's Face," *Wall Street Journal*, 27 October 1995, A10.

[125] Both in Williams, "Wiping Egg Off the Ministry's Face."

[126] Sheryl WuDunn, "Key Official in Japan Quits Finance Post," *New York Times*, 30 December 1995, 41.

[127] Ibid.

[128] Ibid.

[129] "Nomura Honsha Kyōyo" [Namura chief forced out], *Asahi Shimbun*, 6 June 1997, 1; "2 Japanese Bank Officials Are Indicted," *New York Times*, 5 July 1997, 29.

to Koike Ryuichi, a well-known *sokaiya* gangster. *Sokaiya* are racketeers who buy shares in companies and threaten to disrupt shareholder meetings unless the company pays them protection money, an activity known as greenmail. In the 1990s, many Japanese firms took measures to deter the practice, for instance, by planning their annual shareholders meetings all on the same day, but did not succeed in stamping out the practice.[130] The hush money paid to Koike enabled him to buy a major shareholding in Nomura, which he had used to extort money ahead of the 1995 annual shareholders meeting, when Nomura were planning to reinstate to the board the former president and chairman, who had resigned in disgrace following a series of scandals in 1991, partly involving payments to the *yakuza*. Nomura, in turn, had paid protection money to Koike. The affair, when discovered, resulted in the arrests of several senior officials and the suicide of a former chairman of Dai-Ichi Kangyo.[131]

There is some evidence that the authorities were taking seriously their new mandate to pursue fraud, with a steadily increasing number of investigations and cases being brought for financial fraud.[132] In 1996, for example, Sanada Yukihiko, a lawyer, was arrested and charged with insider trading in shares of Nihon Orimono Kako. This was the first time in Japan that someone who did not work directly for the company in question was charged with such an offence.[133] In other words, the SESC was taking its job seriously. But the scandals continued to put pressure on the LDP to do more to clean up the financial markets.

Moreover, in addition to the charges of incompetent economic management came new criticisms of sleazy conduct, involving officials receiving lavish entertainment from the banks and brokers they regulated. Such criticisms were not new: a character in a popular 1987 cartoon book remarks, "When the [MOF] inspectors arrive, the bank has its prettiest female clerks ready to wait on them hand and foot."[134] But what had been acceptable during the Bubble years became grounds for outrage now. The defining moment in the uproar occurred when certain MOF officials were found to have been demanding that bankers and brokers entertain them at the notorious No-Pan Shabu Shabu restaurant. Here, in a lavishly appointed dining room specially equipped with mirrored floors, the traditional Japanese delicacy *shabu-shabu* was served by waitresses wearing nothing under their miniskirts. These revelations represented quite possibly the lowest point for the

[130] For example, 2,355 companies began their meetings simultaneously at 10 A.M. on 27 June 1997.

[131] "Ex-Head of Tainted Japan Bank, Under Inquiry, Commits Suicide," *New York Times*, 30 June 1997, D2.

[132] SESC, *Outline of Activities, 1996* (Tokyo: Securities and Exchange Surveillance Commission).

[133] "Taiho no Bengoshi o Kohatsu" [Lawyer arrested], *Asahi Shimbun*, 1996, 35.

[134] Ishinomori Shorato, *Japan Inc.* (The Comic Book), vol. 2, English language edition (Sunnyvale, Calif.: Lanchester Press, 1996).

reputation of Japan's bureaucrats in recorded history. Administrative reform seemed ever more likely as MOF-bashing became, in the words of one expert observer, "a national sport, rivaling sumo."[135]

The Financial Supervisory Agency

The idea of breaking up the MOF was first seriously aired by Suzuki Yoshio, a former executive director of the Bank of Japan, in 1995.[136] Many senior LDP policymakers agreed with his argument that a new inspection agency responsible for the prudent supervision of finance should be established independently of the MOF, which should retain responsibility for the budget, the management of public finances, and taxation. An LDP spokesman, Kajiyama Seiroku, agreed that the MOF was "somewhat not suited for the current age," that it "tends to protect itself and becomes too conservative," and that it "should be altered to meet international standards."[137] Kato Koichi, secretary-general of the LDP, was also reported to have suggested shifting the ministry's Banking, Securities, and International Finance Bureaus into a separate agency.[138] The minister for international trade and industry, Tsukuhara Shumpei, was reported as saying that close to 80 percent of the Diet "would probably say they are considering something like splitting up the Finance Ministry."[139]

The MOF itself, understandably, was opposed to the idea of a breakup. Vice Minister Ogawa remarked that, "The present system . . . is an appropriate way to guide the Japanese economy."[140] His views were echoed by the minister for finance, Kubo Wataru, who thought that it was "not appropriate" to discuss the breakup at the current time, arguing instead that "What is important now is to review whether there is an institutional problem with the Ministry or simply a management problem."[141] Many younger LDP members and the opposition parties believed that the problem was the former, and pressured Prime Minister Hashimoto into calling a coalition government panel on administrative reform. The Finance Ministry Reform Panel, chaired by Ito Shigeru, secretary-general of the Social Democratic Party, was set up in February 1996.[142]

The panel's recommendation to break up the MOF was accepted by the

---

[135] Robin Radin, "Japan's Big Bang in Historical Perspective," Harvard Law School, Program on International Financial Systems mimeo, 1998.

[136] Suzuki Yoshio, "Reviving Financial Markets with a New Regulatory System," *Japan Echo* 23, no. 1 (1996): 24. This is a translation of the original article, "Kinyu Gyosei wa Torihiki Kanshi Kiko e Utsuse," *Shukan Toyo Keizai*, 2 December 1995, 21–24.

[137] "Finance Ministry under Siege in Tokyo," *International Herald Tribune*, 7 February 1996, 15.

[138] Ibid.

[139] Ibid.

[140] Gwen Robinson, "Profile: Tadashi Ogawa," *Financial Times Survey of Japanese Finance*, 25 March 1997, vi.

[141] "Finance Ministry under Siege in Tokyo."

[142] William Dawkins, "Tokyo Finance Ministry Under Threat," *Financial Times*, 8 February 1996, 1.

Diet and took effect on April 1, 1998. The ministry was effectively split in two, to create one body responsible for fiscal policy and another responsible for regulatory supervision, the Financial Supervisory Agency (FSA). The FSA was formed by merging the inspection divisions of the banking and securities bureaus, the ministry-wide Financial Inspection Department, the SESC, and the Deposit Insurance Corp. The agency was to be independent of the MOF, affiliated with the prime minister's office. The chairman was to appointed by the prime minister, and would ideally come from the private sector. The FSA's supervisory duties included control over the licensing of financial institutions, since the panel believed that control over licensing had historically given the MOF too much power over private firms. The functions of tax and budget policy were left in the newlydownsized MOF, although the term *Okurasho* (Great Storehouse), which had been in continuous use since A.D. 678, was slated for removal by 2001. The blander term *zaimucho*, usually translated Ministry of Treasury, was to be used instead, to the fury of MOF staff.[143] In another potentially severe blow to the bureaucrats' ability to guide the markets informally, the MOF agreed in 1998 to abolish its mass of directives and circulars known as *tsutatsu*. The bureacrats had been able to use these directives, many of which had had the authority of cabinet ordinances, to exercise disretionary power over private firms. Finally, the Bank of Japan Law was revised to give the BOJ independence from the MOF. The reform was a stunning victory for the politicians over the MOF, which had fought hard against the proposals. Even panel Chairman Ito expressed surprise at the success of the reform.[144]

III. Continued Liberalization at the Tokyo Stock Exchange: *Biggu Bangu*

Meanwhile, as Japan's regulatory structure was being overhauled, pressure was building to continue the liberalization of the financial markets themselves. The pro-competitive, liberalizing trend described in chapter 5 had slowed in the early 1990s for reasons described here. By 1996, the pace of reform was to pick up speed again.

The Tokyo stock market crash of 1990 and the subsequent collapse of land prices had severe continuing effects for the rest of the Japanese economy. One of the most serious was a massive bad debt crisis affecting all of Japan's financial institutions, most of which had been lending money recklessly to speculators on collateral artificially pumped up by the Bubble. The collapse of the real estate market created huge problems for those institutions that had borrowed heavily, using the value of their land as collateral.

---

[143] Mary Jordan, "Japan to Alter Name of Powerful Ministry," *Washington Post*, 17 April 1999, E1.

[144] *Nikkei Weekly, Japan Economic Almanac 1997*, 18.

Many companies had used the money they raised for speculation rather than long-term investment and therefore suffered further losses as share prices fell. The total volume of bad loans in the financial system soared. In 1996, the MOF calculated that bad loans totaled ¥38 trillion (approximately $300 billion). This was a conservative estimate, using the most stringent definition of bad loans and figures disclosed by the financial institutions, which were notoriously inaccurate.[145] Others put the bad-loan total at closer to ¥75 trillion.[146] Even at the end of the 1990s, the problem had not been solved. In 1997, the MOF put the figure at ¥27.9 trillion. By then, the big ten banks had written off much of their debt, which was disproportionately held by the smaller financial firms—agricultural cooperatives, savings institutions, small banks, and nonbanks.[147] Bankruptcies among financial institutions—rare for most of the postwar period—rose through the mid-1990s. In 1991, there had been one bankruptcy worth about ¥213 billion. In 1995 there were six bankruptcies, worth a total of ¥4.3 trillion.[148]

The stock market crash, the recession, and the ensuing bad-debt crisis had temporarily put the process of financial liberalization on hold. Trading volumes on the securities exchanges and demand for new bank loans dried up. Banks and securities companies became so involved with their immediate problems that they had no time or inclination to develop new businesses. The MOF's attention was taken up with shoring up the weakened system and defending itself from criticism. Its first response was to avoid structural reform and instead to use large sums of public money to try to solve the problems in the financial system. In part, this strategy was premised on the belief that the system was so fragile that the shock therapy of major reform, which would inevitably entail severe losses and a rash of bankruptcies, would be more likely to kill than to cure the patient. Some in the MOF hoped that, given time and an economic recovery, the banks could grow their way out of the problem in the same way that the big American banks had outgrown the Latin American–debt crisis of the early 1980s.[149]

Accordingly the MOF tried to maintain stability by propping up stock prices through the Price-Keeping Operation described earlier. The PKO may have prevented some financial firms from going bankrupt in the short term, but it did little long-term to solve the debt crisis. The practice was finally ended in October 1996 by Mitsuzuka Hiroshi, appointed minister of finance in the newly elected Hashimoto administration.[150] As the PKO

---

[145] The bankrupt Hyogo Bank was discovered by MOF inspectors to have bad loans worth ¥1.5 billion more than it had previously disclosed.

[146] *Japan Almanac 1997* (Tokyo: Asahi Shimbun, 1997), 25.

[147] "Japan Banks Said to Carry $240 Billion in Bad Loans," *New York Times*, 5 July 1997.

[148] *Japan Almanac 1997*, 24.

[149] Interviews with MOF and BOJ officials, Tokyo, June–July 1994.

[150] Gwen Robinson, "Profile: Hiroshi Mitsuzuka," *Financial Times Survey of Japanese Finance*, 25 March 1997, vi.

failed to deliver recovery, the MOF used public money, usually from the Fiscal Investment Loan Program, to inject funds into weakened banks. Meanwhile, market liberalization slipped in everyone's priorities.

By the mid-1990s, it was becoming clearer that the MOF's strategy of putting off reform and buying time for the financial system was proving to be both expensive and counterproductive. In particular, policymakers were growing increasingly concerned with the "demographic tsunami" of the aging population, and its implications for public finances.[151] The authorities had been aware of problem of *koreika*—the aging of the population—for several years; the Ministry of Health and Welfare had predicted in 1991 that by the end of the decade, the number of Japanese over sixty-five would exceed those under the age of fifteen.[152] What was changing were the financial implications. The continued recession was resulting in the growing problem of the underfunding of both public and corporate pension systems. With fewer taxpayers in the workforce and more elderly people spending their savings and drawing down governmental resources in the forms of pension, health care, and so on, the economy faced a severe long-term structural problem. The extensive attempts at fiscal stimulus to combat the recession had compounded the problem by devastating public finances. In 1990, the Japanese government had run a budget surplus of approximately 3 percent of the GDP. By 1996, the budget deficit had deteriorated to approximately 6 percent of GDP. This structural problem, argued Prime Minister Hashimoto, could only be addressed by the structural solution of financial system reform.

Ironically, the problem was not that Japan was short of savings. On the contrary, Japan had more than ¥1,2000 (approximately $10 trillion) in personal financial assets in 1996. The problem was that lack of competition in the financial sector meant that the returns on these assets were very low. From 1985 to 1995, for example, Japanese pension funds had earned an average 5 percent per year, compared with approximately 15 percent for U.S. pension funds.[153] By 1996, Japanese insurance companies would only guarantee a 2.5 percent return on the pension funds they managed.[154] Once again, poor performance by Japanese financial institutions had been made possible by lack of competition. Early attempts to introduce foreign competition into the pension-fund business resulted in a mass exodus of funds from Japanese to foreign managers. In the five years from 1992 to 1997, the share of Japanese pension funds managed by foreigners more than quadrupled from 1.7 percent to 8.3 percent.[155] Two big changes occurred in

---

[151] The term was coined by Kathy Matsui of Goldman Sachs. Kathy Matsui and Hiromi Suzuki, "Demographic Tsunami: The Pension Dilemma and Equity Market Implications," Goldman Sachs Portfolio Strategy Report, 5 December 1995.

[152] Yoshio Sugimoto, *An Introduction to Japanese Society* (Cambridge: Cambridge University Press, 1996), 73–75.

[153] Richard Katz, *Japan: The System That Soured* (New York: M. E. Sharpe, 1998), 333.

[154] Ibid.

[155] Ibid., 335.

1994: foreigners were permitted to manage up to one-third of a corporate pension fund, and the rules restricting individuals from holding foreign bonds were relaxed.[156] Once again, more liberalization and greater competition in the markets seemed to be the only viable long-term solution to Japan's problems.

Meanwhile, opposition to reform from the brokering community was being eroded by the rapidly deteriorating competitive position of the Tokyo Stock Exchange in world markets. At the height of the Bubble in 1990, share-trading volumes in Tokyo exceeded those in London and matched those in New York. By 1997, the value of shares traded in Tokyo was only one-fifth of those in New York.[157] In addition, investors in Japanese shares were increasingly turning to rival exchanges to conduct business. The proportion of Japanese shares traded on the London Stock Exchange grew from 4 percent in 1992 to 18 percent in 1997, with some estimates putting this figure even higher.[158] Corporate borrowers, too, were known to be dissatisfied with the high costs and poor quality of service they received from Japanese financial institutions.[159] In the face of this loss of business, Japanese securities companies accepted the necessity of deregulation, and the more competitive even welcomed it.[160] This dynamic, of course, exactly parallels the situation in Britain prior to the Big Bang, when British brokers woke up to the threat to their business from New York.

Against this background, authorities in the LDP and the MOF started to accept the necessity of reform. Among the chief architects were Sakakibara Eisuke, the brilliant and outspoken head of MOF's International Finance Bureau, and Nagano Atsushi, chief of the MOF's Securities Bureau. In June 1996, the Securities and Exchange Council, the advisory council to the Securities Bureau of the MOF, worked on a plan to revitalize and internationalize Japan's financial markets, which it completed in June 1997.[161] In the words of Ariyoshi Akira, director of the Research Office of the Securities Bureau and an author of the proposal, "High costs, a restrictive regulatory environment, and lack of dynamic players gradually eroded Japan's role as a major financial center. If a disproportionate amount of transactions of yen-based financial products were being conducted outside Japan, then clearly something had to be amiss."[162]

[156] Robert Steiner, "Tired of Poor Returns, Many Japanese Send Their Savings Abroad," *Wall Street Journal*, 26 December 1995, A1.

[157] William Dawkins, "Last Chance to Catch Up," *Financial Times Survey of Japanese Finance*, 25 March 1997, v.

[158] Ibid. See also Katz, who claims that Japanese shares traded in London were "as much as 30–40 percent of the levels in Tokyo." Katz, *Japan: The System That Soured*, 334.

[159] Ikeo Kazuhito, "A Look Behind the Financial Reform Drive," *Japan Echo* 24, no. 3 (1997): 19.

[160] Aoki Hideyuki, "Financial 'Black Ships' Good for Japan, Says Top Brokerage," *Daily Yomiuri*, 2 September 1997, 16.

[161] Securities and Exchange Council, *Comprehensive Reform of the Securities Market* (Tokyo: Shoken Torihiki Shingikai, June 1997).

[162] Ariyoshi Akira, "The Big Bang Blueprint," *Look Japan* 44, no. 508 (1998): 14.

The Securities Bureau's views of the problem and the proposed solution, greater innovation and competition, were echoed by the Financial System Research Council, representing the banking bureau, and the Insurance Council, representing the insurers. The bureau managed to sell the idea to the rest of the MOF. Prime Minister Hashimoto and Finance Minister Mitsuzuka accepted the call for radical financial reform, and Hashimoto announced the Big Bang in November. He wanted, he said, for Japan's markets to be "Free, Fair, Global." He elaborated that "free" meant "a liberal market based on the market principle" (*Shijogenri ga hataraku jiyuna shijo*). "Fair" meant that clear rules of disclosure would permit trust and confidence to be established (*Tomei de shinrai dekiru shijo*). "Global" meant that the market should lead the way into a new international era (*Kokusaiteki de jidai o sakidori suru shijo*).[163]

The plan took the form of the Financial System Reform Bill, an omnibus bill that ran 977 pages and revised twenty-four financial and tax laws. The Diet passed the bill in March, and it came into effect in December 1998. Among the proposals were to eliminate barriers between segments of the banking sector (e.g., between city, trust, and long-term credit banks); to promote new entry into the banking, securities, and insurance sectors; to expand the range of activities in which financial institutions can engage; to liberalize the currently nonnegotiable commissions for securities trading; to revise the legal system to allow for new financial instruments such as derivatives; to review the restrictions on fund-management services and to improve the disclosure system of such services; to permit investment trusts and pension funds to invest in unlisted companies (to encourage venture business); to permit all forms of holding companies; to eliminate a variety of transactions taxes such as withholding tax on government bonds; to harmonize Japan's accounting system with international standards; and, perhaps most important as a first step, to completely liberalize the foreign-exchange system, allowing institutions to engage in foreign-exchange business without prior permission and without having to go through a bank.[164]

In October 1999, the reform was firmly on track. The lifting of restrictions on foreign-exchange transactions went into effect smoothly in the summer of 1998. The final tiers of fixed commission rates (on deals smaller than ¥50 million) were abolished in October 1999, so that now commission rates on the TSE are completely liberalized. Laws encouraging the market for asset-backed securities were passed in September 1998. Laws allowing holding companies were passed in 1998, further facilitating the entry of financial institutions into new business areas.

The Japanese Big Bang differed from its British namesake in three ways. First, the reforms were far more wide-reaching, encompassing all aspects of the financial services industry. By comparison, the British reform was

---

[163] Hashimoto Ryutaro, "Wagaguni Kinyushisutemu no Kaikaku" [Reform of our national financial system], 2–3.

[164] I am grateful to Robin Radin of the Harvard Law School for this summary of the proposals.

narrowly focused on brokerage commissions and entry to the LSE. Second, the Japanese reforms were to be introduced gradually, over a five-year period from 1996 to 2001, in a deliberate attempt to give the Japanese firms time to adjust. This contrasts with London's Big Bang, in which reform took place overnight. But these first two differences are not as great as they appear. Japanese reforms were more widespread because they needed to be: to reach the stated goal of a "free, fair, and global market" they had further to go and more to do. And although the British reforms were implemented in a sudden fashion, the three-year delay between the Goodison-Parkinson Accord of 1983 and the Big Bang in 1986 gave British brokers almost as much time to prepare for change as their Japanese counterparts were granted.

The final, and perhaps most significant, difference is in the attitudes of the brokering communities and the general public to the reforms. The British, by and large, either welcomed the Big Bang or else didn't know about it. The Japanese plainly did not like their *Biggu Bangu*. For brokers, it was a painful necessity but one from which few financiers expected to come out well. Japanese brokers looked to Britain and perceived that whereas London was booming as a financial center and Britain was benefiting greatly as a result, few British firms were among the leading financial institutions. This observation led, with monotonous regularity, to an invocation of the Wimbledon Effect—the observation that since the All-England Tennis Club had opened its famous tournament to foreigners in the 1930s, no Englishman has ever won the championship.[165] Ordinary Japanese citizens seemed to regard the reform with anything from suspicion to resentment. Some saw financial deregulation as something dictated by the Americans. "First Commodore Perry, then General MacArthur, and now Secretary Summers," was a remark I heard many times. Many Japanese did not, and still do not, believe that the *Biggu Bangu* is going to help them. A poll conducted by the *Asahi Shimbun* in March 1998 found that 32 percent of Japanese individuals believed that Big Bang would affect them positively, compared with 43 percent who believed that it would affect them negatively.[166]

IV. The Changing Face of Japanese Financial Markets

Viewed in terms of numbers of external and internal barriers to entry and of the importance of the market mechanism in setting prices, Japanese financial markets were considerably more liberal in the mid-1990s than they

[165] Englishwoman Virgina Wade's victory in 1977 was usually ignored by those making the analogy.

[166] Asahi Shimbun, 4 January 1998. The data used here were originally collected by the Asahi Shimbun. The data were obtained from the Japan Public Opinion Location Library (JPOLL), Roper Center for Public Opinion Research, University of Connecticut. Neither the original collectors of the data, nor the Roper Center, bears any responsibility for the analyses or interpretations presented here.

were in the mid-1970s, or even the 1980s. However, in studying financial regulation, it is often hard to discern real change from cosmetic adjustment and to detect major trends from a mass of technical and arcane detail. Events can also change with bewildering speed and equally bewildering complexity. This section gives what will inevitably be an incomplete and rapidly dated snapshot, as of 1999, of some of the ways in which Japan's financial markets have been transformed.

The most dramatic change has been in the rapid rise in foreign involvement in the market. Foreign investors now account for almost one-quarter of stock trades on the TSE, and hold almost 10 percent of Japanese shares.[167] (See table 6.1.) Foreign brokers have captured market share relentlessly since they were permitted to compete on Japan's exchanges. Foreigners accounted for approximately 8 percent of share trading on the TSE in 1987, 20 percent in 1992, and 30 percent in 1999.[168] Exactly as happened in Britain, the freer markets promised by the Big Bang resulted in a massive influx of new foreign financial firms seeking to take advantage of the new environment. Foreign direct investment in Japan's financial services sector was $242 million in 1995. By 1998 it had leapt to $8.6 billion.[169] Among the more spectacular deals, the U.S. Travelers Group, Inc., formed a comprehensive tie-up with Nikko Securities in 1998.[170] In 1999, Ripplewood, a U.S. private equity group, was approved to take over the Long Term Credit Bank (LTCB) at a cost of over $1 billion. Other foreign joint-ventures or tie-ups included Dresdner Bank with Bank of Tokyo-Mitsubishi, JP Morgan with Dai-Ichi Kangyo, Deutsche Bank with Nippon Life, Bankers Trust with Nippon Credit Bank, and Merrill Lynch with the failed Yamaichi Securities. Merrill Lynch reportedly refused MOF overtures to take over the failing Japanese brokerage before it went under but hired most of the approximately 2,000-member staff as soon as Yamaichi had declared bankruptcy.[171] GE Capital bought many of the assets of an affiliate of LTCB and began a joint venture with Toho Mutual Life, a major life insurer. Also in the life insurance sector, the French company Atermis bought the assets of the collapsed Nissan Mutual company. None of these deals would have been conceivable at the beginning of the decade.

The abolition of fixed commissions appears to be having the same effect in Tokyo as it did in London. Commission rates are going down for large investors and staying put or increasing for small investors. In the wake of the April 1998 deregulation of commission rates on medium-sized transactions, some brokers cut their fees by up to 90 percent. By contrast, the three

[167] Tokyo Stock Exchange, *Fact Book* (1998).
[168] "Goodbye to All That," *The Economist*, 12 December 1992, and "Once There Were Four," *The Economist*, 27 September 1997, 83.
[169] Gillian Tett, "Foreign Investment in Japan," *Financial Times Survey*, 19 October 1999, 2.
[170] "Financial Realignment Picks up Speed," *Nikkei Net Interactive*, 8 June 1998. <www.nni.nikkei.cosup/>.
[171] "Once There Were Four."

Table 6.1. Foreign participation in the Tokyo Stock Exchange

	1975	1980	1985	1990	1997
Share ownership (%)	2.6	4.0	5.7	4.2	9.8
Share trading volume (%)	4.7	7.4	12.5	9.8	23.3
Number of listed companies	16	15	21	125	60

Source: Tokyo Stock Exchange Fact Book (Tokyo: Tokyo Stock Exchange).

biggest brokers all reported that they had either increased or kept the same fees for retail investors.[172]

Competition has also resultied in an intensive round of cost-cutting, re-trenchment, and consolidation in all sectors of the Japanese financial services industry. There have been several major consolidations, including the massive merger between Industrial Bank of Japan, Fuji Bank, and DKB in August 1999; and between three of the biggest insurance companies in October 1999.[173] With the arrival of competition, the market share and market power of the Big Four (now the Big Three) Japanese brokers has decreased dramatically, and not only because of the bankruptcy of one of their number, Yamaichi Securities, in November 1997. Their share of TSE stock trading slipped from 70 percent in the 1960s to approximately 55 percent in 1985 to 40 percent in 1990. This was due in part to a 1989 rule set by the MOF prohibiting any broker from handling more than 30 percent of the daily trading in any one stock.[174] Their share of trading in 1997 was estimated, at best, at 25 percent.[175] For all Japanese brokers, efforts to cut costs and shed staff have been intense: Yamatane Securities is a typical medium-sized broker that halved its staff from 2,000 in 1990 to 1,000 in 1999 and cut the number of branch offices from 55 to 35.[176]

The end of the convoy system and the genuine possibility of bankruptcy is another sea change in Japanese finance. The failures of Hokkaido Takushokin bank and Yamaichi Securities in 1997 represent a fundamental departure from the MOF's old policy of never letting a major financial institution go bust. In short, the MOF can no longer control either entry or exit from the financial markets.

How have these changes affected Japanese capitalism more generally?

[172] Tomoko Otake, "Deregulation Uncovers New Face of Securities Competition," *Japan Times International*, 1–5 October 1999, 11.

[173] Naoko Nakamae, "Three Japanese Non-Life Insurers Plan Merger," *Financial Times*, 18 October 1999, 17. The firms were Mitsui Marine and Fire, Nippon Fire and Marine, and Koa Fire and Marine.

[174] Wagstyl, "Japan's Scandal-Hit Traders," vi.

[175] "Once There Were Four."

[176] "Securities Firms Outline Plans for Survival in Face of Reforms," *Daily Yomiuri*, 21 September 1999, 1.

Table 6.2. Corporate executives' views on which entities most influence business management in 1977 and their projections for 2002

	Company Executives		Main Banks		General Shareholders	
	1977	2002	1977	2002	1977	2002
Strong Influence (%)	82	77	34	38	12	60
Weak Influence (%)	18	23	66	62	88	40

Source: Japanese Economic Planning Agency, "Questionnaire concerning Corporate Activities," 1977.

One trend is clear: bank lending is declining in importance to Japanese corporations. In 1975, bank loans represented approximately 90 percent of the external funding sources for Japanese nonfinancial institutions. Now, the figure is less than 70 percent, with up to 30 percent of new external funds being raised in securities markets.[177] With this change has come a change in perceptions about the importance of banks to shareholders in terms of their influence on corporate management. A study conducted by the Economic Planning Agency in 1997 found striking results. First, corporate managers overwhelmingly (80 percent of those surveyed) believed that traditional entities, including banks and executives promoted from within the company's ranks should wield the strongest influence over corporate managers. The reasons given are familiar—the old pattern of bank influence encourages stability, long-term planning, and a greater knowledge of the company on the part of those who influence it. In contrast, only 12 percent of those surveyed believed that new entities such as shareholders and institutional investors should have strong or relatively strong influence. However, those surveyed also believed that however desirable the old system, change was inevitable. When asked which entities would more strongly influence managers in five years, over 60 percent believed that shareholders would gain at least relatively strong influence.[178] (See table 6.2.)

The cross-shareholding system also appears to be eroding, albeit at a glacial pace. Exact figures for cross-shareholdings are impossible to obtain but were believed to make up approximately 50 percent of the capitalization of the TSE in 1990. By 1999, the figure was estimated at 45 percent. Moreover, the pace of unwinding appears to be picking up, with ¥2,800 billion ($23 billion) of cross-shareholdings being sold in the first six months of 1999, representing close to 1 percent of the market's ¥350,000 billion capitalization.[179] The real figure for sell-offs may be bigger because many

[177] Japan Securities Research Institute, *Securities Markets in Japan* (Tokyo: Japan Securities Research Institute, 1998), 3.
[178] Economic Planning Agency, *Economic Survey of Japan 1997–1998* (Tokyo: EPA, 1998), 202.
[179] Gillian Tett, "Sharp Rise in Unwinding of Corporate Japan," *Financial Times*, 7 July 1999, 1.

Japanese corporations reportedly sell cross-held shares secretly through for-eign brokers, so as not to upset long-standing relationships with business partners.[180] Sell-offs appear to increase whenever the market rises, which may indicate more to come as the Nikkei recovers.

The long-term effects of this shift in influence from stakeholders to shareholders are unclear, but there is some evidence that the decline in bank influence will enhance managerial efficiency or, rather, reduce management inefficiency. The Economic Planning Agency's study of corporate capital procurement and managerial efficiency found, with many caveats, that "a correlative relationship . . . appears to exist between the degree of main bank dependence and management efficiency, with corporate management more inefficient the higher the main bank financing ratio."[181] In the same vein, U.S. investment bank Goldman Sachs compared the share-price per-formance of Japanese companies with a relatively high degree of sharehold-ers (defined as institutional investors, pension funds, foreigners, etc.; so-called Nifty stocks) with the performance of all the companies represented in the Nikkei 225 index. The survey found that the shareholder-dominated companies overwhelmingly outperformed the average, yielding a return on equity from 1990 to 1999 of 7 percent, compared with the average for the Nikkei 225 of -3 percent.[182]

Another area of fundamental change in Japanese capitalism has been in mergers and acquisitions, which are becoming a much more common fea-ture of the corporate landscape. Both the value and number of mergers and acquisitions mushroomed in the 1990s. From 1994 to 1999, the number of merger-and-acquisition deals grew from 200 per year to close to 1,000, rep-resenting a tenfold increase in volume from approximately $5 billion to ap-proximately $50 billion.[183] The shift has even extended to hostile takeovers, long regarded as antithetical to Japanese-style capitalism: in June 1999, Minister for Trade Yosano Kaoru announced that he supported the ¥70 bil-lion ($565 million) hostile bid for IDC, a Japanese telecommunications company, by the British Cable and Wireless Group.[184]

These changes are well recognized. During the 1995 round of negotia-tions on liberalization of Japanese financial services, the United States noted several areas in which the Japanese had liberalized.[185] These included the re-laxation of rules for bond issuance; the diversification of maturities and in-terest-rate structures for bonds; the diversification of permitted products, such as asset-backed securities or forward agreements; and improvements in transparency through the implementation of the Administrative Procedures

[180] Confidential interview with U.S. investment banker, Tokyo, June 1998.
[181] Economic Planning Agency, *Economic Survey of Japan 1997–1998*, 196.
[182] Kathy Matsui, "Demographic Tsunami," Goldman Sachs (Japan), June 1999.
[183] Michiyo Makamoto, "No Longer Taboo," *Financial Times*, 25 August 1999, 10.
[184] Gillian Tett, "Tokyo to Welcome Hostile Foreign Bid," *Financial Times*, 23 June 1999, 1.
[185] "Measures by the Government of the United States and the Government of Japan Re-garding Financial Services," II (2) a.

Law and of market access by investment advisory companies to employee pension-fund accounts.[186] In addition, both countries noted with approval that private Japanese pension-fund sponsors and managers had made private initiatives to develop standardized performance data along internationally accepted lines in order to allow for better independent performance evaluation.[187]

In summary, the founding of the FSA and the *Biggu Bangu* are two of the clearest pieces of evidence that the Japanese have, perhaps reluctantly, decided to abandon the old financial system that had apparently served them so well during the high-growth era. The founding of the FSA is crucial because it represents the first time in Japanese financial history that the job of regulating financial institutions will be conducted by a different organization than the one charged with protecting the interests of the same institutions. The long-term implications of this change are likely to be as profound in Japan as similar reforms were in the United States in the 1930s. The *Biggu Bangu* is crucial because it represents an unequivocal commitment to the market mechanism, as opposed to bureaucratic control, as the preferred arbiter of entry to and exit from Japanese financial markets and for the correct allocation of prices such as brokerage fees. Both changes mark the end of producer dominance in the regulation of financial services.

[186] "Measures," IV (12) a.
[187] "Measures," III (6) b. i.

The New Politics of
Financial Interdependence

I. Greater Competition, Greater Supervision

Britain and Japan have followed two separate but related pathways of financial reform: the first is toward greater market competition, and the second is stronger supervisory oversight. Both countries have introduced much freer markets in terms of price setting, entry and exit, and product diversity with their individual Big Bangs, heralding the triumph of the market mechanism. At the same time, both have introduced stricter rules and tougher standards of supervision for investor protection. Britain's Super SIB and Japan's Financial Supervisory Agency both represent a fundamental shift in traditional patterns of oversight and supervision. The broad explanation for these trends is the same: in both countries, cartelistic market structures and informal regulatory oversight were incompatible with internationally integrated capital markets. Beyond that, the explanations for each trend are more complex and differ somewhat.

Greater Market Competition
In the early 1980s, Britain and Japan both had protected and cartelistic stock markets, but the pattern of beneficiaries was different. In Britain, fixed commissions, single capacity, and the partnership system benefited small investors at the expense of large investors and brokers. In Japan, fixed commissions also hurt the interests of large investors, but as a result of the producer-oriented nature of the regulatory structure, the beneficiaries were the brokers rather than small investors. From the 1980s on, both countries abolished anticompetitive practices such as fixed commissions and tight restrictions on the new entry of competitors. The result has been a decrease in dealing costs for large investors and a relative increase in dealing costs for individuals. In other words, institutional investors have won out at the expense of brokers and small investors in both countries. A related effect has been that costs have declined and funding options have increased for institutional borrowers.

What explains this trend? I suggest that large-scale users of financial services, both borrowers and lenders, were able to exploit the increased opportunities created by financial market openness either to escape unfavorable domestic regulations or to pressure their governments into reform. It was the threat of exit by institutional investors in the United Kingdom that sealed the fate of the LSE cartel and forced the pace of reform. In Japan, it was the exit of corporate borrowers to the euromarkets that forced the pace of the securities market liberalization in the 1980s. In the 1990s, the exit of investors in Japanese stocks to rival exchanges such as London and Singapore undermined opposition to reform from Japan's brokering community. This dynamic appears to have a self-reinforcing snowballing quality. Exit prompts liberalization, which usually allows further exit, which increases the pressure for more liberalization. Thus we see how lifting restrictions on the foreign management of Japan's pension funds caused a flood of funds to be transferred from Japanese to foreign managers, which in turn stimulated greater demands for more complete liberalization.

The degree to which the brokering communities in both countries welcomed liberalization varied considerably. British stockbrokers were generally far more enthusiastic about the Big Bang than the Japanese were. This could have been a result of a greater belief in the virtues of Thatcherite deregulation or of the distinctly better market conditions prevailing in London in 1986 than in Tokyo in 1996. It may also reflect an overoptimistic assessment by Londoners of their own competitiveness. A popular cartoon strip depicted a group of gung-ho British stockbrokers preparing for the Big Bang 'fired with enthusiasm.' A year later, in the wake of the 1987 stock market crash, the same group were downsized by a gleefully cost-cutting boss and found themselves 'fired, with enthusiasm.' Japanese brokers, as we have seen, tended to regard the *Biggu Bangu* as a painful necessity. But while the two groups had very different opinions about the temperature of the water, they both jumped.

Greater Supervision

The political dynamics explaining the trend toward stricter levels of investor protection are somewhat more complicated, but are remarkably similar in both countries. In the early 1980s, both countries had completely different regulatory structures. In the United Kingdom, investor protection was highly fragmented among various regulatory authorities—the DTI, the LSE, the Bank of England, the Metropolitan police Fraud Squad, and so on. Regulatory supervision was conducted in an informal fashion, often relying on the close social ties between the regulators and the tight-knit brokering community. The main defense against the exploitation of investors was the structural protection of the single-capacity system, although the regulators seemed to be reasonably conscientious and relatively even-handed in their concern for investors and brokers. This system worked reasonably well as long as single capacity was in place and the market remained insular and socially cohesive. In Japan, investor protection was highly centralized in the offices of the Ministry of Finance. Again, supervision was conducted in an informal fashion, although it appears certain that the interests of the brokers were placed far higher than those of the investors. That no one seemed to care about the systematic neglect of investor protection on the Japanese stock exchanges may be because Japanese individuals tended not to place a high proportion of their savings in the stock market. The image of the Tokyo Stock Exchange as, in the words of Ronald Dore, "a haunt of anti-social speculators" presumably also contributed to the lack of concern about proper investment protection.[1]

Neither system proved adequate to cope with the new challenges of liberalization and internationalization. The British authorities sacrificed the structural protection of single capacity on the altar of market efficiency. They discovered too late that informal nod-and-wink supervision, while fine for small, closed, socially cohesive markets, was hopelessly insufficient for open, international, highly competitive ones. Some of the resulting scandals were caused by individuals who came from well outside the social circle of the regulators, such as Agha Hasan Abedi of BCCI, Peter Clowes, or even, arguably, Robert Maxwell. In other cases, such as Guinness or Blue Arrow, the cutthroat competition and greater potential rewards of the new marketplace caused once highly reputable institutions such as County Bank to engage in highly dishonorable practices. Finally, Britain's old regulatory structure was not prepared for the demands of international financial activity. National regulators were ill-equipped to monitor multinational financial firms such as Baring Brothers or BCCI. In Japan, the close links between regulators and brokers were politically acceptable as long as the regulators were believed to be fulfilling the Confucian ideal that bureaucrats are honest and wise guardians of the national interest. The manifold failures of the MOF, including its inability to prevent fraud in cases such as Recruit Cosmos and the loss-compensation scandals, badly undermined the system's legitimacy. The revelation that many bureaucrats were venal as well as incompetent further undermined the old system. And finally, as in Britain, the system of informal supervision was not adequate for an international marketplace. Foreign investors, foreign brokers, and foreign regulators did not accept the MOF's right to do whatever it wanted in the interests of guidance and retaliated strongly when the MOF tried to exercise that right—as the loss-compensation, Daiwa, and Sumitomo scandals show.

Interestingly, both countries tried at first to keep their old supervisory structures intact, even after a wave of scandals had revealed their shortcomings. Britain's Financial Services Act of 1986, with its two-tier system of Securities and Investments Board and Self-Regulatory Organizations, was an attempt to improve on, but not replace, the practioner-based informal and fragmented model of supervision. Japan's SESC, established in 1991, was a compromise in which the MOF succeeded in retaining much of its supervisory power. Both compromises failed, for in neither case had the fundamental problems been addressed. Britain's system was still too fragmented and too reliant on self-regulation. Japan's system was still too centralized, suffering from inherent conflicts of interest. Critics in both countries looked to more viable solutions, and both countries ultimately concluded that the American model of investor protection was the best available. America's

[1] Ronald Dore, *Taking Japan Seriously*, 116.

SEC became the model for Tony Blair's powerful and independent SIB, and for Japan's powerful and independent FSA. Britain consolidated, Japan fragmented, and both reached a similar end point.

The movement toward better supervision and improved investor protection thus combined both international market forces and domestic political pressures. In both cases, the catalyst for reform was a series of mostly domestic scandals that raised public awareness and politicized the usually arcane issue of financial regulation to the point where politicians saw that capital could be made out of it. International pressure from dissatisfied foreign firms and regulators helped to push the reform efforts along and to dictate their final form. Finally, the perceived success of the SEC in its mission exercised a strong bellwether effect in shaping the final outcome. In the issue of regulatory supervision, then, domestic factors explain institutional change, but international factors explain the shape of those changes.

II. Winners and Losers in Interdependent Markets

The recent history of financial reform in Britain and Japan suggests that internationalization and economic interdependence will result in regulatory reforms that will systematically favor the actors holding the most-mobile economic assets. In the context of financial regulation, this group includes both large corporate borrowers and large institutional investors. The reforms described in this book have been deregulatory to the extent that they have tended to increase competitiveness within the industry, but they have also introduced a greater level of state involvement in markets where this was deemed necessary to protect and enhance the property rights of the institutional consumers of financial services. The result has been significant policy convergence between the two countries toward a common set of regulatory institutions that more closely match the preferences of large users of financial services than was the case in either country before the financial globalization of the 1980s. The main tool by which these mobile-asset actors exercised political influence was more often the threat of exit than the exercise of voice, although there were a variety of other pathways through which internationalization transformed domestic politics.

Mobile-asset holders have benefited in a number of ways from regulatory reform. First, and most uncontroversially, they have benefited from increased market competition. Such competition has been encouraged by the lowering of intermarket and intramarket (or internal and external) barriers to entry by producers. Examples include the erosion of Article 65 in Japan, the abolition of single capacity through the Big Bang in the United Kingdom, and the entry of foreigners to both exchanges. Financial service intermediaries, both banks and investment banks/securities companies, are bearing more of the costs and securing fewer rents of transaction. The second, closely related benefit to large investors and borrowers has been the vastly increased number and variety of financial products available. Such products include futures, options, and other derivatives. These have generally lowered transaction costs and given greater possibilities for diversification and speculative trading. The increase in such product diversity has been achieved at the cost of a concurrent increase in the externalities of systemic risk and overtrading, but the risks and costs seem to be borne primarily by the governments. Finally, large users of financial services have benefited from greater clarity in regulations and especially by enhanced investor protection, which is provided decreasingly by structure and increasingly by government-administered regulation, for example through heightened disclosure requirements. In general, the shift has been toward strengthening the power of the shareholders, the group with the the most-mobile assets, at the expense of management, labor, and the holders of less-mobile assets. One example is the institution of fraud rules, which have vastly strengthened the property rights of shareholders relative to other groups. The logic of prohibitions on insider trading, for example, is that private corporate information should be the property of shareholders and not, for example, the managers or employees of the corporation.

Smaller consumers of financial services, in contrast, have also lost out compared to the big institutions. They had in most cases been the beneficiaries of the old systems, benefiting both from cross-subsidization and from the structural regulatory protection given by functional segmentation and high entry barriers. In some instances, it is true, they have also benefited from increased competition or from the improvement in regulatory structures, but usually they have benefited relatively less than the big institutions. In other instances, notably in dealing costs on the London Stock Exchange, they are worse off in absolute, not just relative, terms, since they are now paying more for the same services.

Retail investors have also failed to benefit from the trend in prudential regulation, although this observation is more true for Britain than Japan. Both countries used to maintain systems of structural protection against problems of moral hazard or adverse selection that were of benefit to all investors, large or small. Indeed, given their greater vulnerability to such problems, small investors may be thought of as the prime beneficiaries of such protection. In both countries, however, these structural barriers were lowered or removed in order to allow large investors and traders to reap the benefits of greater competition and therefore lower costs. The reforms that were intended to replace structural protection have proved to be inadequate substitutes: scandals in both countries continued to occur regularly.

Moreover, the deregulation of the use of exotic financial instruments, which has been of benefit almost exclusively to institutional investors and borrowers, has had the consequence of facilitating risky speculative investing. This creates far greater possibilities of systemic risk, which threaten everyone. Governments have done little to improve supervision or control of this type of trading. The collapse of Barings was made possible because Barings was allowed to trade overseas and in the highly volatile futures markets without sufficient regulatory oversight. Similarly, Sumitomo and

Daiwa were both allowed to incur billions of dollars of losses in the futures or commodities markets over a period of several years without regulators noticing or acting. In the Barings case, the bank was small, and the Bank of England was prepared to allow the company to go bankrupt. The main losers would have been the shareholders, depositors, and bondholders. Were a larger British institution to be close to failure, it is far more probable that a taxpayer-financed bailout would be launched.

III. Internationalization and Domestic Politics

Pathways of Influence

How did internationalization translate into increased political power for the users of economically mobile financial services? There are four main pathways of influence through which mobility was turned to political advantage.

Threat of Exit

The first broad group of mechanisms centers on the political consequences of the fact that internationalization gives to some economic actors the opportunity to escape domestic regulations and conduct business in new jurisdictions. This threat of exit plays into political outcomes in a variety of ways, which can be grouped into two broad categories: the first group are those in which the pattern of influence goes directly from the mobile actors to the policymakers. The second group are those in which the new political influence of mobile-asset consumers of services is mediated indirectly through the efforts of service providers, who lobby policymakers on behalf of the mobile-asset consumers whose business the service providers want to keep or to win.

There are three pathways to regulatory reform where direct influence is used. First, mobile-asset actors can explicitly threaten to leave the country as a bargaining chip in negotiating with policymakers. In this way, the threat of exit simply gives mobile-asset actors a louder voice in the political marketplace and translates into more-favorable lobbying outcomes for these actors. But they do not even have to make threats. The mere fact that they are able to leave will be well known to policymakers, who may make preemptive regulatory concessions in order to prevent an ultimately unwinnable political battle. Finally, policymakers may be forced to make reactive regulatory reforms in order to entice back mobile-asset actors who have already exercised their exit option and left the country.

Cases of indirect influence include occasions when the providers of financial services lobby policymakers to reform regulations in ways that will keep their mobile-asset customers from deserting them. Paradoxically, this will result in producer groups demanding regulatory reforms that at first glance appear to be contrary to their interests. The Big Bang accord, in which the LSE cartel asked the government to scrap itself, is the most spectacular but by no means the only example of such indirect influence.

Promise of Entry

The second set of pathways to reform focuses on the influence of foreigners. In a sense, this is the reverse of the previous group: instead of producers and regulators contending with the threat of exit of mobile-asset domestic actors, they are concerned with attracting the business of internationally mobile-asset foreign firms. The path of influence may go directly from the mobile-asset consumers to the regulators, as when policymakers decided to reform their markets so as to make them attractive to foreign businesses. Authorities in both countries were, and still are, quite open about their desire to promote their nations as a international financial centers. This desire is independent from the lobbying by British or Japanese brokers to attract foreign competition. Alternatively, domestic producers may lobby for regulatory reforms that will bring in new business for them. The desire by Japanese industry, who were consumers of financial services, to clean up Japan's stock-market practices by the establishment of a regulatory agency modeled on the U.S. SEC, which would help attract American investment banks, is such a case.

Cross-National Regulatory Activity

The third broad category of influence concerns the changing relationships among national regulators that internationalization prompts. Internationalization produces a host of new opportunities for firms to escape regulatory oversight, which therefore produces incentives for regulators to win back control. In addition, regulators will often be subject to lobbying by domestic constituents who feel they are at a disadvantage because of the regulatory structure in another country in which they wish to conduct business. Such firms will demand that their national governments support them in trying to bring about reform in these other countries. Regulators thus have multiple, sometimes conflicting incentives to pressure their opposite numbers in other countries. They can do so in two ways, either coercively or cooperatively. Instances of coercive pressure included the liberalization of the euroyen market following the yen–dollar talks of 1984; the demands by Britain and the United States that Japan open its stock market to foreign membership; and the insistence by the SEC and the SIB that the MOF improve its supervisory role in the wake of the Daiwa and Sumitomo debacles of 1997. Instances of regulatory cooperation include the increasing use of memoranda of understanding between national regulators to combat insider trading and instances of fraud.

Changing Preferences of Multinational Firms: Hostages and Divided Loyalties

The fourth pathway by which internationalization alters domestic politics concerns the shifts in political allegiance and regulatory preference that private firms undergo when they open branches or subsidiaries in foreign countries. For one thing, these subsidiaries are typically under the jurisdiction and therefore the control of a foreign government. This makes such subsidiaries prime targets as hostages in the event of a regulatory dispute between the host and home countries. The threat by both the Bank of England and the U.S. Treasury that the subsidiaries of leading Japanese securities companies would not be granted dealers' privileges in bond markets unless the Japanese authorities agreed to reciprocal access for British and U.S. firms is one example. The harsh punishment meted out to Daiwa Bank's U.S. subsidiary following the revelations that it had concealed trading losses in New York may be seen as another.

Moreover, as firms expand overseas, their preferences change. Most obviously, firms that conduct business in multiple markets probably prefer that there be at least broadly similar regulations and regulatory institutions in the different countries. Such harmonization presumably lowers both the search costs of trying to find out exactly what is or isn't legal in a new country and the costs of complying with the various regulations. For example, if the accounting standards are not harmonized, then a firm must produce a different balance sheet for each country in which it wants to list shares. If there is one commonly accepted standard, then the firm need produce only one. In addition, firms planning to invest in new markets may want to be assured that their property rights will be protected at least as well as they are back home. This will make markets that assure such rights more attractive to them.

The United States: Hegemony and the Bellwether Effect

Most of the reforms were not caused by the use of threat or coercion by one country to another. Nor did most reforms come about as a result of transnational cooperation on the part of policymakers. This does not mean that the importance of external influence, and in particular of U.S. hegemony, can be dismissed out of hand. There is certainly evidence of some American influence, both active and passive. We see overt American pressure, including direct threats of retaliation against the Japanese, over market access and at the yen–dollar talks. And it was certainly true that the SEC was active in attempting to bring other countries up to U.S. regulatory standards over the issue of insider trading. Even then, this crusade does not seem to have been the only, or even the most important, cause of action by either Britain or Japan. It is more probable that strict insider-trading laws are more attractive to speculative investors and traders. There was thus an unusual confluence of interests between mobile-asset investors and U.S. regulators.[2]

On other issues, U.S. influence was more passive, but greater. The United States provided a model for many of the reforms, especially in the area of investor protection. Britain modeled the new LSE on the NASDAQ system of market makers, not because the United States forced them to do so, but because NASDAQ offered a good working example of a successful market. The SIB and FSA, at least in their final iterations, were explicitly

---

[2] This argument is made by Haddock and Macey, "Controlling Insider Trading."

modeled on the SEC. Thus, U.S. influence is perhaps best understood, in Louis Pauly's term, as the bellwether effect.[3]

The Politics of Interdependence

The conclusion that internationalization will favor mobile-asset consumers at the expense of relatively less-mobile-asset producers and regulators turns on its head Stigler's argument that producer groups will be the prime beneficiaries of regulatory politics.[4] If I am right, then we are seeing a new form of regulatory politics, one not covered by existing theories.

I illustrate the various typologies of regulatory politics in figure 7.1, categorizing them somewhat simplistically as three-actor models with regulators, consumers, and producers. The arrows denote the hierarchy of political power: how influence travels down the hierarchy from the most to the least favored in the battle for regulations. In case 1, the regulatory capture model most commonly associated with Stigler, it is producer groups who dominate the political landscape. They are able to capture the regulators, who in turn write regulations to benefit producers at the expense of consumers. In case 2, it is the regulators who hold most power, which they use to provide regulation that is most beneficial to producer groups and only of secondary benefit to consumers. Such a state of affairs described Japan, according to Chalmers Johnson, who terms it a "developmental state."[5] In case 3, regulators also hold the most power relative to the other actors, but they are more concerned with providing regulations of benefit to consumers than to producers. An instance of this is provided by Goodhart, who argues that the desire to avoid politically damaging scandals motivates regulators to overprovide consumer protection.[6] In case 4, which is perhaps the closest model to what we ordinarily think ought to be the case, consumer groups influence regulators to provide regulation of primary benefit to the consumers, with producer groups forced to adapt accordingly. James Q. Wilson is one of many political scientists who subscribes to this pluralist conception of politics.[7] Case 5 is my model of the politics of interdependence. Here, consumers dominate the political battleground, but they do so only indirectly, by the economic pressure they exert over producer groups.[8] These producer groups in turn are able to influence the bureaucrats to provide regulations that favor the consumers first and the producers second.

---

[3] Pauly, *Opening Financial Markets*, 179.

[4] George Stigler, "The Theory of Regulation," *Bell Journal of Economics and Management Science* 2 (1971): 3–21.

[5] Chalmers Johnson, *MITI and the Japanese Miracle: The Growth of Industrial Policy, 1925–1975* (Stanford: Stanford University Press, 1982).

[6] Charles A. E. Goodhart, *Money, Information, and Uncertainty*, 2d ed. (London: Macmillan, 1989).

[7] James Q. Wilson, ed., *The Politics of Regulation* (New York: Basic Books, 1974).

[8] As I discussed previously, consumers in this context refers specifically to large users of financial services. Although the distinction between large and small consumers is important in my model, I do not think that it affects how the model fits into the typology discussed here.

My conclusions, in other words, are certainly not intended to mean that domestic politics play no role in determining regulatory outcomes. I wish to avoid the sterile debate about the influence of international versus domestic factors in explaining policy outcomes. Such an argument treats the two as mutually exclusive and seeks to come up with an either/or causal account. The gist of my argument is that both are indispensable: changes in the international environment initiate and modify changes at the domestic level, but naturally much or even most of the reform goes on in the domestic political arenas and is therefore subject to domestic political forces. In this way I am in agreement with those who argue that international capital mobility represents a structural constraint on nation-states, but while that fact influences policy choices it does not predetermine them.

The evidence presented in this book is enough, however, quickly to dismiss the characterization of reforms as a competition in laxity. Although this does come close to describing the dynamics of the reform process, as it is usually formulated it does a poor job of describing the outcomes. On issues such as commission rates, market segmentation, market access, and product choice, it is true that there has been deregulation. On other important issues, there is overwhelming evidence that the regulatory race, if there is one, is to the top. Such issues include stricter disclosure laws; new or strengthened watchdog agencies; more precise and expansive definitions of what constitutes fraud, including (but by no means limited to) recent prohibitions on insider trading; stricter penalties for fraud or sharp practices; and a greater willingness by authorities to monitor and prosecute wrongdoing. My argument shares with the competition-in-laxity theory the notion that internationalization is followed by increased opportunities for exit by certain mobile-asset actors and that governments will be forced to take account of their preferences. However, my model adds a more careful and perhaps counterintuitive specification of the preferences of some of these actors, and an examination of the multiple different ways in which the forcing actually plays out.[9]

Internationalization and Japanese Politics: Convergence or Diversity?

My description of financial politics in Japan is in substantial agreement with Rosenbluth's account. Both agree on the appropriateness of Stigler's model in explaining the initial distribution of power and benefits. Both agree on the importance of international market forces in changing preferences, but both recognize that international market forces are mediated through domestic political battles. We disagree somewhat on the theoretical implications, although this may have more to do with the time period studied.

[9] The competition-in-laxity view has also come under recent attack by David Vogel in *Trading Up*, in which he argues that rather than a "Delaware Effect" in which business migrates to the least regulated jurisdiction, there has been a "California Effect" in the fields of international consumer protection and environmental laws, in which business migrates to the best and most highly regulated jurisdictions, forcing less well regulated countries to follow in a race to the top.

Rosenbluth sees the reform process of the 1980s as evidence of the continued applicability of Stigler's theory, while my interpretation is that openness has had and will continue to have a more fundamental influence on the relative power of consumer and producer groups.[10] My conclusions, however, are more squarely at odds with the prevailing literature in the convergence debate.

The contention that British and Japanese financial systems are converging is by no means shared by all scholars of Japanese political economy. Some argue that markets remain as distinct in the 1990s as they ever were. Steven Vogel suggests that reforms in the 1980s served actually to reinforce the national differences in regulatory style.[11] A weaker version of this argument accepts that there has indeed been some convergence in regulatory style, but that markets still remain, in Sobel's words, "distinctly national in character."[12] As discussed in chapter 3, such a position fits squarely into the growing body of comparative political economy that argues for, in Suzanne Berger's phrase, "The resilience of national models."[13] A central feature of either of these positions is that, despite the rhetoric accompanying globalization, the role of domestic politics in shaping domestic political outcomes must still take the primary position in any causal account of the reform process.

In response to the assertion that there has been little or no convergence in regulatory structure, I would refer to the evidence summarized in table 1.1, and discussion presented in section IV at the end of chapter 6. The thrust of policy reform has been the same in both countries, and the most striking variation in regulatory reform has been by issue area rather than by country. It is, of course, true that there have been important differences in the process of change and in the timing and details of many of the reforms. Moreover, as Vogel correctly notes, many important differences remain between the two countries. This observation highlights the need to define "convergence" more closely. I take convergence to mean a growing similarity in the nature and scope of regulations governing market entry and exit, product choice, supervisory responsibility, and the monitoring and enforcement of fair business practice. Under this definition, which stresses market outcomes as opposed to policy processes as such, the evidence for convergence between Britain and Japan—and between both and the United States—is irrefutable. If we define convergence as the complete eradication of any forms of national difference in regulation, then we have not seen convergence. I agree that different national markets retain somewhat different structures, rules, and regulations. I am certainly not arguing that there has

[10] Rosenbluth, *Financial Politics in Contemporary Japan*, 49.

[11] See Steven Vogel, *Freer Markets, More Rules*; Schaede, *Change and Continuity in Japanese Regulation*; and Sobel, *Domestic Choices, International Markets*, as discussed in chap. 3.

[12] Sobel, *Domestic Choices, International Markets*. Vogel, *Freer Markets, Mores Rules*, also takes this position.

[13] Suzanne Berger, Introduction to *National Diversity and Global Capitalism*, ed. Suzanne Berger and Ronald Dore (Ithaca: Cornell University Press, 1996), 19.

been complete, or even near-complete, convergence of Japanese financial regulations with those of Britain or the United States. Such a radical definition, however, reminds us to keep a sense of perspective in what we expect to see. The differences between Japanese and British financial regulations are still marked. On the other hand, there are also marked differences in regulation between the LSE and the NYSE or, for that matter, between the NYSE and Chicago Futures Trading Board. The fact that the Japanese and British economic institutions retain some differences is not surprising given the extreme differences between the two countries as recently as the 1980s. I find it more interesting that there has been a highly significant degree of regulatory reform in Japan and that each step of the reform process has been in the same direction as Britain.

Indeed, the differences between my position and those of the other authors listed above may be less than they appear and be partly reconcilable. For example, Vogel's characterization of the United Kingdom and Japan as maintaining divergent regulatory regimes is based in large part on the processes by which reforms happened, rather than on the outcomes of the reforms. I agree that there is considerably more divergence in the paths by which the two countries have reached the outcomes I have described than there is in the outcomes themselves. There are many different roads two people can take, but I am more interested in the fact that they are both headed to the same destination.

Similarly, I agree entirely with Schaede that the regulatory philosophy prevailing in the Japanese bureaucracy has not changed as much as many of those she describes as "self-satisfied Western journalists" seem to think.[14] Her phrase brings to mind a half-joking remark made by an MOF official at a 1999 conference of Japanese and American bankers and academics:

> In the 1970s we were told there were two ways of doing things: the right way and the wrong way. In the 1980s we found three ways: the right way, the wrong way, and the Japanese way. Now, again, we are told that there are just two ways of doing things: the American way, and the wrong way.[15]

The irony of his remark was not lost on a crowd familiar with the triumphalism of many American observers of Japan's economic problems. Schaede's point is thus worth repeating. There is indeed plenty of anecdotal evidence that as an institution the MOF's regulatory philosophy has not altered much over the past twenty years. It is still reluctant to let the free market determine outcomes, preferring instead to rely on its own best judgment on issues such as who can enter or exit the market and even what the nature of the competition should be. The prolonged attempt to prop up the stock market with the PKO bill and the attempted bullying of Moody's are two

---

[14] Shaede, *Change and Continuity*, 1.
[15] Remarks made at the Harvard Law School Conference on Creating the Financial Architecture for the 21st Century, Kyoto, June 1999.

examples that the spirit of interventionism lives on, and that, as Schaede claims, "changes in regulatory tools and in regulatory intent do not indicate a basic change in regulation philosophy, and they certainly do not signal convergence with other systems of capitalism."[16]

Again, however, this argument is only true and useful up to a certain point, and it risks missing an essential part of the story. What the MOF believes is less important than what it does or what it can do, and on both of these points it has made decisions since the 1980s or so, almost all of which have tended to make Japanese markets look and operate more like American and British ones. This is not, of course, to say that it does not matter at all that Japanese bureaucrats retain a different regulatory ideology at both a practical and a theoretical level. This is important but, I argue, a less important part of the story of national economic and institutional convergence than that of the market changes that have taken place.

To reiterate, the Japanese did not liberalize their financial markets because of a Pauline conversion to the wonders of laissez-faire capitalism. Nor did they do so out of an admiring desire to make their country more like the United States. Instead, Japanese policymakers undertook reforms in a hard-headed and rational fashion in the self-interests of Japanese corporations. Nonetheless, I find it more interesting theoretically and more important substantively that the Japanese undertook pro-competitive, antibureaucratic reforms despite the evident lack of ideological empathy of many in the MOF for these policy choices. For a Japanese corporation wishing to raise funds or a Japanese housewife trying to earn a return on her savings to cover her husband's retirement, the final outcome of reform—the nature of the marketplace—is of greater concern than the policymaking process.

IV. Liberalization and Japanese Capitalism

The implications of this study for Japanese politics are twofold. First, my findings illustrate that, contrary to popular opinion, the Japanese bureaucracy is not all-powerful and has not succeeded in maintaining the regulatory structures that they would have preferred. Even the MOF, the "Ministry of Ministries," has not been immune from the pressures of private economic actors and of the international environment. Nor have the bureaucrats themselves been immune from making serious errors of judgment about policy. Second, I show that, even as Japan retains many unique political and economic institutions, it also has been subject to the global pressures for institutional convergence. Japan is different, but it is not unique. The same could be said of every country.

It has been suggested that the reforms described in this book are more

---

[16] Schaede, *Change and Continuity*, 17.

cosmetic than real and do not really represent any fundamental shift in the way Japanese capitalism works. My response is that institutional reforms, no matter how fundamental they prove to be in the long run, are rarely accompanied by dramatic changes in the economic or political activity the reforms were intended to influence. Structural reforms can take time—often decades—to yield their effects. As an example, look to the experience of Margaret Thatcher's reforms in Great Britain, of which the Big Bang was such an integral part. Most of the key reforms were conceived in the first adminstration and implemented by the mid-1980s, but it was not until the late 1990s that the full effects on the British economy in terms of economic competitiveness were widely accepted.

Another illustration of the lag between reform and result is found in the institutionalization of American capitalism in the 1930s. In fact, the process by which Japan came to clean up the corrupt financial practices in the late 1980s and early 1990s bears an uncanny resemblence to the history of U.S. financial regulation in the 1920s and 1930s. In the United States, the bull market in stocks of 1925–29 was characterized by an array of exploitative practices perpetrated by politically powerful, well-connected, and lightly regulated financial institutions. No one seemed to mind the sharp practices of the brokerages as long as the market was rising. However, the 1929 Stock Market Crash prompted a series of official investigations into wrongdoing. Investors the world over apparently seek tighter regulation only after they have lost money in a crash. The U.S. investigations, most notably the Pecora hearings of the early 1930s, revealed such unsavory practices that the government promptly undertook wholesale regulatory reform. U.S. reformers particularly targeted the cozy relationships between financial regulators and the industry—the beneficiary of one manipulative stock pushing scheme was a former secretary of the Treasury. The result was a raft of legislation including the Banking Act of 1933, the Securities Act of 1933, and the Securities and Exchange Act of 1934. These acts together make up the fundamental blueprint for the U.S. capital-market-based financial system. Yet the acts took years—even decades—to work their way fully into the economic life of the country. To give just one example, the law banning insider trading was passed in the United States in 1934. Yet the first case of criminal prosecution for insider trading was not brought until 1963. By these standards, Japan's financial reforms are having an unusually rapid impact on business practices.

Visitors to Britain are often struck by the social changes wrought by Thatcherism. What is most striking to this particular observer is the growth of a more prosperous, more entrepreneurial, more cosmopolitan, more meritocratic, less class-based, but more unequal society in the 1990s than the 1970s. The story of Nick Leeson, the working-class boy who rose so high in the financial hierarchy that he was able to destroy one of the oldest and most aristocratic banks in England before he was thirty-five, is one of the more compelling legacies of Thatcherism. Will the reforms being undertaken in Japan, of which the Big Bang and the breakup of the MOF are so central, have any deeper, more transformative effects on Japanese society? I am reminded of the time Chairman Mao Tse-tung was asked to comment on the effects of the French Revolution and is reported to have replied: "It's too early to tell." Some marginal effects have already been seen. Western investment banks in Tokyo are one of the few places where well-educated and intelligent Japanese women can make a career with a reasonable expectation of equal treatment. Job-hopping by Japanese executives is becoming more common in the financial services industry, and the attendant institutions of head-hunters, executive renumeration packages, and so on are becoming less taboo. Financial firms are leading the way in experimenting with downsizing and corporate restructuring. These small changes may alter Japanese attitudes concerning the inevitability or perhaps even the desirability of the traditional ways of doing business. Ultimately, changes in financing arrangements from stakeholder to shareholder may create more fundamental changes in managerial practice in Japan. The straws in the wind suggest that such changes are already under way.

Index

access, market, 11, 24, 31, 39–40, 65, 187, 195, 197; and promise of entry, 20, 194. *See also* entry barriers
amakudari ("descent from Heaven" jobs), 114, 115, 160, 174
ARIEL (Automated Real-Time Investment Ltd.), 75–76
Article 65, 11, 21, 118, 137–39, 166, 191
Ashida Jimonsuke, 159, 162

balance of trade, 22–23, 56n56, 59; Japanese, 58, 119, 122, 125–26, 145–46, 174
Bankers' Associations, Federation of (*Zenkoku Ginko Kyokai*; *Zenginkyo*), 107, 136, 143
Banking Act (1933; Glass-Steagall Act; U.S.), 9, 105, 137n149, 201
Bank of Credit and Commerce International (BCCI), 93–94, 97, 190
Bank of England, 20, 21, 23, 189, 195; and ARIEL, 76; and euromarkets, 57, 67; and Financial Services Act, 88, 90, 97; and insider trading, 98; and LIFFE, 69; and LSE, 68, 79, 80–81; oversight by, 39, 66, 67–68; and scandals, 93, 94, 97, 193
Bank of Japan (BOJ), 104, 107, 116, 118, 146, 172, 177
Bank of Tokyo, 104, 107, 143, 174
banks, 10, 26; British, 7, 65–66, 84; and British Secondary Banking Crisis, 68, 86; commercial, 84, 104; commercial vs. investment, 9, 11, 18, 31, 39, 105; foreign-exchange, 104, 107, 125; foreign subsidiaries of, 21, 127; and German-style universal banking, 137, 139; immobile-asset holding, 17–18; international, 59; investment, 65–66; Japanese, 104, 106–7, 110, 118, 122, 126, 127, 137, 144, 146, 174–75; and Japanese Big Bang, 181, 184, 185; and

Japanese MOF, 14n36, 112, 169–70; and Japanese stock market crash, 168, 177–78; loans from, 103, 169, 177–78; merchant, 65–66; securities trading by, 118, 136, 137–39, 144
Barings Bank, 5n13, 12, 28, 80n56, 94, 190, 192, 193
Barlow Clowes scandal, 92, 95
BCCI. *See* Bank of Credit and Commerce International
Benyon, Tom, 96, 97
Big Bang, British, 7, 11, 19, 21, 70–85; beneficiaries of, 191; causes of, 100–102, 193; compared to Japanese Big Bang, 181–82, 183; and competition, 65, 83, 188–89, 201; domestic factors in, 72, 75–81; effects of, 82–85, 102, 129, 201; and Financial Services Act, 90; and insider trading, 98, 99; international factors in, 72–75; reactions to, 180, 189. *See also* London Stock Exchange
Big Bang, Japanese 11, 145, 177–82; beneficiaries of, 103; compared to British Big Bang, 181–82; and competition, 177, 181, 184, 188–89; effects of, 187, 201–2; reactions to, 182, 189
Big Four securities companies (Japan), 107–8, 116, 138, 146, 160–61, 184; and fixed commissions, 131, 133, 134; and scandals, 150–55
Blair, Tony, 85, 92, 101, 191
Blue Arrow scandal, 92–93, 97, 190
BOJ. *See* Bank of Japan
Bond Dealers, Association of International (AIBD), 57–58, 67
bonds: British government (gilts), 22, 70, 76, 129; euro-, 74, 121; euroyen, 120; foreign, 120, 121, 125; futures trading in, 135, 137; in Japan, 105, 122, 126, 137–38, 186, 195; Japanese government (JGBs), 117–18, 130, 135, 136, 137,

bonds (*continued*)
151n20; samurai, 121; and scandals, 155; warrant, 121, 126, 151n20; Yankee, 170

Bretton Woods system, 56, 58–59

Britain: bureaucracy in, 40, 47, 113; as extreme, 23; as financial center, 6, 80, 83, 90, 97, 102, 182, 194; financial services in, 4, 65–67, 69, 81, 83, 85; fragmented regulatory structure in, 40, 87, 112, 189–91; and Japan, viii, 20, 32, 46, 127–30, 139, 144, 156, 170, 171, 172–73; laissez-faire regulation in, 7, 80n56; postwar regulatory structure in, 26, 32, 38–40; regulatory reform in, 5, 6–8, 22, 25, 55, 65–102; social changes in, 201; social relations in, 189, 190; Treasury of, 66, 69, 90, 96, 98, 100; and U.S., 5n13, 34

brokers: in Britain, 66, 70–71, 72, 77; and British Big Bang, 82, 83; and fixed commissions, 131–35; foreign, in Japan, 129–31, 132, 183–84; in Japan, 188, 189, 190. *See also* producers of financial services; securities companies

Brown, Gordon, 85, 97, 101

Bubble Economy (Japan), 110n29, 144, 145–48, 149, 169, 175, 177, 180

Callaghan, James, 72, 77

Campbell, John Creighton, 112, 114

capital markets, 135, 188; international, 5, 60, 120–28; Japanese, 104, 111–12, 118, 119, 144

capital mobility: and British regulation, 100–102; and competition in laxity, 50; and exchange rates, 58, 59; and financial services, 15; historical, 5n13, 44, 55; and internationalization, 55–64; measurement of, 15, 59–64; and national sovereignty, 3, 41–42, 43, 45; perfect, 62, 63n82; and race to the top, 51; and regulatory politics, 1–4, 19–21, 41–42, 197. *See also* mobile-asset holders

capital mobility hypothesis, 42–49, 64; objections to, 44–49

cartels, 5, 13, 14, 33, 37, 134, 188; British, 17, 65, 66, 79; Japanese, 9, 103, 106, 119; LSE as, 7, 19, 20, 72, 77, 78, 189, 193

Chicago, 69, 135, 199

"Chinese walls." *See* fire walls

City, the (British financial center), 65–66, 68, 86, 90, 97, 101, 102

Clean Government Party (*Komeito*), 148n8, 152

Clowes, Peter, 92, 190

collective-action problem, 35, 36, 38, 79

collective goods school, 34–35

commissions, vii, 7, 74, 197; in Britain, 72, 75, 76, 77, 81, 131, 135, 188; and British Big Bang, 82, 83; fixed, 72, 75, 76, 77, 81, 82, 83, 131–35, 145, 183–84, 188; in Japan, 131–35, 145, 155, 187; and Japanese Big Bang, 181, 182, 183–84; in U.S., 73

Committee on Unfair Trading (MOF; Japan), 139, 142

Companies Act (1980; Britain), 92, 99

competition: barriers to, 24, 191; in Britain, 7, 39, 40, 70–71, 72, 74, 75, 76, 78, 80, 101; and British Big Bang, 65, 83, 188–89, 201; and British Financial Services Act, 86, 89, 90; and capital mobility, 15, 16, 17, 18, 21, 191; in financial services, 12; foreign, 60, 113, 179–80; in Japan, 8, 9, 39, 40, 106, 113, 126, 139, 144, 145, 160, 199; and Japanese Big Bang, 177, 181, 184, 188–89; in laxity, 41, 49–51, 52, 55, 197; perfect, 27, 28, 36; and regulatory reform, 10, 11, 12, 31–34, 61–62, 85, 134, 190, 191

conflicts of interest, 8, 16, 18, 30, 33; in Britain, 71; in Japan, 9, 10, 138, 139, 152, 158, 190

Conservative Party (Britain), 68, 69, 95, 99; and Big Bang, 82, 84, 85; and the City, 86, 90; and Financial Services Act, 88, 90; and LSE, 72, 73, 77, 81, 102; and speculative investment, 101–2

consumers of financial services: and competition in laxity, 49–50; costs to, 16, 40; and functional segmentation, 16, 22, 31, 192; immobile-asset holding, 17–18; and imperfect information, 28–29, 30; and information asymmetries, 32, 34; interests of, 1–2, 24; and internationalization, 14, 60; large-scale, 19–20, 24, 26, 32, 34; protection of, 11, 16, 24, 39, 40, 51–52, 158; and regulatory reform, 21–22, 26, 55, 145, 194, 196–97, 198; small-scale, 18, 22, 26, 31, 32, 34; in Stigler-Peltzman model, 35–36. *See also* investor protection; investors; mobile-asset holders

convergence of financial systems, 41, 43–49; arguments against, 45–46; in

Europe, 43, 45, 46; and internationalization, 54, 62, 197–200; in Japan, 47–48, 197–200

costs: of British Financial Services Act, 86, 89–90, 91; and competition, 31, 32, 34, 74, 83; and competition in laxity, 49; to consumers, 16, 40, 192; distribution of, 26, 35; and externalities, 27–28; to government, 16–17, 22, 192; and harmonization of regulations, 195; in Japan, 74; and mobile-asset holders, 15–16, 18; to producers, 38, 191; of regulation, 16–17, 35–38, 71–72, 122–25; and regulatory reform, 22, 129, 184, 191, 192; of securities financing, 122–25; in Stigler-Peltzman model, 35–36

credit associations (shinkin kinko), 104, 107

credit regulation, 45–46, 57, 104; and bank loans, 103, 169, 177–78

Dai-Ichi Kangyo Bank (DKB), 138, 174–75, 183

Daiwa Bank, 21, 171–72, 195

Daiwa Securities, 107, 129, 139, 190, 193, 194; and tobashi scandal, 154–55; U.S. affiliate of, 171–72

Darling, Alistair, 17, 96, 101

Democratic Socialist Party (Japan), 159

Department of Trade and Industry (DTI; Britain), 39, 66, 67, 92, 93, 100, 189

deregulation: and competition in laxity, 52, 197; convergence in, 43; of financial instruments, 192–93; and increased regulation, 1, 5, 7–10, 11, 26, 191; and internationalization, 51, 103; Japanese, 14n36, 22, 23, 103–4, 128, 129; of LSE, vii, 7, 65, 70–85; of NYSE, 72–73, 78, 83, 134

derivatives, 135–37, 142, 192. See also futures trading

Diet, Japanese, 152, 157, 163, 176, 177, 181

disclosure, 7–11, 142, 181, 192, 197

distributional conflict school, 34, 35

dual-capacity system, 84. See also single-capacity system

economic theory, 2n3, 27–38, 55

eigyo tokkin accounts, 150–53

England. See Britain

entry barriers: and Big Bangs, 82, 181, 182, 188; and competition, 31, 191; and internationalization, 24, 60; and investor protection, 29, 192; and

producers, 35, 40; removal of, 20, 184, 187, 194, 198

environmental regulation, 28n5, 37, 38, 51–52

eurocurrencies, 5, 6, 61, 62; and Britain, 57, 67, 70, 74; and Japan, 121, 135–36

euromarkets, 6n22, 48, 56–58; and Britain, 57, 67; and Japan, 14n36, 122, 138, 189

exit option: and Big Bangs, 101, 188–89; in Britain, 20, 101; and competition in laxity, 49, 50; and convergence, 198; financial services, 19; and internationalization, 2, 13, 41, 48, 55, 60, 63, 64, 191, 193; in Japan, 20, 111, 120–28; of mobile-asset holders, 1, 2, 19–20, 43, 64, 197; and U.S. hegemony, 52–53; and voice, 13, 14, 19, 132

externalities, 27–28, 30–32, 195

factionalism, 113, 114–15

Federal Reserve (U.S.), 57n58, 171, 172

FIMBRA. See Financial Intermediaries, Managers and Brokers Regulatory Association

financial instruments, 58, 62, 136; in Japan, 103, 129, 181, 186; and regulatory trends, 10, 11; yen-based, 170, 180; yen-dominated, 119–20. See also product diversity

Financial Intermediaries, Managers and Brokers Regulatory Association (FIMBRA; Britain), 87, 96, 98

Financial Services Act (1986; Britain), 7, 8, 20, 65, 80, 85–98, 100, 190; problems of, 88–91; revisions to, 95–98, 102; and scandals, 91–95

Financial Supervisory Agency (FSA; Japan), 11, 158, 176–77, 187, 188; and MOF, 145, 168; SEC as model for, 191, 195

Financial System Research Council (Japan), 126, 136, 181

fire walls, 8, 9, 71, 136, 139, 142

foreign exchange: in Britain, 126n95; forward transactions in, 126; in Japan, 104, 107, 125, 136, 181; rates of, 56, 58–59, 146; real-demand rule in, 126; and yen, 120

foreign participation, 186, 191; in bond markets, 120, 121, 125; in British markets, 40, 183; and competition, 60, 113, 179–80; and divided loyalties, 21, 194–95; in domestic markets, 39, 61; in euromarkets, 67; investment, 5n13, 57,

foreign participation (*continued*)
61; in Japanese markets, 20, 40, 103, 129–31, 132, 160, 163, 179–80, 182, 183–84, 189; in TSE, 46, 111, 121, 129–31, 144, 183, 184
France, 45, 101, 126n95
fraud, 30, 34, 39, 192, 194, 197; in Britain, 65; definitions of, 11; in Japan, 103, 108, 140–41, 144, 147, 175. *See also* insider trading; scandals
Fraud Squad, Metropolitan (London), 67, 189
free markets, 23, 56, 77, 126, 131, 159, 181, 199
FSA. *See* Financial Supervisory Agency
functional segmentation: and consumers, 16, 22, 31, 192; deregulation of, 197; and fire walls, 8, 9, 71, 136, 139, 142; in Japan, 31, 106, 118, 181; in LSE, 18, 33, 70–71; in U.S., 31, 54
futures trading: in bonds, 135, 137; in Britain, 40, 66, 96, 98, 100, 156; control of, 11, 39; diversity in, 192; and insider trading, 142, 143; in Japan, 40, 103n, 130, 135–37, 144; and LIFFE, 7, 11, 65, 69–70, 135; on LSE, 39, 135; and scandal, 80n56, 94, 135, 136; speculative, 130, 137, 193; and TIFFE, 9, 11, 137; in U.S., 137, 173

Germany, 52, 58, 126n95
gilts (British government bonds), 70, 76, 129
Glass-Steagall Act (1933; U.S.), 9, 105, 137n149, 201
globalization. *See* internationalization
gold standard, 56, 57, 58
Goodhart, Charles, 89, 196
Goodison, Sir Nicholas, 73, 78, 79, 81, 82, 88
Goodison-Parkinson Accord (1983), 182
governments: and competition in laxity, 51; control of capital mobility by, 55n, 56; control of financial markets by, 3–4, 8, 24, 103; debts of, 117–18, 135; and domestic policies, 45–46; and euromarkets, 67; hostages to foreign, 21, 194–95; and internationalization, 43, 45; Japanese, viii, 6, 103, 104, 117–18, 128, 179; as lender-of-last-resort, 32; and professional standards, 29, 33; and public interest, 27, 28; and regulatory reform, 16–17, 22, 191, 192; and risk, 12, 32
Gower, Jim, 80, 86, 88, 89

Gower Report on Investor Protection (1984), 67
Greenspan, Alan, 171, 172
Guinness scandal, 91–92, 190

Hashimoto Ryutaro, 133, 161, 176, 178, 179, 181; and loss-compensation scandals, 151, 152
Hattersley, Roy, 77, 94
Hong Kong, 126n95, 135
Horioka, Charles, 62, 63n82
Horiuchi Akiyoshi, 117, 122
housing loan (*jusen*) industry, 32, 168, 169, 174

immobile-asset holders, 2, 13, 17–18, 19, 21–22, 43
IMRO. *See* Investment Management Regulatory Organisation
Inagawa-kai scandal (1991), 154, 157
Industrial Bank of Japan, 104, 116
inflation, 117, 118, 145–47
information: asymmetries of, 32–34, 71; imperfect, 27, 28–30; technology of, 57
insider trading, 8, 12n, 16–17, 30, 50, 197, 201; in Britain, 17, 39, 65, 95, 98–100, 101, 102, 143; international cooperation on, 21, 194; in Japan, 10, 39, 99, 108, 139–44, 147, 167, 175; and MOF, 139, 140, 142; prohibition of, 11, 22, 65, 99–100, 102, 139–44, 145; and shareholder rights, 192; and U.S., 53, 96, 142, 195
insurance companies, 66, 110, 149n11, 150, 151n19, 181, 183, 184
Interest Equalization Tax (IET; 1963; U.S.), 57, 120
interest rates, 62, 63, 117, 127, 146
internationalization: beneficiaries of, 191–93; and Big Bangs, 101, 180, 181, 188; and Britain, 63, 64, 72–75, 101; and capital mobility, 55–64; and clarity of regulations, 16, 18, 22, 192; and consumers, 14, 60; and convergence, 54, 62, 197–200; and cooperation between regulators, 20–21, 24, 49, 54–55, 194; and deregulation, 51, 103; and domestic politics, 23, 25, 41–64, 191, 193–200; evidence for, 59–64; and exit option, 2, 13, 41, 48, 55, 60, 63, 64, 191, 193; and fixed commissions, 135; and harmonization of regulation, 21, 24, 54–55, 195; and international norms, 143–44; and Japan, 17, 63, 64, 111, 117n65, 119–29, 142–44, 158, 180,

181; and mobile-asset holders, 13, 18–21, 193, 196; and MOF, 120, 125–28; and national sovereignty, 3, 41–42, 43, 45; and regulation, 1–4, 13, 54–55; and regulatory reform, 1–4, 13, 23, 24, 54–55, 119–29, 142–44, 158, 190–91, 197

Investment Management Regulatory Organisation (IMRO; Britain), 87, 95, 96, 98

investor protection, 3, 10, 11, 22; and Big Bangs, 188, 189–91; in Britain, 20, 40, 65, 66, 189–91; and British Financial Services Act, 7–8, 86, 89, 90, 91, 93, 96, 97; and competition in laxity, 50; costs of, 16–17; and entry barriers, 29, 192; in euromarkets, 67; in Japan, 8–9, 40, 103, 106, 189–91; and Japanese Bubble Economy, 145, 147; and laissez-faire regulation, 80n56; on LSE, 70–71, 72, 75, 77, 78, 79, 189; and mobile-asset holders, 12, 18; and social relations, 189, 190; U.S. model of, 190–91, 195–96

investors, individual: in Britain, 79, 84–85, 101, 188; and British Financial Services Act, 85, 90, 96; and domestic savings, 62, 63; and fixed commissions, 133, 134; in Japan, 105, 109–11, 188; on LSE, 22, 192; and privatization, 79; and regulatory reform, 82, 84–85, 145, 192

investors, institutional: as beneficiaries of reform, 21–22, 96–97, 102, 145, 191–93; and Big Bangs, 82, 83, 101, 185, 188; in Britain, 70, 76, 82, 83, 101, 110, 111; and British Financial Services Act, 90, 91, 95; and capital mobility, 15; and fixed commissions, 131, 132, 135; and futures trading, 135, 137; in Japan, 103, 110–11, 185; and LSE, 72, 73, 75–76, 79; and politics of interdependence, 196n8; as shareholders, 186

Ito Shigeru, 176, 177

Japan: and Britain, 20, 127–30, 139, 144, 156, 170, 171, 172–73; bureaucracy in, 4, 40, 47, 103, 105–6, 112–15, 158, 160, 162, 173, 187, 199–200; as consumer, 194; economic miracle of, 129; as financial center, 128, 136, 194; financial markets in, 182–87; financial services in, 4, 38–40, 103–17, 123; industrialization in, 104; mergers and acquisitions in, 186; regional stock exchanges in, 107;

regulators in, 196; regulatory reform in, 8–10, 20, 21, 46–47, 53, 55, 129–44; regulatory structure in, 87, 189–91; and SCAP, 104, 105, 139, 140, 157, 201; structural protection in, 32

Japan Federation of Employers' Associations (*Keidanren*), 125, 159

Japan Securities Dealers Association (JDSA), 149, 151n20, 157, 160, 163

JGBs. *See* bonds: Japanese government

jobbers (Britain), 70–71, 72, 75, 76–77, 82

jusen (housing-loan companies), 32, 168, 169, 174

Kaifu Toshiki, 151, 152, 158, 159, 162

Keidanren (Japanese Federation of Employers' Associations), 125, 159

keiretsu (industrial groupings), 106, 110

kokusaika. See internationalization

Komeito (Clean Government Party), 148n8, 152

Korean War, 115, 140

Labour Party (Britain), 68, 77, 101; and Financial Services Act, 96, 97; and regulatory reform, 72, 81, 85, 102

Large, Andrew, 91, 96

Latin America, 5n13, 178

Lawson, Nigel, 81, 86, 89, 90, 91

Leeson, Nicholas, 94, 171, 201

Leigh-Pemberton, Robin, 79–80, 89

Liberal Democratic Party (LDP; Japan), 48, 133, 158, 180; and MOF, 112, 113, 173–76; and scandals, 148, 149, 152

liberalization. *See* deregulation

Life Assurance and Unit Trust Regulatory Organisation (LAUTRO), 87, 96, 98

LIFFE. *See* London International Financial Futures Exchange

London International Financial Futures Exchange (LIFFE), 7, 11, 65, 69–70, 135

London Metal Exchange (LME), 51n41, 172–73

London Stock Exchange (LSE): and Bank of England, 68, 79, 80–81; and Big Bang, 83–84, 182; as cartel, 7, 19, 20, 72, 77, 78, 189, 193; and the City, 65; and Conservative Party, 72, 73, 77, 81, 102; costs on, 12, 192; deregulation of, vii, 7, 65, 70–85; and euromarkets, 67; and Financial Services Act, 85, 87; and fixed commissions, 131; functional segmentation in, 18, 33, 70–71; futures

London Stock Exchange (*continued*)
trading on, 39, 135; and individual
investors, 22, 192; and insider trading,
98, 99, 100; and institutional investors,
72, 73, 75–76, 79; investor protection
on, 70–71, 72, 75, 77, 78, 79, 189; and
Japan, 9, 180, 189; and LIFFE, 69;
members of, 78–79, 83–84; as model,
136; and NYSE, 73, 78, 101, 199;
pressures to reform, 72–81; U.S. as
model for, 195
long-term credit banks (LTCB; Japan),
108, 183
loss-compensation scandals (Japan; 1991),
109n22, 115, 133, 149–53, 157, 158,
190; foreign reaction to, 155, 156
LSE. *See* London Stock Exchange
LTCB. *See* long-term credit banks

MacArthur, Douglas, 104n9, 182
Maxwell, Robert, 93, 95, 190
Meiji Restoration, 104, 120n76
Merchant Bank Acceptance Committee
(Britain), 66, 75n40
Merrill Lynch (company), 74, 129,
130n108, 183
Ministry of Finance (MOF; Japan): and
Article 65, 137, 139; and banks, 14n36,
104, 112, 169–70; and Big Bang, 180,
181; and bond trading, 118, 121, 122;
and Bubble Economy, 145, 146;
bureaus of, 112, 115, 125, 165–66, 176,
177; Committee on Unfair Trading of,
139, 142; decline of, 103, 184;
dismantling of, 4, 157–58, 168–77,
201–2; dominance of, 9, 10, 47, 112–15;
and *eigyo tokkin* accounts, 150–53; and
exit option, 122; failures of, 168–70,
190; and fixed commissions, 131, 132,
133, 134, 135; and foreign regulators,
170–73, 194; and FSA, 145, 168; and
futures trading, 136; and housing-loan
companies, 32, 168, 169; and insider
trading, 139, 140, 142; and insurance
companies, 110; internal unity of,
114–15; and internationalization, 20,
120, 125–28; and international norms,
143; and LDP, 112, 113, 173–76; and
Moody's Corporation, 169–70, 199; as
Okurasho (great storehouse), 112, 177;
oversight by, 39, 40; philosophy of,
199–200; and PKO, 178–79; and
politicians, 113–14; pressures for
change on, 48, 200; price manipulation
by, 115–16, 168–69; regulation in, 189;

and regulatory reform, 23, 159–60, 184;
and scandals, 114, 150–53, 154, 156–57,
162, 174; Securities Bureau of, 106,
160, 180, 181; and securities companies,
112, 115, 117, 160; Securities
Enforcement Division of, 140; and
SEL, 105; and SESC, 161–63, 164,
165–68; and SIB, 98; and stock market
crash, 144, 178; and TSE, 129, 168–69
Ministry of International Trade and
Industry (MITI; Japan), 112, 126
Mitsuzuka Hiroshi, 178, 181
Miyazawa Kiichi, 148, 149
Mizuhara Toshihiro, 164, 166
mobile-asset holders: as beneficiaries of
regulatory reform, 2–3, 4, 10, 12,
21–22, 65, 102, 145, 191–93; and
British deregulation, 82; costs to,
15–16, 18; exit option of, 1, 2, 19–20,
43, 64, 197; interests of, 24, 55; and
internationalization, 13, 18–21, 193,
196; and Japanese deregulation, 103,
128; large-scale, 24, 65; power of, 14,
43, 64; preferences of, 15–17; and
promise of entry, 20, 194; and U.S.
interests, 195
MOF. *See* Ministry of Finance
Moody's Corporation, 168, 169–70, 199
moral-hazard problem, 17, 28n6, 192
multinational corporations, 15, 26, 194–95

Nakasone Yasuhiro, 119, 148–49
NASDAQ (National Association of
Securities Dealers Automated
Quotation), 82, 195
NatWest Bank, 89, 92–93, 190
Newmarch, Mick, 73, 75
New York Stock Exchange (NYSE), 134,
155, 180; and LSE, 73, 78, 101, 199;
May Day deregulation of (1975), 72–73,
78, 83; as order-driven market, 82
Nikkei Stock Index, 9, 115, 135, 147, 149,
168, 169, 186
Nikko Securities, 107, 138, 152, 154, 155,
156, 183
Nomura Securities, 74, 107, 109, 115,
131, 139, 142; and Britain, 129; and
gangsters, 174–75; and scandals,
150n13, 151, 152, 153, 154, 155, 156
Norton-Warburg scandal (1981; Britain),
86
NYSE. *See* New York Stock Exchange

Office of Fair Trading (OFT; Britain), 72,
75, 77–81, 82, 101

offshore markets, 5, 6n22, 125, 144. *See also* euromarkets

OFT. *See* Office of Fair Trading

oil shocks, 59, 117, 118, 121

Okurasho (the great storehouse). *See* Ministry of Finance

Osaka Stock Exchange, 105, 107, 136, 137, 141

oversight, 11, 24, 33, 194; by Bank of England, 39, 66, 67–68; and Big Bangs, 188, 189–91; in Britain, 39, 40, 65, 66–67, 89; in Japan, 103, 106; by MOF, 39, 40; and speculation, 192–93

Parkinson, Cecil, 81, 82

Pauly, Louis, 43, 53, 196

Pecora hearings (1930s; U.S.), 56, 201

pension funds, 102, 186; in Britain, 61; in Japan, 110, 168, 179–80, 181, 187, 189; and scandals, 92, 93, 94–95

PKO. *See* Price-Keeping Operation

policymakers: and capital mobility, 2–3; and competition in laxity, 50; and interdependence, 196; and internationalization, 5, 19, 20–21, 55, 60; and regulatory politics, 14, 193

politicians: British, 40, 113; Japanese, 47, 113–14, 141, 148, 151n19, 173; and special interests, 37

politics: and campaign finance, 108; domestic, 1–4, 41–64, 117–18, 190–91, 193–200; of interdependence, 196–97; party, 37–38, 47, 48. *See also* regulatory politics

postal savings accounts (Japan), 117, 168

price controls, 7, 10, 11, 18; and Big Bangs, 65, 188; in Britain, 39, 40, 65; in Japan, 8, 9, 39, 40, 182; in LSE, 70–71, 72

Price-Keeping Operation (PKO; Japan), 168–69, 178–79, 199

price manipulation, 10, 36, 139; and Bubble Economy, 147; in Japan, 108, 150, 154, 157; by MOF, 115–16, 168–69

producers of financial services: as beneficiaries of regulation, 26, 35, 37, 38; in closed markets, 14; and competition, 191; and convergence, 198; effects of reform on, 21–22, 145; and exit option, 19; immobile-asset holding, 17–18; and information asymmetries, 32; and internationalization, 60; in Japan, 158, 187, 188; large-scale, 24; power of, 40, 48, 187, 193, 196–97; in Stigler-Peltzman model, 35–36. *See also* securities companies

product diversity, 11, 16, 22, 24, 35, 191–93; and Big Bangs, 188; in Britain, 39, 40, 65; and choice, 31, 197, 198; in Japan, 39, 40, 186

property rights, 15, 16, 21, 22, 51

real estate market, 177–78

Recruit Cosmos scandal (1988), 141, 148–49, 190

regulation, cross-national, 21, 24, 54–55, 195

regulators, 196–97; backgrounds of, 66, 112, 114; international cooperation of, 21, 24, 49, 54–55, 194; U.S., 201

regulatory politics, 34–38, 189–91; actors in, 13–14, 24, 38, 113, 134, 193; and capital mobility, 1–4, 19–21, 41–42, 197; in closed markets, 13–14; in interdependent markets, 14; models of, 13–14, 25, 26, 34–38, 196–97

Rosenbluth, Frances McCall, 14n36, 38n, 47–48, 113, 122n86, 197, 198

scandals, 12, 34, 102, 191, 192; in Britain, 66, 68, 91–95, 190, 193; and British Financial Services Act, 86, 89, 91, 95–96, 97; fear of, 196; and fixed commissions, 133; and futures trading, 80n56, 94, 135, 136; and insider trading, 139, 141, 142; in Japan, 10, 22, 109n22, 114, 115, 133, 148–58, 160, 162, 174, 190; and Japanese Bubble Economy, 145, 147–57; and pension funds, 92, 93, 94–95; U.S. bond-auction, 155

SCAP (Supreme Commander for the Allied Powers), 104, 105, 139, 140, 157

Schaede, Ulrike, 46, 47, 199, 200

SEAQ (Stock Exchange Automated Quotation), 82, 83

SEC. *See* Securities and Exchange Commission

Secondary Banking Crisis (1973-74; Britain), 68, 86

Securities Act (1933; U.S.), 33, 86n82, 105, 139, 201

Securities and Exchange Act (1934; U.S.), 33, 105, 139, 201

Securities and Exchange Commission (SEC; U.S.), 8, 105; and insider trading, 53, 142; and Japan, 140, 155, 159, 171; as model, 20, 95, 97, 98, 102, 152, 190–91, 194, 195–96; profits of, 17n39; and SESC, 10, 159, 161, 163, 164, 165, 167; and SIB, 65, 88, 195

Securities and Exchange Council (Japan), 135, 136, 139, 180

Securities and Exchange Surveillance Commission (SESC; *Shoken torihiki kanshi ii inkai*), 11, 65, 163–68, 175, 177, 190; founding of, 145, 157–58; independence of, 165–68; and SEC, 10, 159, 161, 163, 164, 165, 167

Securities and Investments Board (SIB; Britain), 8, 11, 65, 190, 194; and Financial Services Act, 87, 88–91; and insider trading, 100; and Japan, 156, 173; and SEC, 65, 88, 195; and SESC, 10, 165; strengthening of, 95, 96, 97–98, 191; Super, 188

securities companies, 10, 11, 21–22, 191; and banks, 9, 137–38, 139; in Britain, 66, 71, 180, 182; and fixed commissions, 131, 133; foreign subsidiaries of, 21, 157, 195; and futures trading, 136; and insider trading, 140; in Japan, 72, 107–9, 112, 115, 116, 117, 122, 137, 150, 160, 180, 182; Japanese Big Four, 107–8, 116, 131, 133, 134, 138, 146, 150–55, 160–61, 184; reactions to reform of, 180, 182, 189; saleswomen for, 109; and scandals, 152, 153, 154–55; in U.S., 73

Securities Exchange Law (SEL; *shoken torihiki-ho*; 1947), 104–5, 122, 131, 154, 163; amendments to, 116, 141–42, 157; and futures trading, 136, 137; and insider trading, 141–42

SEL. *See* Securities Exchange Law

self-regulation, 39, 40, 66, 98, 133

self-regulatory organizations (SROs), 8, 58, 67, 163, 190; and Financial Services Act, 87, 91, 96, 97

Serious Fraud Office (Britain; SFO), 92, 93, 94, 95, 96, 173

SESC. *See* Securities and Exchange Surveillance Commission

SFO. *See* Serious Fraud Office

shareholders: in Britain, 85, 96–97; individual, 83, 105; institutional investors as, 186; in Japan, 105, 185; rights of, 8, 10, 11, 12, 22, 192; strengthening of, 12, 192; vs. stakeholders, 101, 186, 202

Shoken Torihiki Kanshi ii Inkai (SESC). *See* Securities and Exchange Surveillance Commission

SIB. *See* Securities and Investments Board

Singapore, 12, 15, 126n95, 189; futures trading scandal in, 80n56, 94, 135, 136

single-capacity system, 70–71, 72, 74–76, 78, 82, 188, 189; abolition of, 21, 190, 191

Slater-Walker scandal (1975-77; Britain), 86

Smith, Adam, 36, 49–50

Sobel, Andrew, 47, 198

Sony Corporation, 120, 141n159

special interests, 36, 37, 45, 48

speculation, 22, 56, 195; and exchange rates, 58, 59; in futures, 130, 137, 193; in Japan, 103, 104, 150; and oversight, 192–93; and short-termism, 101–2

SROs. *See* self-regulatory organizations

stakeholders, 101, 186, 202

Stigler, George, 14, 35, 36, 38, 44n11, 48

Stigler-Peltzman model of regulatory capture, 1–2, 13, 17, 26, 35–36, 48, 55, 196–98

Stock Exchange Council (Britain), 67, 77, 98

stock market crashes, 26, 27, 30–34; of 1929, 53, 56, 105, 201; Black Monday (1987), 146, 151n17, 189; Japanese (1990), 144, 150, 168, 169, 177, 178; and Japanese Bubble Economy, 145, 147

Sumitomo Corporation, 51n41, 110, 172–73, 190, 192–93, 194

Takeover Panel (Britain), 98, 99, 100

Tax Agency, National (Japan), 150, 159–60, 165, 174

taxes, 31n, 101, 118, 181; and MOF, 114, 176, 177; and scandals, 148, 149, 150; U.S., 57, 120

technology, 5, 57, 75–76, 82, 84, 117

Thatcher, Margaret, 6, 72, 73n28, 77n45, 79, 81, 201; and British Big Bang, 7, 189; and Financial Services Act, 88; pressure on Japan from, 129

TIFFE. *See* Tokyo International Financial Futures Exchange

tobashi trading, 154–55, 167

tokkin accounts, 149–50

Tokyo International Financial Futures Exchange (TIFFE), 9, 11, 137

Tokyo Stock Exchange (TSE), 9, 11, 104, 129–44, 145, 190; and Bubble Economy, 146; cross-shareholding in, 185; fixed commissions on, 131–35; foreign participation in, 46, 111, 121, 129–31, 144, 183, 184; futures trading on, 135–37; and Japanese Big Bang, 103, 177–82; and MOF, 129, 168–69; and NYSE, 140; and Recruit Cosmos

scandal, 149; and securities companies, 107, 108; and SESC, 164; surveillance division of, 160; and U.S., 129, 130
Tradepoint (computer-based market), 84, 85
transparency, 8, 9, 10, 11, 15, 32, 33
Treasury (Britain), 66, 69, 90, 96, 98, 100
TSE. *See* Tokyo Stock Exchange

United Kingdom. *See* Britain
United States: arrogance of, 199; and balance of trade, 58; and bellwether effect, 53, 195–96; and Britain, 5n13, 34; and capital mobility hypothesis, 43; and convergence, 46–47, 48, 198–200; and cooperation between national regulators, 194; and euromarkets, 57; Federal Reserve of, 57n58, 171, 172; financial system in, 9, 72, 73, 74, 110, 112; foreign investment in, 57, 61, 126n95, 127; fraud in, 141; futures trading in, 137, 173; hegemony of, 49, 52–54, 195–96; and insider trading, 53, 96, 99, 100, 139, 140, 142, 143, 195; investor protection in, 190–91, 195–96; and Japan, 20, 46–48, 104–5, 119–20, 128, 137n149, 138, 139, 142, 144, 160, 170–72, 182, 186; and Japanese

scandals, 153n40, 155–56; and Latin American debt crisis, 178; as model, 95, 96, 145, 158, 168, 190–91, 195–96; regulatory reform in, 9, 22, 24, 105, 137n149, 187, 201; regulatory structure in, 112; and TSE, 129, 130; and tuna boycott, 52. *See also* Securities and Exchange Commission
U.S. Treasury Department, 21, 129, 137, 172, 195

Vogel, David, 34, 51–52, 197n
Vogel, Steven, 47, 112–13, 198, 199
voice (political influence), 191; and exit option, 13, 14, 19, 132

Wilson, James Q., 26, 37–38, 196

Yamaichi Securities, 107, 116, 129, 183, 184
Yen-Dollar talks (1983-84), 20, 53, 54, 119–20, 126, 170, 194, 195

Zaibatsu (financial cliques), 104, 105, 109
zaiteku (innovative financing techniques), 141, 146n3, 149n11
Zenginkyo (Federation of Bankers' Associations), 107, 136, 143

CORNELL STUDIES IN POLITICAL ECONOMY
A series edited by Peter J. Katzenstein

Border Games: Policing the U.S.-Mexico Divide
by Peter Andreas

National Diversity and Global Capitalism
edited by Suzanne Berger and Ronald Dore

The Price of Wealth: Economies and Institutions in the Middle East
by Kiren Aziz Chaudhry

Power, Purpose, and Collective Choice: Economic Strategy in Socialist States
edited by Ellen Comisso and Laura Tyson

Transforming Europe: Europeanization and Domestic Change
edited by Maria Green Cowles, James Caporaso, and Thomas Risse

The Political Economy of the New Asian Industrialism
edited by Frederic C. Deyo

Rivals beyond Trade: America versus Japan in Global Competition
by Dennis J. Encarnation

Enterprise and the State in Korea and Taiwan
by Karl J. Fields

National Interests in International Society
by Martha Finnemore

Democracy and Markets: The Politics of Mixed Economies
by John R. Freeman

The Misunderstood Miracle: Industrial Development and Political Change in Japan
by David Friedman

Patchwork Protectionism: Textile Trade Policy in the United States, Japan, and West Germany
by H. Richard Friman

Ideas, Interests, and American Trade Policy
by Judith Goldstein

Ideas and Foreign Policy: Beliefs, Institutions, and Political Change
edited by Judith Goldstein and Robert O. Keohane

Monetary Sovereignty: The Politics of Central Banking in Western Europe
by John B. Goodman

Politics in Hard Times: Comparative Responses to International Economic Crises
by Peter Gourevitch

Cooperation among Nations: Europe, America, and Non-tariff Barriers to Trade
by Joseph M. Grieco

Nationalism, Liberalism, and Progress, Volume I: The Rise and Decline of Nationalism
Volume II: The Dismal Fate of New Nations
by Ernst B. Haas

Pathways from the Periphery: The Politics of Growth in the Newly Industrializing Countries
by Stephan Haggard

The Politics of Finance in Developing Countries
edited by Stephan Haggard, Chung H. Lee, and Sylvia Maxfield

Rival Capitalists: International Competitiveness in the United States, Japan,
and Western Europe
by Jeffrey A. Hart

Reasons of State: Oil Politics and the Capacities of American Government
by G. John Ikenberry

The State and American Foreign Economic Policy
edited by G. John Ikenberry, David A. Lake, and Michael Mastanduno

The Nordic States and European Unity
by Christine Ingebritsen

The Paradox of Continental Production: National Investment Policies in North America
by Barbara Jenkins

The Government of Money: Monetarism in Germany and the United States
by Peter A. Johnson

Corporatism and Change: Austria, Switzerland, and the Politics of Industry
by Peter J. Katzenstein

Cultural Norms and National Security: Police and Military in Postwar Japan
by Peter J. Katzenstein

Industry and Politics in West Germany: Toward the Third Republic
edited by Peter J. Katzenstein

Small States in World Markets: Industrial Policy in Europe
by Peter J. Katzenstein

Norms in International Relations: The Struggle against Apartheid
by Audie Jeanne Klotz

International Regimes
edited by Stephen D. Krasner

Disparaged Success: Labor Politics in Postwar Japan
by Ikuo Kume

Business and Banking: Political Change and Economic Integration in Western Europe
by Paulette Kurzer

Power, Protection, and Free Trade: International Sources of U.S. Commercial Strategy,
1887–1939
by David A. Lake

Money Rules: The New Politics of Finance in Britain and Japan
by Henry Laurence

Why Syria Goes to War: Thirty Years of Confrontation
by Fred H. Lawson

Remaking the Italian Economy
by Richard M. Locke

France after Hegemony: International Change and Financial Reform
by Michael Loriaux

Economic Containment: CoCom and the Politics of East-West Trade
by Michael Mastanduno

Business and the State in Developing Countries
edited by Sylvia Maxfield and Ben Ross Schneider

The Currency of Ideas: Monetary Politics in the European Union
by Kathleen R. McNamara

The Choice for Europe: Social Purpose and State Power from Messina to Maastricht
by Andrew Moravcsik

Collective Action in East Asia: How Ruling Parties Shape Industrial Policy
by Gregory W. Noble

Mercantile States and the World Oil Cartel, 1900–1939
by Gregory P. Nowell

Negotiating the World Economy
by John S. Odell

Who Elected the Bankers? Surveillance and Control in the World Economy
by Louis W. Pauly

Opening Financial Markets: Banking Politics on the Pacific Rim
by Louis W. Pauly

Regime Shift: Comparative Dynamics of the Japanese Political Economy
by T. J. Pempel

The Politics of the Asian Economic Crisis
edited by T. J. Pempel

The Limits of Social Democracy: Investment Politics in Sweden
by Jonas Pontusson

The Fruits of Fascism: Postwar Prosperity in Historical Perspective
by Simon Reich

The Business of the Japanese State: Energy Markets in Comparative and Historical Perspective
by Richard J. Samuels

"Rich Nation, Strong Army": National Security and the Technological Transformation of Japan
by Richard J. Samuels

Crisis and Choice in European Social Democracy
by Fritz W. Scharpf, translated by Ruth Crowley and Fred Thompson

Winners and Losers: How Sectors Shape the Developmental Prospects of States
by D. Michael Shafer

Ideas and Institutions: Developmentalism in Brazil and Argentina
by Kathryn Sikkink

The Cooperative Edge: The Internal Politics of International Cartels
by Debora L. Spar

The Hidden Hand of American Hegemony: Petrodollar Recycling and International Markets
by David E. Spiro

Fair Shares: Unions, Pay, and Politics in Sweden and West Germany
by Peter Swenson

Union of Parts: Labor Politics in Postwar Germany
by Kathleen Thelen

Democracy at Work: Changing World Markets and the Future of Labor Unions
by Lowell Turner

Fighting for Partnership: Labor and Politics in Unified Germany
by Lowell Turner

Troubled Industries: Confronting Economic Change in Japan
by Robert M. Uriu

National Styles of Regulation: Environmental Policy in Great Britain and the United States
by David Vogel

Freer Markets, More Rules: Regulatory Reform in Advanced Industrial Countries
by Steven K. Vogel

The Political Economy of Policy Coordination: International Adjustment since 1945
by Michael C. Webb

The Myth of the Powerless State
by Linda Weiss

The Developmental State
edited by Meredith Woo-Cumings

International Cooperation: Building Regimes for Natural Resources and the Environment
by Oran R. Young

International Governance: Protecting the Environment in a Stateless Society
by Oran R. Young

Polar Politics: Creating International Environmental Regimes
edited by Oran R. Young and Gail Osherenko

Governments, Markets, and Growth: Financial Systems and the Politics of Industrial Change
by John Zysman

American Industry in International Competition: Government Policies and Corporate Strategies
edited by John Zysman and Laura Tyson